Praise for *Leadership from the Inside Out*

"*Leadership from the Inside Out* is a major paradigm shift in leadership development. It gives you the tools to go directly to the heart of all significant leadership transformation: growing as a person to grow as a leader."
—**Paul Walsh, former Chairman and CEO, Diageo**

"*Leadership from the Inside Out* gets to the heart of what we face as global leaders in today's complex world: the ability to have people reach beyond themselves, achieving great results by integrating purpose, knowledge, and personal growth."
—**Daniel Vasella, MD, Chairman Emeritus and former CEO, Novartis AG**

"Every CEO is faced with the same basic challenge: how to inspire enduring performance. Cashman's *Leadership from the Inside Out* is an invaluable resource to awaken purpose-driven performance in yourself, your team, and your organization."
—**Thomas Ebeling, CEO, ProSeibenSat.1 Media**

"What is more important than bringing our gifts to infuse life in all those around us? Cashman can give you the pragmatic tools to profoundly and purposefully do this. Get this book to serve all those you touch."
—**Brian McNamara, CEO, GSK Consumer**

"Cashman helps you to pause on purpose to serve all the stakeholders in your life. Use this book so you can lead forward with greater authenticity and impact."
—**Stuart Parker, CEO, USAA**

"If you seek a purpose-driven life and purpose-driven leadership, Cashman is the inspiring, insightful guide who can bring you there."
—**Ludwig Hantson, CEO, Alexion Pharmaceuticals, Inc., and former CEO, Baxalta**

"In today's complex and ambiguous world, the need for clarity and agility has never been greater. Cashman will help you sort out clarity of purpose and the power of authenticity to transform volatility into vision."
—**Paul Laudicina, Chairman, Global Business Policy Council, and Chairman Emeritus, A. T. Kearney**

"*Leadership from the Inside Out* was honed in a very real-world laboratory coaching and developing thousands of leaders. I have personally seen Cashman's work touch the lives of hundreds of leaders. Use this book to inspire your own personal journey to transformative leadership."
—**Steven Baert, CHRO, Novartis AG**

"In today's constantly changing marketplace, finding the constants of authenticity, purpose, and values-driven performance is critical. *Leadership from the Inside Out* gives you the personal resources to navigate change from an enduring inner foundation."
—**Liam Condon, CEO, Bayer Crop Science**

"I consider my friend and colleague Kevin to be the leading leadership philosopher today. He blends the research, wisdom, and practicality of leadership into one beautiful package. I learned from the first edition, and I learned even more from this revision. I love the concept of going deep and going long on authenticity. The Buddha would be pleased."

—**Bob Eichinger, bestselling coauthor of** *The Leadership Machine, FYI, and You* **and cofounder of Lominger International**

"Cashman's *Leadership from the Inside Out* enables you to gain clarity of your purpose in life—the key to authentic leadership, true fulfillment, and doing your best for the greater good. Savor this book to become a purpose-driven leader in all aspects of life!"

—**Kurt Graves, Chairman and CEO, Intarcia Therapeutics**

"Cashman's latest work can help you to inspire yourself and others to realize your purpose-filled dreams."

—**Patrick Thomas, CEO, Covestro**

"Inspiring purpose-driven performance is a worthy, challenging pursuit. Cashman and *Leadership from the Inside Out* can help you meet this critical challenge with courage and conviction. It has worked for me."

—**David Meek, CEO, Ipsen**

"*Leadership from the Inside Out* is an inspiration to lead from a deep knowledge of one's core purpose, creating value with true authenticity."

—**Deborah Dunsire, MD, CEO and President, XTuit Pharmaceuticals**

"Achieving results with integrity is the challenging call of CEO leadership. Cashman can help you find the value-creating sweet spot of deep purpose and high performance."

—**Steven Reinemund, retired Chairman and CEO, PepsiCo**

"In today's hyperpaced, hyperperforming world, it is critical to provide a purposeful context in which we can dedicate our precious energies. Cashman challenges us to courageously be our most authentic selves as we passionately serve the unending human needs in our society."

—**Aaron Hurst, CEO, Imperative, and author of** *The Purpose Economy*

"Cashman can help you sort out two critical realities: transactive management to ensure success now and transformative leadership to create the future. *Leadership from the Inside Out* will give you the agility needed to bridge the dynamics of short-term performance and long-term innovation."

—**Jack Stahl, former CEO and President, Revlon**

"*Leadership from the Inside Out* gives you profound resources for truly inspiring and enduring leadership."

—**Deborah Yates, CHRO, Reckitt Benckiser**

"In the decades I have known Kevin Cashman, he has consistently made his work a masterpiece in the art of leading on purpose. His new edition is an intriguing guide to this art, and it inspires us to take it to the next level."

—**Richard J. Leider, founder of Inventure—The Purpose Company, author of** *The Power of Purpose*, **and coauthor of** *Repacking Your Bags* **and** *Work Reimagined*

"Kevin Cashman's message of staying resilient is critically relevant in today's high-change, high-stress marketplace. *Leadership from the Inside Out* provides a set of tools for managing energy and personal engagement, crucial to stay ahead of the game of leading and living."

—**Jim Loehr, CEO, Johnson & Johnson Human Performance Institute, and coauthor of *The Power of Full Engagement***

"If you want personal transformation, then buy *Leadership from the Inside Out*. It will guide you through the unexplored territories we often miss in our frenetic-paced business world."

—**Trudy Rautio, former CEO, Carlson Companies**

"Today's top talent can spot a phony a mile away. Trust is hard to build and easy to lose. Cashman's resounding message is one of truth and honesty, critical enablers of trust, commitment, and ultimately, great performance."

—**Michael A. Peel, former Vice President, Human Resources, Yale University**

"Some books are noteworthy in and of themselves. Others serve as signs that something important is happening in the world. Kevin Cashman's *Leadership from the Inside Out* meets both criteria. Throw in the fact that it is well-designed for reading and for doing the exercises throughout, and you have a real mind opener."

—**Perry Pascarella, Contributing Editor, *American Management Review*; former Editor-in-Chief, *Industry Week*; and coauthor of *Leveraging People and Profit***

"Kevin Cashman knows people can change, but to really improve the outside, every person needs to understand what's on the inside. This book walks you through a step-by-step process of self-discovery. Anyone who is serious about personal improvement should contemplate the questions posed by this book."

—**Joseph Folkman, coauthor of *The Extraordinary Leader***

"Sooner or later, all leaders who would like to lead more effectively find themselves blocked. Kevin Cashman's book illuminates how we can find the means within ourselves to identify and remove these barriers in order to fulfill our leadership destiny."

—**J. P. Donlon, Editor Emeritus, *Chief Executive* magazine**

"*Leadership from the Inside Out* has produced something any manager should admire: long-term value. As a former bestseller and perennial member on our monthly bestseller list, Cashman's classic has provoked positive change in leaders of all types and backgrounds for years. This revised and expanded work takes the timeless principles first introduced years ago and brings them to life for the next generation of leaders through new examples, new research, and new meaning."

—**Jack Covert, founder and President, 800-CEO-READ**

"*Leadership from the Inside Out* is a testament to the too often forgotten reality that leadership success comes from living your deepest purpose and values as you earn followers, starting with the person in the mirror."

—**Vance Caesar, PhD, CEO, The Vance Caesar Group, and Professor, Pepperdine University**

LEADERSHIP
FROM THE INSIDE OUT

LEADERSHIP
FROM THE INSIDE OUT

Becoming a Leader for Life

THIRD EDITION

KEVIN CASHMAN

Berrett–Koehler Publishers, Inc.
a BK Business book

Berrett-Koehler Publishers, Inc.
1333 Broadway, Suite 1000
Oakland, CA 94612-1921
Tel: (510) 817-2277   Fax: (510) 817-2278   www.bkconnection.com

Ordering Information
Quantity sales. Special discounts are available on quantity purchases by corporations, associations, and others. For details, contact the "Special Sales Department" at the Berrett-Koehler address above.
Individual sales. Berrett-Koehler publications are available through most bookstores. They can also be ordered directly from Berrett-Koehler: Tel: (800) 929-2929; Fax: (802) 864-7626; www.bkconnection.com
Orders for college textbook/course adoption use. Please contact Berrett-Koehler: Tel: (800) 929-2929; Fax: (802) 864-7626.

Distributed to the US trade and internationally by Penguin Random House Publisher Services.

Berrett-Koehler and the BK logo are registered trademarks of Berrett-Koehler Publishers, Inc.

Leadership from the Inside Out and *The Pause Principle* are service marks of Kevin Cashman. *Executive to Leader Institute*, *Chief Executive Institute*, *LeaderSuccession*, and *LifePlan Institute* are all service marks of Korn Ferry.

Printed in the United States of America
Berrett-Koehler books are printed on long-lasting acid-free paper. When it is available, we choose paper that has been manufactured by environmentally responsible processes. These may include using trees grown in sustainable forests, incorporating recycled paper, minimizing chlorine in bleaching, or recycling the energy produced at the paper mill.

Library of Congress Cataloging-in-Publication Data
Names: Cashman, Kevin, author.
Title: Leadership from the inside out : becoming a leader for life / by Kevin Cashman.
Description: Third edition. | Oakland, CA : Berrett-Koehler Publishers,
[2017] | Includes bibliographical references and index.
Identifiers: LCCN 2017019304 | ISBN 9781523094356 (pbk.)
Subjects: LCSH: Leadership. | Executives--Conduct of life. | Executive ability.
Classification: LCC HD57.7 .C373 2017 | DDC 658.4/092--dc23
LC record available at https://lccn.loc.gov/2017019304

Third Edition
23 22 21 20 19 18   10 9 8 7 6 5 4 3 2

TEXT DESIGN: Peggy Lauritsen Design Group   PROOFREAD: Kay Mikel and Lunaea Weatherstone
COVER DESIGN: Studio Carnelian/Dan Tesser   INDEX: Paula C. Westby-Durbin
EDIT: Peter Berry   PRODUCTION: Linda Jupiter Productions

*Dedicated to those value-creating leaders
with the courage to commit to authentic
personal transformation and the passion to
serve the world on-purpose.*

TABLE OF CONTENTS

CHAPTER FOUR: INTERPERSONAL MASTERY

CHAPTER FIVE: CHANGE MASTERY

Chapter Eight: Coaching Mastery

Merging Three Interrelated Coaching Mastery Steps

Coaching Mastery Step One: Building Awareness

Reflection: Building Awareness

Coaching Mastery Step Two: Building Commitment

Reflection: Building Commitment

Coaching Mastery Step Three: Building Practice

Reflection: Building Practice

The Art of Coaching Others

Coaching Others to Build Awareness

Coaching Others to Build Commitment

Coaching Others to Build Practice

Best Practices for Practice

Parting Thoughts for Your Journey Ahead

WHY A NEW EDITION?

It has been two decades since the original writing of *Leadership from the Inside Out*. It is both humbling and fulfilling to know that the book has been integrated into the curricula at more than 150 universities, became a number-one best seller, and continues to influence numerous leadership programs. Occasionally I wonder, "Why did this book catch on?" Was it simply because it was one of the first leadership books to deeply connect personal growth to leadership effectiveness? Perhaps. But, on deeper reflection, I think its resonance was built on the foundation of timeless, enduring principles of human development and life effectiveness. These principles, including authenticity, self-awareness, courage, and purpose, are not simply values that are *nice to have*. They are enduring precepts, deeply woven into the fabric of life, that produce tangible, measureable, cause-and-effect relationships. They serve both parties—people on each side of the dynamic equation—and they tend to sustain their life-enriching impact for the long term. These time-tested core concepts are not fleeting fads, ephemeral fixes, or charm-school interventions. They are fundamental to who we are as human beings and essential to our effectiveness as leaders.

For more than thirty years, we have based our global CEO and Executive Development practice on these same foundational ideas. Since writing the original *Leadership from the Inside Out*, mounting research has caught up with and validated many of these principles. It has been really satisfying to see the work in our real world, client-centered leadership laboratory being supported by research inside and outside of our organization.

Jim Collins, in *Good to Great*, has identified and correlated the principles of authenticity and enduring value creation with his substantial research on "Level 5 Leadership." John Zenger and Joseph Folkman, in *The Extraordinary Leader*, confirmed through their analysis of nearly 400,000 360° assessments that balancing people effectiveness with results orientation produces quantum leaps forward in leadership effectiveness. Daniel Goleman's research studies on emotional intelligence and focus have greatly influenced and supported our work. Korn Ferry Institute researchers David Zes and Dana Landis recently reported groundbreaking research correlating the self-awareness of top leadership with tangible, meaningful financial results.

The Center for Creative Leadership and Korn Ferry have shown that Learning Agility is a greater predictor of potential than raw intellectual intelligence. After assessing more than seven million leaders worldwide, our studies also have demonstrated that effective leaders must move from task-focused, decisive content to strategic and collaborative context to thrive at the top. In addition, emerging research from multiple sources is making the significant connection between purpose-driven leadership, engagement, and performance. It is no longer possible to discount these principles as *soft*; they produce quantifiable results, and they are essential to substantial leadership, team, and organizational success.

Since the last edition, our access to research and thought leadership has expanded exponentially. Why? The Hay Group and PDI Ninth House have become part of the Korn Ferry family, establishing the largest database on leadership effectiveness in the world. It is hard to fathom, but monthly we touch the careers of over 100,000 people. With this huge sample of people and organizations, we can more precisely identify significant patterns. We have incorporated key elements of this important research, learning, and best practice in this edition. We are honored to be a part of the thought leadership lineage at Korn Ferry, which now draws on the distinguished work of Richard Ferry and Lester Korn on executive recruitment and transition; Gary Burnison on leadership and transformation of the talent industry; Bob Eichinger and Michael Lombardo on leadership competencies; Lowell Hellervik, Stu Crandell, and RJ Heckman on leadership assessment and development; Terry Bacon on power, influence, and character; David Dotlich on leadership and executive transitions; Andrés Tapia on inclusive leadership; Edward N. Hay on people and organizational dynamics; Daniel Goleman on emotional intelligence and focus; the late David McClellan on motives, styles, and climate; and Deb Nunes and the late J. Richard Hackman on senior teams.

Since our last writing, we have worked with thousands of leaders in more than eighty countries. We have advised hundreds of CEOs and senior-level executives worldwide in both our *Executive to Leader Institute* and *Chief Executive Institute*. We have custom-designed leadership programs for thousands more high-potential leaders. We have taken scores of senior leadership groups through transformative team programs. Since the first edition, thanks to our Korn Ferry connection, we have grown from one office in one country to over 130 offices globally, and from thirty employees to 7,000. The breadth and depth of this expansion and its commensurate learning has greatly influenced this writing.

In this edition, we have added a new chapter, Story Mastery, which explores the profound ability of narratives to inspire both self-awareness and purposeful influence. Stories are the language of inspirational leadership, so learning how to comprehend, express, and inspire with this "new language" is critical. As you will experience, Story Mastery helps connect Personal Mastery, Purpose Mastery, and Interpersonal Mastery into a more holistic development experience. We also have revamped Action Mastery, crafting it into Coaching Mastery, so that you can learn how to powerfully coach yourself and others to greater leadership transformation. Along with refreshing the research, stories, and quotes in all the other chapters, this edition seeks to be an even more integrated leadership development experience.

In our consulting work, we seek to align personal leadership, team leadership, and organizational leadership to optimize purpose-driven performance. At the core of these levels of leadership is the distinction we make between managers and leaders. *Managers improve what is; managers enhance what is; managers move forward what is. Leaders go beyond what is.* Indeed, if the experience of leadership is like being at the edge of an unfamiliar chasm, the act of leadership is building a bridge across that chasm. *What is the bridge, then, from the known area of transactive management to the unknown area of transformative leadership? How do we build that bridge?* This book will help you address these questions, as well as others, and offers the tools that will help you and your organization transcend what is and grow to the next level of personal, team, and organizational success.

Rich with new insights and inspiration, this new edition of *Leadership from the Inside Out* promises to set you on a provocative, inspiring, and challenging leadership journey. Whether this is your first or your fifth reading, welcome to our shared, courageous journey to authenticity, self-awareness, and purpose-driven leadership from the inside out.

How to Use This Book

. . . from the Inside Out

Leadership from the Inside Out guides you through a reflective journey to grow as a whole person in order to grow as a whole leader. We will not simply analyze the external act of leadership, breaking it down into a simplistic formula of "ten easy-to-follow tips." Instead, you will experience and embody the learning, growth, and transformation to become a leader for life.

You need not rush. As a matter of fact, I encourage you to set aside the urge to plow through the pages. Instead, when a thought or feeling surfaces, pause. Close the book, put up your feet, and explore the insight. If you have a breakthrough, take the time to capture it by writing it down. Instead of just reading the book, experience it, digest it, and integrate it into your life.

You've probably read all sorts of personal and professional development books; treat this one differently. Savor it as you would a walk with an old friend on a calm, sunny afternoon. There is no need to hurry, to anticipate, or to reach the end of your journey. On the contrary, your true reward is in pausing frequently and immersing yourself in the experience itself.

On days you feel like taking a short walk, just skim the quotes. You'll find one or two that speak to your needs that day.

If you are ready to begin, let's take a walk together down the eight pathways to mastery of *Leadership from the Inside Out*.

THE BEGINNING OF THE JOURNEY

It is a magical night—one of those rare December evenings when the cold and the warmth mix just right to blanket everything with big, fluffy, crystalline flakes of snow. Everything looks so perfect; everything feels so silent. As the snow deepens, so does the silence in the atmosphere. I could be viewing this mesmerizing winter scene from a chalet in Switzerland, but I'm not. I'm in bumper-to-bumper traffic on a Minneapolis freeway, and oddly enough, I'm enjoying every minute of it.

Being in a car at rush hour can be a prison or a monastic retreat. It all depends on your perspective. Does it really matter that I'm going to be late? Even though I could feel stressed, I don't. I could use this time to peek at e-mails, catch up on calls, or listen to a podcast. Instead, I welcome the opportunity to sit in the quiet and to reflect. As I sink into a meditative state, I begin to think about my day. And a meaningful day it was—a rich mixture of purpose, passion, emotion, and concentrated learning.

Our consulting team finished guiding a senior executive of a major company through our *Chief Executive Institute*. It was an intense, rewarding three days. We helped the client pull together a profound, integrated plan to better leverage his whole person to impact the whole enterprise. In a way, we helped him step back and observe himself, just as I was observing the snowfall—clearly, objectively, and appreciatively.

At the end of the last session, he said, "You know, I've been through all sorts of assessments, coaching, and development programs. This is the first time things have really made sense to me. I've gotten pieces of the puzzle before, but never the whole picture. I clearly understand where I'm at, where I'm headed, and what I need to do to really enhance my leadership and life. What would my organization be like if a critical mass of leaders mastered the same sense of conviction and clarity that I have now?"

As the snow picks up, I'm feeling very blessed. To occasionally help people connect to their purposeful potential would be lucky. But to coach thousands of leaders, teams, and organizations for more than thirty years and play a role in helping people and organizations actualize their potential is a privilege. I'm feeling very blessed, when suddenly I snap out of my thoughtful state and catch a glimpse of the clock. I'm an hour late! When the heck is this snow going to let up!?

My good fortune goes beyond playing a role in the growth and development of leaders, teams, and organizations. Possibly the greatest blessing is the depth of co-learning along the way. I've had the opportunity to witness the essential human dynamics supporting sustainable success, fulfillment, and effectiveness. But one learning is very clear: these principles are not reserved for a few exceptional leaders. They are fundamental insights available to guide and to inspire us all.

> *Give me beauty in the inward soul; may the outward and inward man be at one.*
>
> —Socrates

While reading this book, you may think, "Is this book about leadership, or is it about personal development?" The answer is yes. It is about both. As much as we try to separate the leader from the person, the two are totally inseparable. Unfortunately, many people tend to split off the act of leadership from the person, team, or organization. We tend to view leadership as merely an external act. We only see it as something people do. This book attempts to expand that view. Leadership is not simply something people do. It comes from a deeper reality within us. It comes from our values, traits, principles, life experiences, beliefs, motives, and essence. Leadership is an intimate expression of who we are; it is our whole person in action. Andreas Guenther, CHRO of Bayer, shared this perspective: "For leadership development programs to be meaningful and lasting in influence, they must be designed to develop the whole person in order to serve the whole business. When leadership programs find this important intersection of the whole leader and the whole business, then great things are possible."

We lead by virtue of who we are. Some people reading this book will make breakthroughs and then lead their own lives more effectively. Others will develop themselves and passionately lead major organizations to new heights. Whether we are at an early stage in our career, a midlevel manager, or a senior executive, we are all CEOs of our own lives. The only difference is the domain of influence. The process is the same; we lead from who we are. The leader and the person are one. As we learn to master our growth as a person, we will be on the path to mastery of *Leadership from the Inside Out.*

What does *mastery* of leadership mean to you? To many people it is mastery *of* something: mastery *of* the skill to be a dynamic public speaker; mastery *of* strategic planning and visioning; mastery *of* consistent achievements and results. Instead of being an ongoing, internal growth process, mastery is usually seen as mastery *of* something outside of ourselves. When you think about it, it's no wonder our ideas about mastery and leadership tend to be externalized. Our training, development, and educational systems focus on learning about *things*. We learn *what* to think, not *how* to think. We learn *what* to do, not *how* to be. We learn *what* to achieve, not *how* to achieve. We learn *about things*, not the *nature of things*. We fill up the container of knowledge but rarely consider comprehending it, expanding it, or using it more effectively.

In organizations, this external pattern continues. As leaders of organizations and communities, we receive recognition for our external mastery. Our success is measured by the degree to which we have mastered our external environment. Revenue, profit, new product breakthroughs, cost savings, and market share are only some of the measures of our external competencies. Few would question the value of achieving and measuring external results. That isn't the real issue. The core questions are: *Where do the external results come from? Is focusing on external achievement the sole source of greater accomplishment? Could it be that our single-minded focus on external results is causing us to miss the underlying dynamics supporting sustainable peak performance?* Malcolm Forbes said, "Only a handful of companies understand that all successful business operations come down to three basic principles: People, Product, Profit. Without TOP people, you cannot do much with the others."

Our definitions of leadership also tend to be externalized. Most descriptions of leadership focus on the *outer manifestations* of leadership (i.e., vision, innovation, results, drive, etc.) instead of getting to the foundational principles of *leadership itself.* For years, many companies came to us with their beautifully crafted leadership models. One day I had a meeting with representatives from one of these companies. When they walked into my office, I noticed that they were carrying an imposing, massive document. They dropped it onto my desk with a thud. When I asked them what it was, they said with obvious pride, "This is our leadership competency model." A bit taken aback by its size, I said, "Gee, it looks pretty big. How many competencies are in there?" With a knowing

> *The two most important days in your life are the day you were born and the day you find out why.*
>
> —Mark Twain

confidence, they said, "Eighty-four." Not sure how to respond to this, but wanting to provoke their thinking, I asked, "Have you ever met one?" The certainty in their eyes disappeared. Their faces twisted into puzzlement, and they asked, "What do you mean?" I explained, "In the whole history of your career and experience in organizations, do you know of anyone who has all these qualities at all times in all circumstances? In your current organization, does anyone possess all these qualities?" They said that they hadn't, and I pressed further. "But you want everybody to develop all eighty-four competencies, right?" We went back and forth like this, settling into a more realistic view of leadership. Companies create perfection myths about what they want or expect of leaders. While aspiring to all those competencies may be a noble growth goal, we have yet to meet the "perfect, fully developed leader."

We are not saying that we do not support competency models. In fact, we help companies globally build leadership competency models directly correlated to their business strategies. But when competency models are perfectionistic, and disconnected from business needs, they are counterproductive.

As a result of seeing too many of these unrealistic competency models, we decided to step back and look at the most effective clients we had assessed, advised, and coached over the last thirty years. After reviewing thousands of leadership assessments, we challenged ourselves with the questions, "What is foundational to the most effective, results-producing leaders? What supports their various competencies or styles on the surface?" Three patterns became clear:

1. *Courage and Authenticity:* Having the courage to authentically be our whole selves, complete with strengths, vulnerabilities, and differences; having the courage to authentically show up with openness and integrity.

2. *Influence:* Purpose-driven communication that inspires self and others to do what is genuinely important and meaningful for the long term.

3. *Value Creation:* Serving multiple constituencies—self, team, organization, family, community, and world—to sustain enduring performance and contribution.

Continuing to evaluate and test these emerging principles over an extended period of research, we landed on what we think is an essential definition:

> *Leadership is courageous, authentic influence that creates enduring value.*

The implications of this definition are potentially far-reaching. From this new perspective, leadership is not viewed as hierarchical; it potentially exists everywhere in organizations. The roles of leadership change, but the core process is the same. Anyone who is courageously and authentically influencing to create enduring value is leading. Some may influence and create value through ideas, others through systems, and yet others through people, but the essence is the same. Deep from their core, leaders courageously bring forward their talents, connect with others, and serve multiple constituencies.

Courage is foundational to all moments of authentic leadership:

- courage to authentically be ourselves
- courage to be vulnerable
- courage to risk judgment and rejection
- courage to stand for the difficult and the unpopular
- courage to explore the new and the different
- courage to do the right thing
- courage to risk our own safety, security, image, and comfort in service to others
- courage to change and be changed

Reacting to this definition of leadership, Paul Laudicina, Chairman of the Global Business Policy Council and former Chairman and CEO of A.T. Kearney, shared, "Leadership is so much more than a hierarchical role. It is how we courageously and authentically show up to serve all those we touch. Real leadership involves inspiring people at all levels to serve something much bigger than themselves."

Using this definition, we acknowledge that there are an infinite number of ways to manifest leadership. There are as many styles of leadership as there are leaders. Viewing leadership from this vantage point, we will be exploring three essential questions to enhance the impact of our leadership:

- How can we enhance our *courage* and *authenticity* as a leader?
- How can we extend our *collaborative, inspiring, purpose-driven influence*?
- How can we create more *enduring value* inside and outside our organization?

Leadership from the Inside Out is about our ongoing journey to discover and develop our purposeful inner capabilities to make a more positive contribution to the world around us.

Bill George, Harvard Business School professor and former Chairman and CEO of Medtronic, shares this view: "As leaders, the more we can unleash our whole capabilities—mind, body, spirit—the more we can create within and outside of our organizations."

Mastery of *Leadership from the Inside Out* is not merely a function of achieving things. It is principally about achieving one thing—consciously and courageously making a bigger difference by fully applying our potential. This does not mean that we only lead from the inside out. On the contrary, we lead just as much—and sometimes more—from the outside in. Leadership involves a constant dynamic between the inner and the outer. We are emphasizing the inside out dynamic because too often it is overlooked. We tend to focus too much on the outside. We are in a continuing flow, a dynamic relationship with ourselves and the constituencies we seek to serve: employees, customers, investors, vendors, local and global communities, and the planet.

> *We convince by our presence.*
> —Ralph Waldo Emerson

Ultimately, we want a balance of leading from the inside out and the outside in. Our decisions and actions are in a dynamic loop from us to others and back again. To practice leadership at its highest level, we need to take responsibility—personal and social responsibility. We need to be equally vigilant about the "I" and the "We" of effective leadership. Daniel Goleman's work precisely identified this inner-outer/outer-inner dynamic as representing the two interactive qualities of emotional intelligence that must connect: awareness of self and awareness of others.

The purpose of this book is to help you master eight ways to lead more effectively. We will do this by sharing our distilled insights from working with thousands of leaders. Although the subsequent chapters will elaborate, here are several essential themes that consistently surface as we help people master their leadership contributions:

- As the person grows, the leader grows. The missing element in most leadership development programs is actually the "Master Competency" of *growing the whole person to grow the whole leader*.
- Most definitions of leadership need to be strengthened from the inside out, moving from viewing leadership only in terms of its external manifestations to seeing it from its internal source as well. Balancing leadership from the inside out and from the outside in gets to the critical dynamic of genuine leadership development.

- Leaders who learn to courageously bring their core talents, core values, core beliefs, and core purpose to conscious awareness experience dramatic, exponential increases in energy, effectiveness, and impact.
- Leaders who balance personal power and results power with relational power, through the power of shared purpose, greatly enhance sustainable performance.
- Leaders who courageously work on authenticity—alignment of their real values and their actions—are more energetic, trust-inspiring, resilient, influential, and interpersonally connected.
- Transforming leadership development programs from a series of fragmented, content-driven events to an integrated, inside out/outside in growth process greatly enhances leadership, team, and organizational excellence.
- Helping leaders move from transactive management focused on speed, accuracy, and performance to transformative leadership, which fosters significance, authenticity, and purpose, greatly accelerates the agile leadership needed today.

Kevin Wilde, longtime Chief Learning Officer for General Mills, who was named "CLO of the Year" by *Chief Learning Officer* magazine, put it this way, "Ultimately, leadership development has to integrate the depth of the inner self-awareness work with the breadth and complexity of external marketplace and cultural dynamics. Enduring leadership development brings together both of these inner and outer realities."

Leadership from the Inside Out involves clarifying our inner identity, purpose, and vision so that our lives thereafter are dedicated to a more conscious, intentional manner of living and leading. This inner mastery directs our diverse intentions and aspirations into a purposeful focus, and increased effectiveness is a natural result. As we move to a more fulfilled manner of living and leading, our attention to purpose transforms our single-minded focus on external success. This purposeful intention and action serves as the energetic, inspiring basis for enduring leadership effectiveness.

> *Try not to become a man of success. Try to become a man of value.*
>
> —Albert Einstein

Unfortunately, I've lost track of the number of times I've met with a CEO, business owner, or corporate executive who had lost connection to this inner core of success.

John, a founder and CEO, approached me a while ago. By all external measures, he was a great success. He had a thriving business. He recently built a new facility to house his expanding operations. But something was missing. When he sat down with me, he opened up immediately by saying, "You know, everyone thinks I'm a big success. My neighbors, friends, and my family look at me, and they see a success. My employees around the globe think I have it all together. But you know what? I'm miserable. I'm unhappy in what I'm doing. My whole life I've been just successfully reacting to circumstances. I got my degree and that defined my first job. That job defined my second job. The same with the third, and so on. Before I knew it I had this business, a family, a mortgage. Recently, I 'woke up' and said to myself, 'Is this me? Is this my life or just a series of circumstances I've successfully reacted to?' I'm not sure what to do, but I have this sense of urgency that I need to take my life back."

> *For this is the journey that men make: to find themselves. If they fail to do this, it doesn't matter much what else they find.*
> —James Michener

From a developmental perspective, many leaders of organizations are like John. We are like naturally gifted athletes who have mastered our external performance capabilities but neglected the inner dynamics supporting our ongoing success and fulfillment. What happens to some of the most gifted athletes who become coaches? They often have an extremely difficult and frustrating time. Why? Most often it is because they have not comprehended, from the inside out, how they become great. As a result, it is challenging for them to mentor others to greatness, and it is equally challenging to be consciously aware of how to replicate their own success in the future. This is why most significant growth and development must begin with self-leadership—mastery of oneself.

When we define our identity and purpose only in terms of external results, the circumstances of our lives define us. In this externally driven state of identity, life is fragile, vulnerable, and at risk. Everything that happens to us defines who we are. We are success. We are failure. We become our circumstances. Life defines us. Our core identity and passionate purpose are overshadowed by the events of our lives. Success may even be present, but mastery has escaped us. Unintentionally, we have chosen to "major" in the "minor" things of life. *Can we lead when we don't see beyond the immediate external circumstances surrounding us?*

Bill, a potential CEO successor in a global company based in Europe, was caught in this external trap, but he didn't know it. His career had been a fast and consistent ascent to the top. He had the "right degree." His background was with the "right companies," and his results were always outstanding. However, his single-minded pursuit of success had great costs. Without intending to, he left a wide wake of frustrated people in his path to success. As a result, he had few close supporters, and team morale was low. At earlier stages in his career, this was not an issue, but as he advanced, it became an increasing problem.

One day the CEO approached him and said, "Bill, your results are outstanding, but we need more than that. The way you're getting results is starting to diminish your effectiveness here." Bill was shocked. A flood of thoughts came to mind: "What do you mean my results are not enough? Since when has my style been an issue? Am I missing something here?" Bill's externally built façade of success was being questioned by his boss and by Bill himself. This jolt was exactly what Bill needed to jumpstart his development to the next level.

After a few days, Bill arrived in my office for leadership development. The shock of his boss's comments and his need to reconcile them with his limited self-understanding had put him in a reflective mood. "I've been avoiding this. If I'm honest with myself, I know I have to do some work. Not the type of work I'm accustomed to, but work on me. But, I'm totally at a loss. My whole life has been focused on achieving at all costs: getting the grades at school, winning in sports, getting results in business. When I'm faced with changing, doing things differently, growing . . . whatever you call it, I'm lost. I'm even beginning to wonder what's really important to me anymore. My life has been invested in getting results. Now that's not enough. What do I do?"

After a couple months of intensive work, Bill began to turn things around. He started to sort out what was really important to him. He began leading more from his core values. He built relationships with people. He asked more questions instead of assuming that he had all the answers. He started to master the power of self-aware, purposeful leadership. His team environment responded to his newfound sense of service. His boss, coworkers, friends, and family all felt that something significant, something of real substance, had begun.

It's important to note that we didn't try to change Bill by taking him through some sort of "charm school." We helped him wake up. He woke up to his identity. He woke up to the influence that he was having on people. He woke up to his values, purpose, and vision. He woke up to how others perceived him. This inside-out and outside-in mastery authentically reconnected him to himself, to others, and to the world around him. It had been there the whole time, but he needed to connect to it. Like Bill, we all fall into a metaphorical slumber at times. Rarely questioning where we are going and why, we go about our business and relationships day after day. Unfortunately, it often takes a traumatic event—a death, a termination, a divorce, a disease, or some other crisis—to bring us out of the depths of our deep sleep. But why wait for a shocking wake-up call? Why not make a more conscious choice to awaken to new potentialities now? If you are up for it, let's begin this journey of awakening together.

REFLECTION

CONSCIOUS WAKE-UP CALL

Go to your favorite spot to sit. Get comfortable. Close your eyes but don't lie down. (Remember, this is an awakening exercise, so our goal is to wake up, not to sleep!) Listen to your internal dialogue and chatter: "This is a dumb exercise!" "Why did I buy this book?" "I'm hungry." "I'm tired." "I'm worried about . . ." Observe the dialogue in a non-judging way. Don't mind your thoughts and feelings; just let them pass in and out. Let your thoughts settle down. This will happen naturally in your non-judging state.

Start to listen. Listen for your inner voice, not the one in your head with the dialogue and thoughts. Listen for the one in your gut, the impulse that speaks to you through feelings, inspirations, intuitions, and possibilities.

From that place, ask questions and listen: "What is really important to me? Is this the life I want to live? What gives passion, meaning, and purpose to my life? How can I better serve, to make even more of a difference? How can I live connected to these inner values?" Pause deeply. Let the questions and answers come to you easily and spontaneously. Enjoy your purposeful pause.

There are many ways to open up to this state: listening to music, taking a walk, going on a run, or sitting in your favorite chair. Use whatever way works for you, and practice this wake-up reflection regularly. If you're a bit uncomfortable or tense at first, don't worry about it. Over time you will settle into it, and your discomfort will pass. *Waking up to the next layer of authentic living and authentic leading is an ever-present and ever-relevant journey.*

When was the last time you woke up in the morning feeling thankful, fulfilled, and happy to be alive? On these days, the sun seemed brighter, your sense of self stronger, your life's purpose clearer, and your mental and physical energies more abundant. These moments did not happen by accident. Several aspects of your life "came together." Your self-recognition, sense of purpose, relationships, career, health, and lifestyle were all "more alive" at these times. As a result, you found yourself thinking, feeling, leading, and achieving in a more positive and energizing way.

> *Only that day dawns to which we are awake.*
>
> — Henry David Thoreau

For at least a brief period of time, each of us experiences these masterful moments. How can we experience them on a more consistent basis? Unfortunately, there is not a simple answer. There are no quick-fix programs in leadership development. Programs that take shortcuts may get some immediate results by temporarily masking acute symptoms, but the chronic situation remains. Over time, the person returns to an even more difficult condition. "Quick fixes" may be quick, but they don't fix anything.

The people I've worked with over the years are looking for something more: courageous mastery of excellence over the long haul. These people are not interested in getting "psyched up" by a motivational speaker; they are interested in substance, results, process, and research-based solutions. They want to reach a deeper, more comprehensive level to master their lives as a whole. They want a holistic, integrated view of leadership.

Leadership from the Inside Out is about unfolding eight mastery pathways to our growth and development. As illustrated here, these mastery areas are not stages of development arranged in a sequential or hierarchical order. Rather, they are an ongoing, interrelated growth process in which each mastery area reinforces the others. When arranged together, we can think of them as an integrated whole, with each mastery area supporting progress toward a more fulfilling destination: *making an enduring difference by bringing forth our gifts to serve others.*

Now it's time to begin our journey. Each of the following chapters offers you pragmatic torches to illuminate your pathways to become a leader for life.

CHAPTER ONE

PERSONAL MASTERY

Leading with Courage, Authenticity, and Awareness

I once heard a poignant story about a priest, who was confronted by a soldier while he was walking down a road in pre-revolutionary Russia. The soldier, using his rifle to block the path of the priest, commanded, *"Who are you? Where are you going? Why are you going there?"*

Unfazed, the priest calmly replied, "How much do they pay you?"

Somewhat surprised, the soldier responded, "Twenty-five kopecks a month."

The priest paused and, in a deeply thoughtful manner, said, "I have a proposal for you. I'll pay you fifty kopecks each month if you stop me here every day and challenge me to respond to those same three questions."

How many of us have a "soldier" confronting us with life's tough questions, pushing us to pause, to examine, and to develop ourselves more thoroughly? If "character is our fate," as Heraclitus wrote, do we step back on a regular basis to question and affirm ourselves and to reveal our character? As we lead others and ourselves through tough times, do we draw on the inner resources of our character, or do we lose ourselves in the pressures of the situation? Are we relentlessly pushing to a better future but forgetting to be our best selves in the present?

BREAKING FREE OF SELF-LIMITING PATTERNS

Joe Cavanaugh is founder and CEO of Youth Frontiers. During one of his powerful character development retreats, Cavanaugh told a moving story about Peter, an elementary school student who suffered burns on 90 percent of his body. Peter's burns were so severe that his mouth had to be propped open so it wouldn't seal shut in the healing process. Splints separated his

> *The ultimate measure of a man is not where he stands in moments of comfort and convenience but where he stands at times of challenge and controversy.*
>
> —Martin Luther King, Jr.

fingers so his hands wouldn't become webbed. His eyes were kept open so his eyelids wouldn't cut him off from the world permanently.

Even after Peter endured one year of rehabilitation and excruciating pain, his spirit was intact. What was the first thing he did when he could walk? He helped console all the other patients by telling them that they would be all right, that they would get through it. His body may have been horribly burned, but his strength of character was whole.

Eventually, Peter had to begin junior high at a school where no one knew him. Imagine going to a new school at that age and being horribly disfigured. Imagine what the other kids would say and how they would react. On his first day in the cafeteria, everyone avoided him. They looked at him with horror and whispered to one another. Kids got up and moved from tables that were close to him. One student, Laura, had the courage to approach him and to introduce herself. As they talked and ate, she looked into Peter's eyes and sensed the person beneath the scarred surface.

Reading her thoughts, Peter, in his deep, raspy, smoke-damaged voice, said, "Everyone is avoiding me because they don't know me yet. When they come to know me, they'll hang out with me. When they get to know the real me inside, they'll be my friends." Peter was right. His character was so strong that people eventually looked beyond the surface. People loved his spirit and wanted to be his friend.

When I consider Peter's situation, I'm not so sure that I would be able to come through his experience with the same courage. But that's the beauty of Personal Mastery. Peter was challenged to awaken his extraordinary strength and to walk down his particular path. It was his path to mastery—not yours, not mine. Somehow his life had prepared him to walk that path with dignity. Each of us is challenged to master our own unique circumstances, although usually under less dramatic conditions than Peter's. *Each of us is being called to lead by authentically connecting our own life experiences, values, and talents to the special circumstances we face.*

Our ability to rise to this challenge depends on our understanding of our deepest, most authentic gifts, as well as the courage to use them despite inner and outer voices that may try to dissuade us. As Maya Angelou so wisely expressed, "You may encounter many defeats, but you must not be defeated. In fact, it may be necessary to encounter the defeats, so you can know who you are, what you can rise from, how you can still come out of it." *Transactive managers strive for single-minded success; transformative leaders extract significant learning from every experience.*

INTEGRATING ALL OF LIFE'S EXPERIENCES INTO A MEANINGFUL CONTEXT

Personal Mastery is not a simplistic process of merely affirming our strengths while ignoring our weaknesses. It is, as Carl Jung would explain it, "growth toward wholeness." It is about acknowledging our talents and strengths while facing the underdeveloped, hidden, or shadow sides of ourselves. It is about honestly facing and reconciling all facets of self. Personal Mastery involves appreciating the rich mixture of our life experience. Peter Senge, in *The Fifth Discipline*, wrote, "People with a high level of Personal Mastery are acutely aware of their ignorance, their incompetence, their growth areas, and they are deeply self-confident. Paradoxical? Only for those who do not see the journey is the reward."

Research originally conducted by Lominger International, now a Korn Ferry company, indicates that defensiveness, arrogance, overdependence on a single skill, key skill deficiencies, lack of composure, and unwillingness to adapt to differences are among the "top ten career stallers and stoppers." A research study by Kenneth Brousseau, Gary Hourihan, and others, published in *Harvard Business Review*, connects the significance of agile growth—an evolving decision-making and leadership style—to leadership and career advancement. This global research on 180,000 managers and executives demonstrated that if people don't develop both strategic and collaborative skills, it is much more challenging to advance.

In a more recent study, researchers David Zes and Dana Landis analyzed 6,977 assessments of managers and executives to identify blind spots and compared the results to the financial data of the 486 publicly traded companies in which the subjects operated. After tracking stock performance over a thirty-month period, Zes and Landis found that organizations with a higher percentage of self-aware leaders (fewest blind spots) had the strongest financial performance. Companies with the least self-aware leaders (most blind spots) had the lowest financial performance. This was a groundbreaking study, the first to correlate self-awareness with financial performance. Despite the research, some leaders still relegate self-awareness to backseat status, regarding it as a soft skill, not critical to business performance. Growing evidence like this makes it difficult to cast self-awareness aside. *Self-aware leaders have the strong, authentic foundation on which to build sustainable performance.*

DEEPENING AUTHENTICITY FOR SUSTAINABLE LEADERSHIP

Of all the principles supporting sustainable leadership, authenticity is one of the most important. It also can be one of the most challenging. Most people never realize that it's an area of their lives that needs attention. In more than three decades of interacting with thousands of leaders, I've yet to meet an executive for coaching who comes to me lamenting, "I'm having real trouble being authentic." If authenticity is so important, why don't we recognize it as an issue within ourselves? The answer is both simple and profound: we are always authentic to our present state of development. We all behave in perfect alignment with our current level of emotional, psychological, and spiritual evolution. All our actions and relationships, as well as the quality and power of our leadership, accurately express the person we have become. Therefore, we conclude that we are "authentic," because we are doing the best we can with the information, experience, competencies, and traits that we have at this time.

There is a big catch, however. *While we are authentic to our current state of development, we are inauthentic to our potential state of development.* As Shakespeare wrote so eloquently in *Hamlet*, "We know what we are, but know not what we may be." As humans and as leaders, we have an infinite ability to grow, to be, and to become. Our horizons are unlimited. If there is an end point to growing in self-awareness and authenticity, I certainly have not seen it.

To deepen authenticity—to nourish leadership from the inside out—takes time, attention, and courage. In today's world, the amount of distraction and busyness we all experience keeps us from undertaking the inward journey and engaging in the quiet reflection required to become more authentic human beings. By middle life, many of us are accomplished fugitives from ourselves. In *Self-Renewal: The Individual and the Innovative Society*, John Gardner writes:

> Human beings have always employed an enormous variety of clever devices for running away from themselves. We can keep ourselves so busy, fill our lives with so many diversions, stuff our heads with so much knowledge, involve ourselves with so many people and cover so much ground that we never have time to probe the fearful and wonderful world within.

To courageously penetrate the commotion and distraction of our lives, to explore the depths of ourselves, is the prerequisite for self-awareness and authenticity. So what is authenticity? Based on our experience assessing and coaching thousands of leaders over the years, we define *authenticity* as the continuous process of building self-awareness of our whole person, as well as being transparent with others about our whole person—both strengths and limitations. This heightened self-awareness allows us to predict our likely responses to a variety of situations. As a result of this awareness, more often than not, the authentic person's beliefs, values, principles, and behaviors tend to line up. Commonly referred to as "walking the talk," authenticity also means embodying your talk at a very deep level.

> There is nothing noble in being superior to your fellow man; true nobility is being superior to your former self.
>
> —Lao Tzu

Authenticity is so much more than simply being true to ourselves; it also requires being true to others. Authenticity carries a much bigger responsibility to speak up, to light up the darkness, and to "shake the spiritual tree," as Ken Wilber puts it. "You must let the radical realization rumble through your veins and rattle those around you," Wilber elaborates. Authenticity is rarely complacent. It is clear about what is important and what needs to change. It is not attracted to convention but is more compelled by courageous conviction. With genuine authenticity, we shake ourselves free from the restrictions of the past and courageously express alternative futures.

Another prominent feature of highly authentic individuals is openness. Whether they come to authenticity naturally or work hard to attain it, the most real, genuine, sincere leaders tend to have the courage to be open about both their capabilities and their vulnerabilities. They have an inner openness about their strengths as well as their limitations. They know who they are and don't apologize for their capabilities. They also have an outer openness about their whole selves. They try neither to cover up their weaknesses nor to "hide their light under a bushel." They have managed to avoid the pitfall that Malcolm Forbes described: "Too many people overvalue what they are not and undervalue what they are." Self-compassion—being open and receptive to our vulnerabilities—is an important aspect of authenticity. By acknowledging our own vulnerabilities and appreciating our whole selves, we can truly be compassionate to others. As David Whyte, poet and author of *The Heart Aroused*, beautifully wrote, "We need to learn to love that part of ourselves that limps."

In *Good to Great*, Jim Collins explains that his research identified the interesting duality in "Level 5 leaders," who are both modest and willful, humble and fearless, vulnerable and strong, interpersonally connected and focused—in short, leaders who "had grown toward wholeness." Their "compelling modesty," as Collins puts it—their authenticity, as we would term it—draws people to come together to achieve.

Authentic people—people on the path to Personal Mastery—have dual awareness of their strengths and vulnerabilities. This more complete self-awareness allows them to focus on the team, organization, and marketplaces—not on themselves. Personal Mastery allows us to transcend our egos and move into authentic service and authentic contribution. As Collins elaborates, "Level 5 leaders channel their ego away from themselves and into the larger goal of building a great company. It's not that Level 5 leaders have no ego or self-interest. Indeed they are incredibly ambitious, but their ambition is first and foremost for the contribution, not for themselves." Level 5 leaders—authentic leaders—see their purpose beyond their limited selves as passionate instruments of service and contribution. As the late David McClelland elucidated in *The Achieving Society*, effective leaders use their Socialized Power in service to a more purpose-driven achievement motive. *Authentic leaders harness their gifts to serve something greater.*

> *The privilege of a lifetime is to become who you truly are.*
>
> —Carl Jung

In Daniel Goleman's extensive research on emotional intelligence in the workplace, Goleman cites self-awareness—"attention to one's own experience," or mindfulness—as the primary competence in his framework for managing ourselves, which is a prerequisite for managing others. In *Primal Leadership: Learning to Lead with Emotional Intelligence*, Goleman and his coauthors, Richard Boyatzis and Annie McKee, assert, "A leader's self-awareness and ability to accurately perceive his performance is as important as the feedback he receives from others." The flow of crucial information to develop our courageous authenticity comes from the inside out and from the outside in.

While most leadership research does not suggest authoritarian leadership approaches as ideal in what Thomas Friedman has coined as today's "flat" world, I have seen some authoritarian leaders with substantial authenticity outperform leaders who strove to be collaborative, yet lacked authenticity. I've seen leaders low in charisma and polish get in front of a group and stumble around a bit, but their personal authenticity and substance were so tangibly established that they inspired the group members and moved them to a new level of excellence. Could such leaders benefit from working on their leadership approaches? Certainly. But how much would it really matter, compared with their trust-inspiring authenticity? "The individual who does not embody her messages will eventually be found out," warns Howard Gardner in *Leading Minds*. "Even the inarticulate individual who leads the exemplary life may eventually come to be appreciated."

THE AUTHENTICITY AND COURAGE TEST

Challenges to our authenticity come in small and big moments. Every day, possibly in every leadership moment, our authenticity is tested. Do we put a little spin on an explanation to make it look better? Do we risk sharing an emotional, inspiring story? Do we slow down and show care and concern in the heat of performance? Do we reveal a vulnerability to build trust and connection? Do we take advantage of people or situations because we can? Small but significant tests of authenticity and courage await us from moment to moment.

Sometimes, truly big moments test and reveal our authenticity and character. Steve Reinemund was Chairman and CEO of PepsiCo during a period of extraordinary growth. Earnings grew 90 percent. But the focus of the business was on more than results; they constantly preached *"Winning the Right Way."* This mantra resonated deeply in the culture.

Recently, Steve reflected on this time and shared with me an interesting story:

> One day, a mysterious envelope arrived at the Pepsi headquarters, marked for one of our key executives. His administrative assistant opened it and was surprised to find that it was filled with trade secrets from a prominent competitor. Someone had anonymously sent them. Within an hour, the administrative assistant had packed up the envelope with its contents and had delivered it back to our competitor's headquarters. Fortunately, she knew the right thing to do. Yes, it would have been highly advantageous for us to possess those documents. But it would have been "winning the wrong way." We gave the administrative assistant a Chairman's Award as a demonstration of our pride and gratitude in how well she embodied our company's values.

This was truly a big authenticity test, a big leadership moment. In that moment, their years of investing in their authentic values paid off. "Winning the right way" had become the only way. *Transactive managers do things right; transformative leaders do the right thing.*

EXPLORING BELIEFS

One of the most effective ways to take this journey to a more integrated, authentic understanding of ourselves is to intentionally explore our personal belief systems. Few psychological dynamics are as fundamental as our beliefs. Beliefs literally create our reality; they are the lenses or filters through which we interpret the world. Some of these "lenses" focus and open up new horizons; others dim our view and limit possibilities. Beliefs are transformational. Every belief we have transforms our life in either a life-enriching or life-limiting way. As Bruce Lipton wrote in *The Biology of Belief*, "Our beliefs control our bodies, our minds, and our lives." In a sense, beliefs are the "software of leadership," our deeply personal operating system that runs the show on the surface.

One of the most dramatic examples of the transformational power of beliefs comes from heavyweight fighter George Foreman. In the 1970s, Foreman was renowned for being one of the toughest, nastiest human beings on the planet. Angry and antisocial, he often came across as a mean, uncommunicative person, not at all the person you see today. He was not known for social graces, self-awareness, or his big smile. However, immediately following his surprising loss to Jimmy Young in Puerto Rico, George went to his dressing room, lay down on the training table, and reportedly had an overwhelming spiritual experience. After that experience, George changed. He changed his entire life, everything: his personality, his relationships, and his life purpose. He transformed them all into a more life-affirming direction.

George peeled the onion of his personality, and the delightful, humorous, self-effacing "George" came forward. The important thing to note here is not whether George Foreman actually had a spiritual revelation. Many medical professionals said he suffered from severe heat exhaustion, and that's what caused his "experience." That's not the issue. The key principle is that George Foreman believed that he had a spiritual transformation, and that belief changed his life. *What we believe, we become.*

Through our years of coaching people, we have consistently observed two distinct types of belief systems operating in people: *Conscious Beliefs and Shadow Beliefs.* Conscious Beliefs are the explicit, known beliefs we have. When asked what our beliefs are about ourselves, about other people, or about life in general, we can articulate many of them. Even though it may take some effort to access and to clarify some of these beliefs, they are accessible to us on an everyday level. Examples of Conscious Beliefs someone might have are, "I believe in treating people with respect; I fear trying new things; I am creative and resilient; many

people are untrustworthy; hard work brings results." Although we can acces
a conscious level, this does not mean we are always aware of them. We can,
easily enhance awareness of Conscious Beliefs and of whether or not we are li
dance with them.

Recently, we guided the chairman of the board of a fast-growing public company through the process of bringing his beliefs into conscious awareness. As a result, the sixty-year-old chairman remarked, "Most people probably think I had this all figured out. What I discovered is that my beliefs were operating, but not consciously enough. After more than thirty years in leadership roles, I realize that unknowingly I've been holding back aspects of myself, crucial to continued leadership success. Once I saw it in my work, it was easy to see that I was doing the same thing at home with my family."

Elena was an executive in a global service firm in the United Kingdom. Her intelligence, energetic work ethic, results orientation, and excellent relationship skills had supported her pattern of success. She prided herself on how connected the people on her team were, with both her and each other. However, team members conducted themselves carefully, and they rarely engaged in conflict.

> *There is but one cause of human failure and that is a man's lack of faith in his true self.*
>
> —William James

One day, during a one-on-one with her boss, Elena was taken aback when her boss said, "Elena, you've been on the team for a while now, and you never disagree with me. I don't really know if you are really invested in all these new changes we're making, or if you are just going along with them. You're too nice! I need you to step forward more powerfully and challenge me."

Ingrained in Elena from a young age was the fear of rejection, which was fueled by the belief that being liked and accepted was the only way to really get the acknowledgment and respect that she craved. Elena's boss encouraged her to see that speaking up—being more open—is not only more respectful but also more authentic. After working with Elena for a while, we were able to help her break free of Shadow Beliefs around rejection and to see that fostering more open discussions, even constructive conflict, surfaces unspoken issues and produces more trust, respect, innovation, and acknowledgment.

Although we access Conscious Beliefs somewhat easily, Shadow Beliefs are subtler and much more challenging to uncover. Doing so, however, is crucial to high performance. Taken from the Jungian concept of shadow, Shadow Beliefs are manifestations of hidden, unexplored, or unresolved personality dynamics. A Shadow Belief is cast when we are unable to deal with something. When a deep-seated fear, loss, or trauma is ignored or hidden, a Shadow Belief is operating beneath the surface.

We all have Shadow Beliefs. If we don't think we do, then a shadow is probably operating at precisely that moment by obscuring some aspect of ourselves. Jeff Patnaude, in his work *Leading from the Maze*, writes, "The leader must be awake and fully alert. Like a nighttime traveler attuned to every sound in the forest, the leader must be aware of all possibilities lurking in the shadows. For we can neither challenge nor transform what we cannot see."

> *The spring wakes us, nurtures us and revitalizes us. How often does your spring come? If you are a prisoner of the calendar, it comes once per year. If you are creating authentic power, it comes very frequently.*
>
> —Gary Zukav

On a personal level, some of my Shadow Beliefs have to do with exceptionally high standards for others and myself. From a young age, I evaluated myself by this external, often critical, yardstick. As a result, I developed a series of Shadow Beliefs: "I'm never quite good enough; I have to work twice as hard to be valued; if something is not exceptional, it is not worthwhile; I am afraid to fail." As you can see, these beliefs have some value. They have fueled a drive to achieve. On the other hand, some of these same beliefs cast a shadow on my behavior and relationships at times. However, when I am actively committed to fostering my awareness of these shadows, I've been able to shed some light on them and hopefully minimize their limiting influence on others and me, particularly in stressful times.

Transforming Shadow Beliefs to Conscious Beliefs is crucial to Personal Mastery. This is not to say we don't struggle continually with them. We do. The difference is that we consciously and courageously engage them rather than unconsciously being driven by them. What happens to us if we don't deal with Shadow Beliefs? We pay a high price. Addictive behaviors, difficulty in relationships, achievement overdrive, a domineering or weak leadership voice, imbalanced lifestyles, and health problems can be some of the costs. Shadow Beliefs are not scary; not dealing with them is.

While I was coaching Edward, the divisional president of a multibillion-dollar glo
zation, a Shadow Belief that was limiting him surfaced. Let me preface this story by
that Edward was not referred to us because he had some-
thing "to fix." He was wildly successful in his current role.
His consumer products firm was number one in revenue
and market share globally for four consecutive years. It was
his success that was starting to be a problem for him. He
had this nagging anxiety: "Can I continue to top my past
achievements?" Each time we would explore future plans,
he would conjure up all sorts of disaster scenarios. As I got
to know him better, I understood that he had internalized a hidden belief that no matter how hard he worked or
what he achieved, it could all go away tomorrow.

> *To leave our self-defeating behaviors behind, we must use our conscious minds to undermine the destructive but unconscious beliefs that cause us to defeat ourselves.*
>
> —Milton Cudney and Robert Hardy

On one level, this Shadow Belief served him well; it gave
him the drive to achieve many goals. However, because he wasn't aware of it, his fear of failure was actually inhibiting him from risking new experiences and new learning. It also was
squeezing the life out of his team, a side effect totally inconsistent with his values and intentions. Finally I asked Edward, "You don't get it, do you?" Surprised, he looked at me and said,
"Get what?" I responded, "Edward, look at your life. You succeed in all areas of your life: your
career, your family, and your relationships. What evidence do you have that you are going to
fail at your next endeavor?"

It was a defining moment for Edward. He saw the shadow and brought it into the light. He
moved from trusting his fear to trusting his real value. He transformed a Shadow Belief into a
Conscious Belief. Before that moment, he wasn't aware of its presence. It had been controlling
him, and now he was beginning to take control of it. A few months later, describing his experience, he said, "This one insight has opened a doorway for me. It has given me the peace of
mind to trust myself and to lead from who I am. I now know that no matter what I attempt, I
will make it a success, and if not, I will adapt, learn, and make something new work."

REFLECTION

CONSCIOUS BELIEFS

Take a few minutes to explore some of your Conscious Beliefs—the self-conversations we have that reveal what we hold to be true, important, and of value:

- What do you believe about yourself?

- What do you believe about other people?

- What do you believe about your teams?

- What do you believe about life?

- What do you believe is your impact or influence on others?

- What do you believe about leadership?

SEVEN CLUES THAT BRING SHADOW BELIEFS TO LIGHT

How often have you heard the expression that "an overdeveloped strength can become a weakness"? Although there is some truth to this statement, there is also a deeper underlying dynamic. Why do some strengths turn into weaknesses? Usually because some Shadow Belief is operating in parallel with the strength. *Leaders either shed light or cast a shadow on everything they do. The more conscious their self-awareness, the more light leaders bring. The more limited their self-understanding, the bigger the shadow a leader casts.*

Let's say we have a Shadow Belief that "we only have value if we are doing and achieving." If we are unaware of this Shadow Belief, our drive and determination will soon turn into workaholism and lack of intimacy, with profound negative implications for our health and relationships. Let's say we have intelligence and self-confidence as strengths, combined with a Shadow Belief that "we always have to be right." Without sufficient awareness, our self-confidence will turn into arrogance, abrasiveness, and self-righteousness. Here are some other examples of how shadows can potentially turn strengths into weaknesses:

STRENGTH	+	SHADOW BELIEF	=	WEAKNESS
Energy		"I can never give up."		Hyperactive
Charm		"I must succeed no matter what."		Manipulative
Conscientiousness		"I can always do better."		Compulsive
Focus		"I must know every detail."		Micro-managing
Courage		"I must always achieve more."		Foolhardiness
Influence		"I must always be seen as exceptional."		Self-Focused

Because our shadows are often hidden from our own view, how can we bring them to light? Over the years, we've developed seven clues to indicate when a shadow may be operating:

- *Shadow Clue One:* If other people often give us feedback inconsistent with how we see ourselves, a shadow is likely present.
- *Shadow Clue Two:* When we feel stuck, blocked, or at a real loss as to what to do next, a shadow may be holding us back.
- *Shadow Clue Three:* As strengths become counterproductive, some hidden dynamics need to surface.
- *Shadow Clue Four:* When we are not open to new information, new learning, or other people's views, a shadow may be limiting us.
- *Shadow Clue Five:* If we react to circumstances with emotional responses disproportionate to the situation, we are likely operating under a Shadow Belief.
- *Shadow Clue Six:* When we find ourselves forcefully reacting to the limitations or differences of others in a critical, judgmental way, our shadow is likely projecting our limitations or fears onto others.
- *Shadow Clue Seven:* If we often experience pain, trauma, or discomfort in our body, a shadow may be attempting to rise to the surface to seek reconciliation. Listen to the wisdom of your body as you look to uncover Shadow Beliefs.

Craig, an executive we worked with, was caught in the executive syndrome of "having it all together." He feared that revealing any of his limitations would result in others perceiving him as weak or inadequate. He also honestly believed others didn't perceive his underdeveloped side. After we examined his 360° assessment together, he realized others saw his limitations even more clearly than he did, and the coaching process began.

Fortunately, after he had experienced several months of coaching, a major business crisis surfaced. Here was the perfect opportunity for Craig to practice what he had learned. Clearly, he had made some mistakes leading up to the crisis. Rather than continuing the old pattern, he faced the troops, acknowledged his mistakes, and asked for their support. His coworkers were shocked and understandably hesitant at first, but they admired his courage and stepped forward to solve the crisis. Commenting on his experience, Craig told me, "I thought my power was in being *right*. Now I understand my power is in being *real*." Authentic Personal Mastery had begun.

THE COURAGEOUS PRACTICE OF AUTHENTICITY

What happens when we are around highly competent people who have the courage to be real and open about themselves and the situations they face? We trust them. Their authenticity, vulnerability, and Personal Mastery have made them trustworthy, and we rush to their side.

> *Personality can open doors. Only character can keep them open.*
> —Elmer Letterman

When asked by Charlie Rose, "What's the most important quality today for leadership?" Howard Schultz, CEO of Starbucks at that time, replied, "To display vulnerability." In his book *Pour Your Heart into It*, Schultz says, "Although they can hire executives with many talents and skills, many CEOs discover that what they lack most is a reliable sounding board. They don't want to show vulnerability to those who report to them." He advises, "Don't be afraid to expose your vulnerabilities. Admit you don't know what you don't know. When you acknowledge your weaknesses and ask for advice, you'll be surprised how much others will help."

David MacLennan, Chairman and CEO of Cargill, one of the world's largest private companies with $107 billion in annual revenue, shared this perspective on authenticity:

> A critical part of transparency and a real test of leadership authenticity is having people come up to you and say, "Hey, this is what I think is wrong. Were you aware of this?" as opposed to, "Look out. There's the CEO. I better not speak up." Your real "authenticity

audit" is the degree to which people are open to you, because you have been open, vulnerable, and honest with them.

When people know you will deeply and authentically listen to them, people will be authentic and honest with you. When asked to clarify his key authenticity practices, David shared ten principles:

- Be comfortable in your own skin; don't ever try to fake realness.
- Never take yourself too seriously; it is not usually about you.
- Share stories of personal failure, vulnerability, and learning; authenticity shows the full picture of who you are.
- Don't believe your own press or focus too much on your accomplishments. Remember, you really are that "kid inside," just trying to do your best.
- Surround yourself with people who will give you feedback. I once was told, "You look tired and you need a haircut." Authenticity is a pragmatic and profound gift.
- Earn the right to be trusted by being courageously truthful. Engage in caring, direct, and courageous conversations. Authenticity is a two-way exchange; it multiplies trust with all those it touches.
- Encourage diversity, and encourage everyone to bring the best in themselves to work; authenticity is inclusive.
- Narrow the gap between your work self and your private/home self; authenticity is being the same person everywhere, in all situations.
- Stay humble to learn, and stay confident to serve; authentic leaders know when to listen, when to be bold, and when to be a learner.
- Dedicate yourself to purpose-driven service. Authenticity is all about service to all stakeholders in all leadership moments.

Toward the end of our conversation, David reflected, "Cargill is so much bigger than I am. I am the ninth CEO in a 150-year history. One day I will be another 'oil painting' on the wall that people barely remember. Authenticity is knowing that life, leadership, and the organization are all so much bigger and so much more important than I am."

In the end, authenticity requires courageous action. David was one of the first CEOs in the United States to be brave enough to publicly speak out against potentially restrictive trade and immigration policies. During a CNN interview on the need for CEOs to weigh in with authenticity and courage on major policy issues, Jeffrey Immelt, former Chairman and CEO of General Electric, asserted, "It is insincere to not stand up for those things that you believe in. . . . We are cowards if we don't take a position on those things that are consistent with our mission and where our people stand."

LEADING IN CHARACTER . . . LEADING BY COPING

If leadership from the inside out is an authentic and courageous influence that creates enduring value, how do we go about expressing ourselves more authentically? Authenticity requires a lifelong courageous commitment to self-discovery, self-observation, and self-authorship. Because the word *authenticity* comes from the same Greek root as the word *author*, I'm sure no one would be surprised that authoring your own life is a continuous journey.

However, in coaching leaders to develop more authentic dimensions of self, we have found some helpful practices to bring out the essence of who we are. When a leader approaches the question, "How authentic am I?" it is often helpful to ask some other questions first: "Where is my leadership coming from? Where are my beliefs and values coming from?" We need to constantly consider the origin of our leadership in various circumstances. Is our leadership serving only ourselves—our career and success—or is it also focused on our team and organization? Is our leadership arising from our *Character*, which is driven to serve others? Or is it derived from a pattern of *Coping*, where we tend to react to circumstances to elicit a more immediate or self-serving result?

Some approaches to leadership are reactive, consume energy, and produce unsustainable or undesirable results. Other approaches are transformative, add energy to the undertaking, and create value for the short and long term. The former approaches come from qualities of Coping, and the latter approaches derive from Character.

Terry Bacon, a colleague and the author of *The Elements of Power*, has conducted research on the personal sources of power. His findings identify five personal power sources: knowledge, expressiveness, history, attractiveness, and character. Significant in his research, "character is the only source of power that can add to or subtract from every other source. You can be very knowledgeable, eloquent, attractive and have existing relationships with the people you are trying to influence, but if they perceive that your character is flawed, your power to lead and influence them will be greatly diminished." On the positive side of character, Bacon writes, "Being recognized as a person of character enhances your capacity to lead and influence others because they trust your intentions, are more confident in your leadership, and see you as a person worth emulating."

In a 2017 research study conducted by James Lewis and Stu Crandell of Korn Ferry Institute, assessment results from 1,110 managers and executives were analyzed to discern the leadership competencies that differentiated C-suite executives from midlevel managers. Research was reviewed across thirty-eight leadership competencies and five industry sectors. Which competency rose to the top as the differentiator in multiple environments between senior leadership and midlevel management? Courage.

The ideal is in thyself; the impediment, too, is in thyself.
—Thomas Carlyle

Interestingly, courage is one of those rare leadership characteristics, like trust, that is both a competency and a character trait. *Courage and trust are foundational to progressive and sustained leadership performance; courage gives us the strength to create the future, and trust keeps us together as we venture into the unknown.* Therefore, courage and character are not merely desirable, more ethical ways to lead; they are fundamental to leading versus managing. *Transformative leaders create the future with courage and character; transactive managers ensure present performance with control.*

Character works to transform and open up possibilities and potential. When we are leading from character, we exude qualities of authenticity, courage, purpose, openness, trust, congruence, compassion, and service. We have the ability to transform circumstances, open up possibilities, and create lasting value for ourselves and for others. *The Character-driven leader tends to emphasize service over self.*

Coping protects us and helps us get through challenging circumstances. In this sense, it has value and, if used sparingly and appropriately, will serve very specific needs. Coping works like a muscle. We need to use it at times, but if we overuse it, the muscle will collapse. Qualities of Coping include concern for image, safety, security, comfort, or control. The Coping leader may get results but also exhibits defensiveness, fear, withdrawal, or a desire to win at all costs. He or she may exclude certain people or information. *The Coping-driven leader tends to emphasize self over service.*

Both Character and Coping are present in most leadership situations. However, we need to ask ourselves, "Which one is my master, and which one is my servant?" When we make

Character the master of our leadership and Coping the servant, we move toward better relationships and create lasting value.

QUALITIES OF CHARACTER AND COPING

As leaders, it is essential to learn how to build our awareness of when we are being guided by Character and when we are being guided by Coping. The following table illustrates some of the behaviors that indicate whether we are in a Character pattern or a Coping pattern:

LEADING BY COPING	LEADING IN CHARACTER
Reacts to Circumstances and Spends Energy	*Transforms Circumstances and Multiplies Energy*
GUIDED BY	**GUIDED BY**
Serving Self	Serving Others
Fear	Courage
Control	Collaboration
Building Image	Building Authenticity
Safety-Security-Comfort	Purpose
Short-Term	Long-Term
Exclusion	Inclusion
Winning at All Costs	Serving at All Costs
Focus on Silos	Focus on Enterprise
Destructive Conflict	Constructive Conflict
Distraction	Presence
Uncomfortable Demeanor	Calm Demeanor
Overwhelmed by Circumstances	Above Circumstances
Criticism/Judgment	Tolerance/Openness
Dogmatism	Wisdom
Arrogance	Humility
Entrenchment	Transcendence

Let's explore three examples:

*1. **Building Image vs. Building Authenticity:*** When we care a bit too much how we look to others and focus on getting their approval, adulation, or acceptance, our leadership may be guided by an Image Coping pattern. We are in this image persona when we try too hard to "look great"; when we present ourselves as more than we are; when our brand is more important than our substance; and when we misrepresent values, beliefs, or other information to win acceptance.

> *Character is like a tree, and reputation its shadow. The shadow is what we think of it; the tree is the real thing.*
>
> —Abraham Lincoln

Recently, I was coaching the CEO of a firm along with one of his key executives, Michelle. Although the CEO needed to work on a few crucial growth areas, authenticity was not one of them. Michelle, however, was unknowingly caught up in her image. At a critical point in one of their interactions, as Michelle was overanalyzing all the political implications of a recent, highly public failure, the CEO calmly and compassionately asked, "Michelle, do you want to look good, or do you want to make a difference?"

Michelle fell silent. Of course she wanted to make a difference. She needed someone to shock her out of investing herself fully in Coping and into shifting her awareness to leading from Character. In *The Corporate Mystic*, Gay Hendricks and Kate Ludeman reinforce this practice: "It is as important to challenge people about their personas as it is to love and cherish their true essence. In the business world it is dangerous to ignore people's personas. Genuinely caring for people means seeing them as they are, not blithely overlooking fatal flaws."

*2. **Safety, Security, and Comfort vs. Purpose:*** If our actions are principally guided by safety, security, and comfort, we are in a Coping pattern. This is a big one for most of us. It is also subtle. We are usually unaware of how staying safe is actually limiting new experiences and possibilities. How often have most of us thought, "When I build up enough assets, then I'll go do what I really want to do"? This is the voice of Coping. In the executive ranks, this can be a major issue. While we, as senior executives, seek to become more comfortable (financially and otherwise), do we continue to risk innovative, meaningful, out-of-the-box initiatives? Or, worse, do we postpone our real purpose and contribution for that mythical future moment when we will be safe and secure enough to fully express ourselves?

I was working with a senior marketing executive who was caught in this Coping pattern. The first day I met Jack, he told me he had lost his passion for his work and was preparing to leave his organization to seek a new opportunity. After spending some time together, he shared his career-life vision: to accumulate assets in order to replace his current income and, in five years, start his own business. On the surface, it sounded all right. As we went deeper, however, it became apparent that he had sacrificed his purpose on the altar of security and comfort. Driven by his need to accumulate money in an attempt to build his inner sense of security, he had gradually lost touch with what really gave him meaning: *using his creativity and insight to help others achieve their potential.* Once Jack reconnected to his purpose, he returned to his work with renewed passion, perspective, and boldness.

When we are caught up in Coping, we seek solutions outside ourselves, like changing a job, accumulating enough money to feel secure, or changing a relationship. Too often we seek solutions in the "Whats" instead of the "Hows" or "Whys." Jack needed to relearn how to show up in his life in a renewed way. He learned how and why it was vital to clarify purpose and to lead in Character.

3. *Control vs. Collaboration:* If our energies are absorbed in having the world conform to our will, with a desire to avoid nearly all surprise, then we are likely leading from a place of Coping. This is particularly challenging if we are moving from managerial to leadership roles in an organization. *Managers control by virtue of their heroic doing; leaders collaborate by virtue of their generous being.* When we are rapidly alternating between management and leadership, as is often the case, the relationship between control and openness is a constant dynamic.

> *Character also means putting the greater good of the organization and society ahead of self-interest. It's about worrying about "what is right" rather than "who is right."*
>
> —Noel Tichy and Warren Bennis

Tracy, a senior-level executive for an international service firm, was clearly operating in a Control Coping pattern. It was actually her "winning formula." She viewed herself as an exceptionally competent person, and by all external measures, she was. Based on a series of outstanding achievements in sales and marketing, she had been on the fast track in her company. She was known for always exceeding the need. If the organization wanted something done exceptionally well, Tracy was the one recruited for the job. Some would say she had mastered her profession, maybe even mastered some aspects of her external environment. But her external success was not based on internal mastery. Her obsessive need to control everything around her had created strain in all her relationships. Her marriage wasn't surviving her need to control. Without understanding why, she gradually drove away nearly everyone around her. For many years, her external competence had been sufficient to help Tracy face her life and career demands. However, her expanding life and leadership demands involved competence of a different order. Tracy was a leader whose take-charge, task-focused style worked well in her career—up to a point. If she had been unwilling to pause for awareness and growth, she could easily have become among those executives whose careers hit the wall and got stuck, falling short of their potential.

Before Tracy could move to the next stage of her leadership and life effectiveness, she needed to access a platform of internal competence and character. It took a few months of coaching, but to her credit, she slowly came to the realization that her excessive need to control was based on a Shadow Belief. She had come to believe that just being herself and trusting that things would work out was not an option. At a crucial point in our coaching, she said, "If I stopped controlling everything, my life would fall apart!" The instant she said it, the paradox hit her with full force. Her life was falling apart *because* she was so controlling, yet she felt that control was her only savior. Over time, she gained the Personal Mastery to begin trusting and to be more open to change. As her self-awareness, self-trust, and openness grew, Tracy's ability to trust and to appreciate others grew as well. She had begun leading in Character.

REFLECTION

CHARACTER AND COPING

Take some time to review and reflect on the qualities that guide Character and Coping listed on page 30.

Think about the qualities of Coping as you consider these questions:

- Particularly in times of stress, which of these qualities of Coping are most prevalent for you?

- What is going on during those times? Inside you? Outside you?

- How do you feel? What do you notice in your body? What do you notice in your relationships?

- What fears, limitations, inadequacies, or beliefs arise when you are in a Coping pattern?

Now reflect on the qualities of Character, and consider these questions:

- Which of these Character qualities are more prevalent for you?

- What is going on when these Character qualities are present?

- How do you feel?

- How can you continue to lead from Character in more situations?

As we have seen, Character transforms, whereas Coping tends to be more of a reactive survival mode. When we are in a Coping pattern, we tend to see the problems of life as existing outside ourselves. We say to ourselves, "If I could only change this person or that situation, then everything would be fine." But life's problems are rarely resolved by only changing the external situation. Lasting solutions involve dealing with our internal situation in order to transform the external circumstance.

To illustrate the difference between Character and Coping responses, imagine Nelson Mandela many years ago saying, "I think I need to leave South Africa. The situation here is just too big a problem. These people just don't get it. I need to go to a more comfortable, accommodating country." It is absurd even to imagine this scenario with a person of so much courage and Character. When Character and purpose are weak, then our initial Coping response is usually to leave or escape our situation. When purpose is strong, leaders transform many of the circumstances they encounter. Obviously, there may be times when we need to leave or walk away from a situation for self-preservation. However, if our first response is consistently to exit challenging circumstances, then we probably need to work on leaning into Character more often.

> *Corporate Mystics develop a kind of double vision, at once able to see the mask and the essential person inside. . . . They know that we all have personas that are wrapped around our true essence, but they also know that we are not our personas.*
>
> —Gay Hendricks and
> Kate Ludeman

It's important to note that Personal Mastery is not about eliminating Coping. It is about increasing Character to such a degree that Character is primary and Coping is secondary. Coping exists for a reason—to protect us and deal with threatening situations—so we don't want to eliminate it completely. It serves a purpose. But we do want to favor Character so that this more substantial way to lead becomes the master of our behavior. To have Character the master and Coping the servant—the inner supporting the outer—is the goal of Personal Mastery.

Leading with Character is not easy. The CEO of a rapidly growing firm shared this comment with me: "I hate to admit it, but most organizations reward Coping. We talk about Character, but we reward Coping. We extol the values of trust, inclusion, and adding value, but we consistently reward control and image. Most of us are unwilling to do the hard work and to take the personal risk to lead in Character."

Unfortunately, some executive coaching programs reinforce Coping rather than fostering Character. Executives are coached *how to act* instead of *how to be*. It's a charm-school process that produces only superficial, short-term results. Executives are coached to polish the

> *The wisest mind has something yet to learn.*
> —George Santayana

exterior, but rarely does any real, substantial, and sustained growth take place. Under sufficient stress, all the old patterns return. Coaching the whole person, light and shadow, sustains real leadership development.

UNDERSTANDING OUR OWNER'S MANUAL

Many of us know more about our favorite vacation spot, sports team, or running shoes than we do about ourselves. To break out of old patterns and grow as a whole person, we need to answer, "Who am I?" As we take on this question, we may stir up our internal critic, or we may return with a quick answer that superficially reflects the roles we play instead of who we really are.

The other day I sat down with a CEO for an initial coaching session. With a bit of nervous bravado, the executive proclaimed, "Kevin, you know, I know myself pretty well." Honestly, I've been in situations like this so many times I envisioned a subtitle across his chest that read, "He doesn't know himself very well." On the other hand, when I meet with someone who admits, "You know, I understand some aspects of myself, but others are still a mystery to me," then my envisioned subtext says, "This person knows himself pretty well."

Perhaps the reason most people think they know themselves well is that their perception of their inner world is restricted to very narrow boundaries. Few people would claim that they know everything outside themselves. We all understand how unfathomable external knowledge and information is. We see the external world as huge. Our inner life, however, is defined too often in a very restricted way. When we get on the path to Personal Mastery, we begin to glimpse how deep, broad, and unbounded our inner life really is. When people casually say, "I know myself," all too often they are really saying, "I know my limited state of self-knowledge." There are no limits within us. There is no end to Personal Mastery; it is likely as vast and grand as the external world that we observe. Begin your journey by considering life's big questions: *"Who are you? Where are you going? Why are you going there?"* That soldier just crossed our path again, didn't he?

Personal Mastery is about comprehending the vehicle that brings us to our destination. There's just one problem: We've temporarily lost the "owner's manual." It's like buying a high-performance sports car without learning how to drive it. Sure, we know how to drive, but we don't understand how to drive *that* vehicle. How are we ever going to arrive safely at our desired destination when we don't understand that taking a curve at sixty-five miles an hour on a wet road at midnight with a certain suspension system is an invitation for disaster? That's exactly how many leaders lead—barreling down the freeway of life without any real mastery of their unique vehicle. So how can we start to understand our owner's manual? How can we begin to uncover our identity and maneuver this "vehicle"? Let's take a moment to begin the courageous journey to authenticity and self-awareness.

REFLECTION

CLARIFYING OUR STRENGTHS AND GROWTH AREAS

Take your time. Be thoughtful. These questions are designed to be insight-provoking, so don't rush through them. Read all the questions first, and begin the exercise by answering the ones that come easiest. Use a notepad or digital device to capture your responses.

1. Imagine yourself observing a dear friend talking about you with heartfelt love and admiration. What would your friend be saying?

2. When you are energized and inspired, what particular personality traits or strengths are you expressing?

3. What are some of your Conscious Beliefs?

4. What are some of your Shadow Beliefs?

5. When you are leading with Character, what qualities come forth? Do certain situations inhibit or express your character more?

6. When you are leading by Coping, what qualities come forth? What beliefs or fears are generating a reactive state of mind, emotion, or behavior?

7. What do other people consistently tell you that you need to work on or develop? What new behaviors are you committed to practicing?

8. At the end of your life, what do you hope people will thank you for contributing?

9. If you decided to take a new approach to living or leading, what would this new approach be?

As we will continue to explore throughout this book, Personal Mastery is not a localized phenomenon; it has far-reaching implications. The presence or absence of Personal Mastery will create or diminish long-term value. Our Hay Group research has shown that leaders account for 70 percent of team climate and that team climate, in turn, accounts for 30 percent of performance. Personal Mastery that serves the team and the enterprise creates tangible, sustainable value.

EIGHT PRINCIPLES OF PERSONAL MASTERY

Keep in mind the following principles as you begin to master your ability to lead courageously with more awareness and authenticity:

1. Take Total Responsibility: Commit yourself to the path of Personal Mastery. Only you can commit to it, and only you can walk your own path to it. No one else can motivate you. No one else can do it for you. A mentor cannot do it for you. Your organization or clients cannot do it for you. As Hermann Hesse wrote in *Demian,* "Each man had only one genuine vocation—to find the way to himself." Personal Mastery is the one life experience we must give ourselves. No one else is "in the loop." Walt Whitman wrote, "Not I—not anyone else—can travel that road for you; you must learn to travel it for yourself."

> *The leader for today and the future will be focused on how to be—how to develop quality, character, mind-set, values, principles, and courage.*
>
> —Frances Hesselbein

No matter what life or leadership challenges we face, no matter what circumstances we encounter, we are responsible. As we advance, we notice that we are more self-validated, self-recognized, and self-trusting. As we increasingly assume responsibility for the life we are creating, we are prepared to assume responsibility for leading and serving others. The foundation of authentic, value-creating leadership is built with self-leadership, self-responsibility, and self-trust.

2. Bring Beliefs to Conscious Awareness: Commit to the process of clarifying your Conscious Beliefs and your Shadow Beliefs. Practice by pausing to reflect on how some of these beliefs open you up and how others close you down. Practice reinforcing the ones that open up possibilities and energize you and others. Reconsider the ones that limit possibilities and drain energy. Remember: beliefs are the operating system underpinning your leadership behaviors.

3. Develop Awareness of Character and Coping: Develop an awareness of when you are leading with qualities of Character and when you are being led by qualities of Coping. Instead of overinvesting in Coping, commit your energies to leading with Character. Doing so requires that you courageously examine the beliefs, fears, and limitations generating the qualities of Coping. Facing these limiting filters will free up energy to experience new learning from the outside and to express new potential from within. Be abundant with Character and very selective with Coping.

> *Leadership and learning are indispensable to each other.*
>
> —John F. Kennedy

4. Practice Personal Mastery with Others: Practicing Personal Mastery requires risk and vulnerability. It means placing ourselves in situations where we may not be accepted or validated by others for who we are or for what we think or believe. If we do not take this risk, we too often will be led by the expectations of others. As a result, we might unknowingly compromise our integrity. As you practice Personal Mastery with others, keep these thoughts in mind:

- Listen to your authentic inner voice for what you really think and feel versus what others want you to think and feel.
- Be mindful when "creating others in your image."
- Be mindful when "being created" by others in their image.
- Practice the strength of vulnerability; notice how it opens up relationships and teams.
- Practice sharing your genuine thoughts, feelings, joys, successes, concerns, and fears with people. Let your openness be the catalyst to open up the culture around you.

5. Listen to Feedback: Even though Personal Mastery is self-validating, sometimes other people hold valuable keys to our self-knowledge. As Edith Wharton wrote, "There are two ways of spreading light: to be the candle or the mirror that reflects it." How often have we resisted the input of others only to realize later that their comments were right on target? Is it possible their insights were greater than we were prepared to assimilate at the time? Rather than spending our energy defending a rigid state of self-awareness, we can think of Personal Mastery as a continuous, lifelong learning process. Life experiences are opportunities to learn and to develop. Colleagues are there to coach and mentor. Consider all input from others as potentially instructive. Those around us may be holding the torches to light our path to Personal

Mastery. *Personal Mastery involves a delicate, discerning reconciliation of openness to learning from others while evolving our authentic core.*

6. Consider Finding a Coach: There is nothing "wrong" with getting support. In fact, in my experience, most companies now use coaching to optimize performance rather than to "fix" problems. Having a coach as your partner during your growth process might be the most "right" thing you ever do. You might be pleasantly surprised to know how much an objective, experienced coach can accelerate your personal and leadership progress. Coaching can free self-awareness and facilitate some helpful directions for growth. Be sure to take some time to find the best coach for you. Initially, experience personal sessions with a few coaches. Share your story. Then gauge your chemistry and connection with each potential coach, as well as his or her level of experience with your type of situation. Quality, professional support can offer a significant growth experience; it is a time to be yourself and to get clarity. It is an opportunity to more objectively explore and practice new ways to lead and live.

7. Avoid Confusing Self-Delusion with Self-Awareness: In a survey of business executives, published in *Businessweek*, executives were asked, "Are you in the top 10 percent of leadership performance?" Their responses: 90 percent said yes. Hmmm. Someone has to be wrong here! Self-assessment can be the least accurate assessment. To remedy this, use grounded, validated assessments with a solid history to ensure that your growing self-awareness is real. Using instruments like Korn Ferry Assessment of Leadership Potential®, KF4D®, Hay Inventory of Leadership Styles®, Global Personality Inventory®, Hogan Personality Inventory®, Hogan Development Survey®, California Personality Inventory 260®, and Zenger/Folkman 360-Degree Assessment®, among others, can accelerate your self-awareness. Auditing your self-assessments against these research-based assessments can challenge your personal growth to new levels. However, be aware that no one tool can capture your entire profile. Assessment instruments can be very helpful, but they are most effective if they are part of an overall leadership development and coaching process. Be sure to have at least one tool that is inside out (personality, values, or preference assessments) and one that is outside in (360° assessments and/or 360° interviews).

8. Be Agile: Sometimes the strengths that helped you lead in your present state of development may hamper your future chances of success. You may have seen the photos of Karl Wallenda's final high-wire performance, as he attempted to cross between two tall buildings.

As he made his way on the wire, using his famous balancing pole, an intense wind came up. Everyone watching immediately understood Wallenda's dilemma. As the wind blew him off the wire, he clutched onto his balancing pole. All he needed to do was to let go of the pole and grab the wire. But, because the pole had saved his balance so many times before, he held on to it even as he fell to the ground. He held on to what he knew best even when it no longer served him. Understand and appreciate your strengths, but also be flexible and adaptable. Many strong winds may be coming your way.

> *Let's burn our masks at midnight*
> *and as flickering flames ascend,*
> *under the witness of star-clouds,*
> *let us vow to reclaim our true selves.*
> *Done with hiding and weary of lying,*
> *we'll reconcile without and within.*
> *Then, like naked squint-eyed newborns,*
> *we'll greet the glorious birth of dawn;*
> *blinking at the blazing, wondrous colors*
> *we somehow failed to notice before.*
>
> —John Mark Green

LEADERSHIP GROWTH PLAN

PERSONAL MASTERY

It's time to step back. Shift out of "I'm reading a book" mode. Instead of treating this book as an intellectual exercise, sit back and capture some insights and commitments that can make a genuine difference in your life and in your leadership. Pause to identify some areas to Build Awareness, Build Commitment, and Build Practice. (For more on Building Awareness, Commitment, and Practice, see Chapter Eight, Coaching Mastery.) Aim high. Also, note potential obstacles and success measures. As you do this, keep asking yourself: *What will really make a difference to enhance my courage, authenticity, and self-awareness?*

1. Areas for Building Awareness:

- _____
- _____
- _____

2. New Commitments to Make:

- _____
- _____
- _____

3. New Practices to Begin:

- _____
- _____
- _____

4. Potential Obstacles:

- _____
- _____
- _____

5. Timeline and Measures of Success:

- _____
- _____
- _____

LEADERSHIP GROWTH PLAN

PERSONAL MASTERY EXAMPLE

1. Areas to Build Awareness: Image and control are more prevalent than I thought; I need to build awareness of my shadow belief regarding "never achieving/doing enough."

2. New Commitments to Make:

   A. Move from control to trust to let others participate more.

   B. Let go of some of my image needs.

   C. Explore my need to do so much.

3. New Practices to Begin:

   A. Do 360° feedback.

   B. Find a coach.

   C. Get colleagues and spouse participation/feedback.

4. Potential Obstacles:

   A. Fear of change.

   B. Fear of failure if I change things too much.

   C. Will colleagues and the organization accept changes?

5. Timeline and Measures of Success:

   A. In three months, have people acknowledge that I am less controlling and more trusting.

   B. In six months, have several people notice that I am dropping my image and being more authentic. Re-do the 360° to measure progress.

   C. In one month, get home before 6:30 p.m., four nights a week.

CHAPTER TWO

STORY MASTERY

Leading with Inspiration

Stop for a moment and visualize basketball great Shaquille O'Neal—a monumental professional athlete, 7 feet tall, 300 pounds of muscle, and wearing a billboard-size neon smile—alongside his legendary college coach, Dale Brown—older, past his prime, more than a foot shorter, sagging a bit in the middle, and sporting his own, more diminutive grin. It's hard not to be amused, isn't it? They were an odd, comical-looking duo. But despite their superficial contrasts, these two men, player and coach, shared what I think of as an unexpected love story.

I became aware of their sweet, endearing connection and compelling love for each other while I was watching an ESPN documentary. As the story unfolded, it struck me that most couples in romantic relationships do not possess the electricity and loving connection that these two men, mentor and mentee, enjoyed.

It was clear that Dale had become a second father to Shaq during his formative years at Louisiana State University. It wasn't because Shaq was hungry for someone to be a father to him. As it happens, Shaq had a strong relationship with his biological father. What was stunning to me was Shaq's great fortune to have not just one but two outstanding "fathers." The uniqueness of this revealed a hole in my heart and moved me to tears. I found myself wondering what it would have been like to have even one devoted father role model in my early life. How would I be different today? How would I see myself and my life differently? Shaq and Coach Dale's story revealed a wound in me, a deeply submerged longing for a more emotionally engaged paternal relationship.

But there was another level of resonance to the story. Dale also reminded me of one of my dear mentors and business partners, Sidney Reisberg. Sidney was an older, expressive, Jewish guy from New York City, who could not have been more different from my young, reserved, Scandinavian self. In many ways, he was my Coach Dale. He took me under his tough, loving wing, and with his characteristic intelligence and humor, Sidney changed my life. He helped me strengthen my voice, and he helped fill an emotional gap, for which I will be forever grateful.

> *There is no agony like bearing an untold story inside of you.*
>
> —Maya Angelou

Realizing the deep connection in the two stories—Shaq's and Dale's, mine and Sidney's—I watched more of the film. I cried tears of pain and joy, and I understood once again the potential of other people's stories to inspire our own insight and growth. As one very self-aware CEO reflected toward the end of his career, "I am always amazed how stories multiply human energy. My story catalyzes others, and their stories energize me."

THE LANGUAGE OF LEADERSHIP

While spreadsheets are the language of management information, stories are the language of leadership inspiration. Stories can activate our deepest, best selves; they are certainly one of the most transformative of all leadership tools. Powerful narratives can bridge the authentic, essential depth of a leader to the complex breadth of strategy, culture, values, and purpose. The best stories are like concentrated, potent mantras that resonate with our shared humanity and enliven our collective aspirations.

Yet despite the nearly universal recognition of their inspirational impact, rarely do we examine and master their effective and affective use in leadership development. If a leader even considers stories as a leadership development device, often it is only for the superficial reason of "storytelling" as a skill. Rarely do we engage in story comprehension and story embodiment to connect self-awareness to service. The essential plot of this chapter is going deep to touch hearts.

Humans are story beings. From cave paintings and oral histories to novels, films, dance, and digital media, we are driven to create, share, and absorb stories. "There have been great societies that did not use the wheel, but there have been no societies that did not tell stories," author Ursula K. Le Guin reflected. However, in the crush of our hyperactive world, we have drifted away from our storytelling heritage. We rarely pause to sit "around the fire" together to recount the values-filled stories of the day and to envision what could be.

The late Joseph Campbell was a well-known philosopher and sage and the author of *The Hero with a Thousand Faces*, which articulates the "Hero's Journey," the basic structure of all inspiring stories about becoming a leader. Campbell would say that we have lost the "power of myth"—not the unreal aspect of myth but the deepest archetypes supporting meaning and purpose that course through the veins of our daily experience and nourish what is enduring, significant, and uniquely human. Anthony de Mello, the spiritual teacher and writer, put it beautifully when he wrote, "The shortest distance between a human being and the truth is a story." Likewise, the shortest distance between a leader and collective inspiration is a heartfelt story.

This is why I love the provocative and evocative power of documentaries: real stories, real drama, real emotions, real issues, and real dilemmas. As a story medium, documentaries are an artistic form of leadership; they illuminate what is important. The highly awarded film-maker Ken Burns said, "People seem to coalesce around stories that are transcendent." Done well, they elevate what makes us uniquely human and heroic. Philip Pullman, who wrote the epic fantasy-adventure trilogy *His Dark Materials*, captured the essence of story: "After nourishment, shelter, and companionship, stories are the thing we need most in the world."

FROM INFORMATION TO INSPIRATION

Stories elevate the mind and the heart to go beyond what is, to mobilize us and others to reach new possibilities. Annette Simmons, group process consultant, understood this dynamic when she wrote, "People do not want information. They are up to their eyeballs in information. They want faith—faith in you, your goals, your success, in the story you tell." Science has demonstrated that stories, especially stories that sustain our attention with a narrative arc and some tension, have the unique force to move us intellectually and emotionally at the same time.

> *To be a person is to have a story to tell.*
> —Isak Dinesen

In an article, "Why Your Brain Loves Good Storytelling," published in *Harvard Business Review* in 2014, scientist Paul Zak explains that his lab discovered more than a decade ago that the neurochemical oxytocin is necessary for humans to feel safe. Zak says, "It does this by enhancing a sense of empathy." Our brain produces more of it each time we experience kindness and trust.

More recent research by Zak's lab explored how to tap into oxytocin in people's brains to motivate them to engage in cooperative behaviors. Researchers did this by testing people's blood to measure their oxytocin levels before and after they watched narrative videos. They found that character-driven stories produced more oxytocin, and more oxytocin in the blood was a predictor of how willing people were to help others, for example, by donating to a charity linked to a story they saw. Zak, who specializes in neuroeconomy, concludes that we can leverage stories to engage employees to feel empathy for customer struggles and pleasure at the role they play in resolutions. His research demonstrates that we are attracted to stories in which people overcome challenges and discover new capabilities, like the archetypal Hero's Journey described by Joseph Campbell.

> *We all live in suspense, from day to day, from hour to hour; in other words, we are the hero of our own story.*
>
> —Mary McCarthy

Zak also suggests that organizations tell their own founding story more often to connect people to what he called "transcendent purpose"—to engage people with the original passion behind the enterprise. He writes: "These are the stories that, repeated over and over, stay core to the organization's DNA. They provide guidance for daily decision-making as well as the motivation that comes with the conviction that the organization's work must go on, and needs everyone's full engagement to make a difference in people's lives."

I witnessed this inspiring principle while in Europe to deliver a keynote with Liam Condon, CEO of Bayer Crop Science, and his top 100 leaders. During this program, Liam revealed multiple career stories that aligned and amplified the purpose-driven aspiration of Bayer: *"Science for a Better Life."* The authenticity and relevance of Liam's stories palpably energized the entire room. It was a visible demonstration that stories about purpose trigger oxytocin-induced inspiration.

A TALE OF TWO CEOs

A while ago, I was working with two CEOs, who were running two different global enterprises. One had honed his skills as an inspiring leader, and the other one was a more analytical, "only the facts" kind of person. Each was about to roll out his recently refreshed set of organizational values to support the cultural and leadership shifts needed to achieve his strategic goals.

The fact-oriented leader went to the stage and stood before 3,000 associates / new agenda. They were primed for something new, ready to hear fresh, diff ing ideas. The CEO was not ready to satisfy their deep hopes and longi his job was merely to inform, he dryly, rationally listed the five critical values with pr.... Value 1 . . . Value 2 . . . Value 3 . . . Value 4 . . . Value 5 . . . all supported by a well-crafted PowerPoint projected on a large screen behind him. The group was stunned. A resistant quiet blanketed the room. People moved back from the edges of their seats and leaned into their seatbacks with a disappointed, resigned thud. Doubt filled the room. Where excitement, energy, and engagement should have drawn everyone to the leader and to each other, instead there was disconnection and disillusionment. The underlying buzz was unmistakable. *Is this all you have? Do you really care about these so-called values, or are you just mouthing the words from HR? These sound just like the empty values at my last soulless company! Do I really want to attach my career and creative energies to this leader . . . to this organization?*

Sensing the flat response, the CEO tried to rally. "Okay. Let me list these values again." And again he went through them, one at a time, with analytical precision. As you can imagine, not even a glimmer of inspiration or engagement remained. Instead, cynicism and sarcasm took root, securing a hopeless and draining feeling within most people present. (Likely, many LinkedIn profiles were updated that evening.)

The other CEO, the one with a more developed talent for touching people's hearts with sto-ries, took a different approach. Yes, he had five core values too, which he listed for everyone with the help of a PowerPoint on a screen behind him. And yes, some of the values were identical to our other CEO's values. However, instead of reading them off as a list, he took his time, and he told an authentic, real-life story for each one. As he did, the PowerPoint melted into the background, and each of the core values came to life.

To present the first value, he told a moving story of a health crisis experienced by his teenage son and how the trauma of this tough journey made the value real for him. For the second value, he shared the story of a failure that he had faced early in his career and how the expe-rience still keeps him humble, compassionate, and open to learning. He illustrated the third value by sharing a story of a mentor-boss who took a chance on him before he was really ready for a role and its challenges, reminding him that we need to take chances on people and see their potential before they do.

You can imagine the audience perched on the edge of their chairs, absorbed in the authenticity and relevance of the CEO's inspired messages. Not only did they hear the CEO and feel the realness of the values presented, but the stories also awakened the audience's own. The CEO had tapped into the collective brain and the collective heart of the organization, and the connection resonated in the room. Oxytocin was pumping through the entire group!

> *The fact of storytelling hints at a fundamental human unease, hints at human imperfection. Where there is perfection there is no story to tell.*
>
> —Ben Okri

Deep authenticity intersected with profound relevance and brought shared inspiration through the power of stories. Patrick Thomas, CEO of Covestro, the highly successful IPO spin-off of Bayer, is a true believer in the power of stories. Patrick recently shared, "Stories have the unique power to engage the hearts and minds of individuals and to move them as a collective body from the mundane to the meaningful." *Stories move us from intellectually transmitting information to emotionally inspiring transcendence.*

THE STORY OF TEAMS

High-performing teams share and tell inspiring stories. For years we have accelerated the intersection of personal, team, and strategic performance by helping team members share stories of their most meaningful personal and career moments. Before coming together as a business team, most teams need to come together as people. Teams need to make a deeper connection. Business context is crucial, but teams also need personal context to build the trust needed for meaningful performance.

In a 2016 *Harvard Business Review* article, "Teams Who Share Personal Stories Are More Effective," Francesca Gino, behavioral scientist and professor at Harvard Business School, writes about research findings that demonstrate the power of personal narrative. Gino and her co-researchers, Dan Cable of the London Business School, Julia Lee of the University of Michigan, and Brad Staats of the University of North Carolina, found that the process of sharing "relational self-affirmation" through narrative and stories can heighten team members' contributions and team outcomes. Through story, team members can more clearly experience their own strengths and more deeply appreciate the contributions of others on their team. These results are worthy of reflection. You might consider the following questions as you and your team seek to elevate performance:

- What brought you to this team, and what keeps you here?
- What are you most passionate about, and how can that show up more on this team?
- Who influenced your leadership the most? How can you better bring that influence to this team?
- What success or failure stories can this team share with the broader organization that will bring to life its values and strategic priorities?

Managers tell a story of past performance by recounting numbers; leaders tell stories of purpose to envision new futures.

NOT ALL STORIES ARE CREATED EQUAL

Some stories work, and some backfire. Why? The best, most inspiring stories catalyze at the crossroads of authenticity and relevance. The following four-box model illustrates this dynamic:

Story Mastery Dynamics

HIGH

Personal Authenticity

LOW

Self-Absorbed Leaders

Inspirational Leaders

Disconnected Leaders

Manipulative Leaders

LOW   HIGH

Relevance to Others

> *Inspiration is the most radiant and flourishing expression of our authenticity.*
>
> —Elaina Marie

The model illustrates what we've all experienced at some time in our lives. The sweet spot of stories is where deep, personal authenticity meets high relevance for others. Great stories operate at the intersection of the authentic "I" and the deeply connected "We." Pitfalls happen when personal authenticity and/or relevance for others are not sufficiently developed. Jack Stahl, former Chairman and CEO of Revlon and author of *Lessons on Leadership*, recently shared with me, "The best leaders today are both deeply authentic and highly relevant in all situations. As they maintain the depth of their authenticity, they also flex to serve the relevant needs of the situation and the people involved. They recognize when to engage at the strategic level and when to dive deep into the nitty-gritty." Great things happen at this intersection of authenticity and relevance.

Take a moment to reflect on when your stories worked or when they did not. Can you remember the feeling of connection, the depth of authenticity, and the relevance to others when a story hit the engaging sweet spot? When stories fell flat, was it lack of personal depth or lack of relevance that tripped you up?

Like all aspects of leadership growth, Story Mastery is a combination of art and science that can be learned, developed, and practiced. It begins from the inside out with finding our own stories. This begins the transformative experience, but its real potential for transformative impact is in connecting people and ideas to something much larger, more important, and more purposeful. This energizes the feedback loop from both the inside out and the outside in.

THE RED THING

In the basement of our family home was something we called "the Red Thing." The Red Thing was a brightly painted, high wooden bench that happened to be located directly across from where my mother would stand to do the ironing. My sister Karen, my brother Patrick, and I all wanted time on the Red Thing, but it wasn't really about the Red Thing at all.

What we sought was the sage advice and encouragement of our mother. Because she only allowed one of us at a time on the Red Thing, time there with her was highly coveted. Our mom was an amazing listener, coach, teacher, and facilitator. Although we always wanted her to give us answers, which she did occasionally, more often she taught us how to reflect and build our own awareness by looking at different sides of an issue, situation, person, or group. She helped us to think, to process, and to land on our own clarity. She appreciated each of our unique talents and accomplishments, but she also challenged us to explore, excel, and exceed. She was particularly challenging when we were certain that we knew something or when we were judgmental about people.

I was not aware at the time what she was doing; I was only aware of the benefits of it. I did not realize that she was modeling a process, a way to reflect on yourself and the challenges you face. She had this incredible natural ability to use questions to get us to look at something from different perspectives, to help us better understand who we were, why we were going in a particular direction, and how to consider alternatives. She balanced encouragement with a push for excellence. She was intolerant of a lack of openness. She was a master coach. She ignited a passion in me to help people grow.

What are your "Red Thing" stories, in which mentors or loved ones informed and helped bring out your gifts? What are the "Red Things" that have honed the values and learning in your life? The following short stories of pivotal transformation may inspire your reflection on the most critical times and influences in your life.

SOME SHORT STORIES THAT INSPIRE

No matter how many stories we see on film, read in books, or hear in person, if the story is told with heart and touches universal values, we hear every story as singularly inspiring. Here we offer a couple of clients' stories, one from a prominent figure in my community, and one of my own to help you reflect on your own stories and explore how they may spark important emotions, memories, values, and influences.

The Book Revolution

Imagine receiving orders from your local government authorities: "You are no longer permitted to work at your profession. You must abandon your home in twenty-four hours and forfeit your possessions. You may take what you will need for basic survival. You are being relocated to a remote village for reeducation. You must learn to survive." Hard to imagine, isn't it? But this was the childhood reality for Joanne, an executive client of ours, who endured the later years of the Cultural Revolution in China.

Joanne never knew her grandparents or even saw a photo of them. They were property owners and intellectuals, and because of their positions and accomplishments, they suffered repeated denouncements and persecution in many forms. Her mother's father was executed, and her father's father was imprisoned. To minimize risk of more persecution, her parents destroyed all photographs of their beloved parents, who were deeply shamed for their privilege.

The daughter of a professor, Joanne remembers her early years in her family home, with its modern conveniences, and busy life in the city and at the university. She went to school, and her home was filled with books. That all changed when the Chinese government forced her family—her mother, father, sister, and brother—to leave their home and their city life and move to a small village in the mountains.

Joanne's father had a tough decision to make: what do we take with us? Most families packed up food, clothing, and blankets. Joanne's father decided to take minimal necessities so that he could carry what he believed was their most valuable possession: books. Merely possessing books was a risk. It could get them killed by government forces, and filling their boxes with books instead of food also meant that they might starve. Undaunted, he held fast to his conviction that their potential long-term nourishment was well worth the risk.

The family trekked under the cover of night to their assigned reeducation village in a mountainous area. Arriving in the deep darkness, they went to sleep, exhausted. When Joanne awoke that night and could not find a light switch to light the way to the bathroom, her mother gently told her, "No, dear. There is no light, no electricity, and no bathroom." The new darkness of their lives surrounded them. But the books, stacked in the corner, sat latent, ready to illuminate their lives.

Joanne walked each day with her mother to get fuel and water and sometimes to forage for mushrooms and other edible plants for their meals. There was no town and no shops, and the school was very far. It would have been a long, treacherous walk back and forth for her each day. So, what did she do? When she was not helping her family survive, she read. Her father's books became her passion, her nourishment, and her life.

After a few years, the Chinese government eased some restrictions. Joanne's family was allowed to return to the city. However, the associated stigma and shame of her grandparents continued to limit Joanne's choices, even after Mao's death. She could apply to college, but only to certain ones. After all this time out of school, would she pass the entrance exam, or was she too far behind her peers? Amazingly, she scored way beyond her grade level. Her father's "book revolution" had paid off.

Joanne entered college, studied medicine, and later was accepted into a fellowship program at Johns Hopkins University School of Medicine. This opportunity opened Joanne's eyes and was the critical beginning of her leadership journey. What would have happened if they had not taken those books with them on that long trek to the mountains? Would Joanne still be living in a small village with her childhood friends? Instead of saving lives as a medical researcher in a global company, would she be merely surviving and wondering what might have been if she had finished school?

> *With storytelling we enter the trance of the sacred. Telling stories reminds us of our humanity in this beautiful broken world.*
>
> —Terry Tempest Williams

Commenting on her story, Joanne reflected, "The vision, values, and courage of my father remind me daily what true leadership is: maintaining your dignity; staying true to yourself and what is important; caring for others at great personal risk; and courageously challenging authority when your deepest values are at stake. I know deep in my heart why I am so passionate as a leader about learning and helping others grow. It literally saves lives and creates unimaginable future opportunities. It is core to me and why I lead. It is my continuing leadership revolution."

REFLECTION

STORY REFLECTION

Did this story touch you in some way?

_____

_____

_____

_____

_____

Do you have a story in your life that resonates with this story?

_____

_____

_____

_____

_____

The following emotional story was shared with me by Diana Pierce, the iconic broadcast journalist and news anchor of KARE 11 News, Minneapolis, Minnesota.

The Deeper Voice Within

When people ask me what my favorite story has been through my thirty-plus years of being a broadcaster, I tell them about Joe Dilts. In 1998 I met Joe, who was diagnosed with Lou Gehrig's disease, also known as amyotrophic lateral sclerosis (ALS). It's a disease that progressively weakens a person's muscles and strips away their physical abilities. There is no cure. Joe and his wife Linda graciously agreed to let our cameras document their lives for over a year.

Until age thirty-five, Joe Dilts was a regular "Joe," a mechanic with the Metropolitan Transit Authority. But dropping wrenches and stumbling on the job led to a doctor's visit and the diagnosis. Within two years, the hideous disease robbed Joe of his ability to walk. Then, he couldn't hug his children anymore. The disease even took away his voice. However, Joe found a new voice via a computer. The camera caught Joe's great patience as he moved his cursor around, slowly tapping out words and sentences with just a slight head movement. Then with a simple click, his computerized voice would fill the room. When I asked him what he wanted people to know about his daily life, he answered that he wanted people, especially his friends, to know he was still here. Even though his body was failing him in every way, his mind was still sharp and he still wanted his thoughts to be known. His computer voice replied, "Imagine if your hands, feet, and mouth were duct taped. But you can still hear and think for yourself. That's how it is." He continued, saying he was sad that when friends stopped by to say "Hello," they didn't wait long enough for his computer responses, and instead of talking to him directly about football or hockey, they would talk directly to his wife and ignore him, "as if I am just a green plant in the corner of the room."

> *Storytelling reveals meaning without committing the error of defining it.*
> —Hannah Arendt

That was a stunning revelation for me as a broadcaster, as I reflected on how hurt and angry I would feel if friends and family stopped talking to me and started talking around me as if I didn't exist. What Joe showed me was a different type of strength and tenacity in his desire to be heard, recognized, and validated even though his means and method of talking had changed. His honesty also reminded me of why I became a broadcast journalist: *to light people's stories up to educate and inspire.*

REFLECTION

STORY REFLECTION

Did this story touch you in some way?

_____

_____

_____

_____

_____

Do you have a story in your life that resonates with this story?

_____

_____

_____

_____

_____

The Gift of Life in a Year of Struggle

We've all had those days when it feels like everything is happening at once, and it would take nothing less than a miracle to get out from under the crushing burden of crisis. Only it wasn't a day or even a week or a month for Brian and his family. It was a year of relentless, life-or-death health crises, requiring more courage, strength, and fortitude than any of them had ever mustered.

The year was 1994. Brian was twenty-eight years old. His career was taking off. In January, he and his wife, Kathy, learned that they were pregnant. Good news, right? They were happy. When they learned a few weeks later that they were pregnant with twins, they were in shock and a little intimidated, but thrilled. Twins! Wow! It took them a little while to wrap their heads around it, but they'd be ready.

In March, Brian's brother became ill with a kidney disease. Dialysis wasn't working. Brian saw clearly that his brother needed a transplant, and Brian was a 100 percent match. Despite his brother's persistent objections, Brian was determined to be the donor and give his brother one of his kidneys. Fibbing a little, Brian assured his brother that he knew what he was doing. One thing Brian did know was that a 100 percent match kidney from your brother had a higher rate of success than a cadaver kidney. For Brian, it was a no-brainer. But with twins on the way, time was an issue. They coordinated calendars and decided to do the surgery in June. When June came along, Brian was confident that it would all work out.

However, life sometimes throws very unexpected curve balls. The night before Brian was supposed to fly to New York for a couple of days of pre-op and then the surgery, Kathy's mother had a stroke and died. This was totally out of the blue, and Brian wanted to be with his wife, so he changed his flight plans and the scheduled pre-op work. He would figure out a way to do that out of town, which he did. In between the funeral and being with family, Brian ran to the hospital for blood tests, drove to the only place that would ship blood at the time, and somehow, he got it all done. He flew into New York in time for the kidney transplant. Whew! The surgery went well, but Brian had underestimated the physical impact of the surgery on himself. The sixteen-inch incision from belly to spine and the removal of a couple of ribs to get at his kidney had him down for the count. He wasn't mobile for four weeks and couldn't return to work for six.

By early September, Brian was recovered and home when his company offered him a new role: a good one, but it required moving to Maryland. Brian and Kathy decided to go on a surveillance trip to check things out and go house hunting. They wanted to have things set up so that they could have the babies and then move soon after. The doctor reassured them that she could fly: No worries. She had ten more weeks. Plenty of time. On September 16, they flew, checked into their hotel, and went to sleep.

First thing in the morning, another curve ball came flying. Kathy's water broke. She was in labor. With the little information they had, they got in the car and headed to a recommended hospital. Their twins were born an hour later after an emergency C-section at twenty-nine weeks. At two and a half pounds each, the girls weren't much bigger than your hand. Their hearts were developed, but their lungs were not, so they had to be in intensive care, where their parents went every day, taking turns holding their babies and supporting each other. Calls came in the middle of the night for emergency procedures, and Brian would need to go in to sign releases. Kathy was understandably struggling under the stress of having premature twins, being in a strange city, and not knowing anyone. Who wouldn't feel overwhelmed!

When the girls finally came home from the hospital, they were six weeks old and four pounds each. They had to have two ounces of milk every two hours. No matter how long it took them to get those two ounces down, Brian and Kathy had to do it. Brian went back to work, and for weeks he and Kathy slept and fed the girls in shifts until each one attained a weight that ensured survival.

> *You'll never find a better sparring partner than adversity.*
>
> —Golda Meir

This year-long experience goes to the depth of who Brian is as a leader, husband, father, son, brother, and friend. At some point after that critical year, something shifted in Brian. He stopped focusing on success and instead focused on the significance of "being a great leader and father." To him this meant knowing yourself, being yourself, and living your values and what you stand for all the time, in every situation of his life. This realization freed him to be more candid and open with people, a trait that has drawn people to him and inspired trust and collaboration. The experience also instilled a deeper confidence in him that has enhanced his leadership influence.

Brian's leadership is grounded in the learning that emerged from that crazy year. That kidney he gave his brother twenty-two years ago? It's still going strong. His twins? They are happy, healthy young women who are thriving. And there isn't a day that Brian isn't clear that his courage, confidence, and willingness to push the boundaries is based on the battles of that year and the hard-fought gift of life. By the way, Brian is now CEO of a $10 billion global organization.

REFLECTION

STORY REFLECTION

Did this story touch you in some way?

_____

_____

_____

_____

Do you have a story in your life that resonates with this story?

_____

_____

_____

_____

The Compassionate Thing

My telephone rang at 2:00 a.m.—rarely a good sign. Startled, I wondered who it was and what bad news awaited me. Sitting up in bed, I reached for the phone. Putting it up to my ear, I heard my mother's shaken voice saying, "There's been a terrible accident. Your father is unconscious. He's in intensive care. Kevin, you have to go to the hospital."

I reacted, "No way. I'm not going." I'm not proud of my response, but it was honest. It was the way I felt. I knew that my mother couldn't handle going either. She and my dad had been separated for some years.

She insisted. "This is your father, Kevin. You have to go."

We need the courage to learn from our past and not live in it.
—Sharon Salzburg

Grudgingly, I pulled on my clothes and drove to North Memorial Hospital. The entire drive I held onto my resentment, resisting what awaited me. When I walked into intensive care and saw him—bruised, bloody, unconscious, vulnerable, and attached to a web of cords and devices—unexpectedly, I felt something different. Resentment, at least partially, fell away. My mind said, "No," but my heart was surprisingly saying, "Yes." In this conflicted state, I moved forward and held his cool hand. As I did so, I remembered his familiar smell and our common DNA. While he was not a great father, I understood that he was my father. His story and mine were intertwined.

I stayed as long as I could and returned the next day, and the day after that. Every day I held his hand, talked to him about anything that I could think of and hoped that he would either make his way back or have a peaceful transition, whichever he preferred. This routine continued daily for six months, until one day, as I was dozing off, he squeezed my hand twice. He was back, and we were both shocked.

Over the next couple of months, I continued to be there for him, and eventually I became my father's guardian. I was twenty-three years old, and I cared for him for the next twenty-three years. Let's take a pause here for a moment. This is not a simple story of growth and reconcil-

Stories have to be told or they die, and when they die, we can't remember who we are or why we're here.
—Sue Monk Kidd

iation. It is far from that. I was very conflicted. At times, yes, I was compassionate. But other times, I resisted. Resentment reared up, and I wasn't ready to let go of the past. I particularly did not want to be the father to the father I felt I never had. Occasionally, I found myself shouting inside my head and heart, "Why am *I* now responsible for *him*?!"

Slowly, things changed. Very gradually I began to release my child-desperate longing for an idealized father, who had never been there in the first place. As I did, something new and liberating emerged. I began to see my father as a person, not as a parent. I began to see and appreciate his story, his difficult childhood, and how he did the best he could with what he had. I was growing up fast, and he was giving me this gift.

As I began to see his whole story in a more objective, mature way, I started to see more of his whole person, too. Memories of his humor, energy, and zest for living started to counterbalance some of the darker, previously dominant ghosts. I more clearly saw the pluses and minuses of both parents. As my image of him became more whole, I became more whole, too. Was the father I thought I never had actually the one giving me the growth experience I really needed?

While there were innumerable challenges along the way, our story culminated on the day before he passed away. After years of caring for him with little appreciation in return, I was shocked when I came to see him that day. As I entered his room, he immediately came to life. His eyes opened wide with excitement. He reached lovingly for me with his remaining strength, and he smiled as though the most important person in his world had just entered the room. It was an amazing, emotional, unexpected, and heart-healing moment. Had I become the most important person in his life? Possibly. It had never entered my mind that I might be. But his whole being said so, and it filled the deep hole in my heart, which I had forgotten was even there. Who would have imagined that the person I struggled with the most in life was the one who would show up in the end to be the appreciative father I had always sought?

To this day, I still marvel at the power of loving versus being loved and serving versus being served. "The Compassionate Thing" may be the only thing that gives real transformation a chance.

REFLECTION

STORY REFLECTION

Did this story touch you in some way?

_____

_____

_____

_____

_____

Do you have a story in your life that resonates with this story?

_____

_____

_____

_____

_____

Now let's bring to the surface your most powerful, formative stories by creating your StoryLine.

REFLECTION
CREATING YOUR STORYLINE

Step back and consider the most significant highs and lows of your life. Consi... the most formative moments or periods of your personal and professional life. Who has made the biggest difference, both positive and negative, in your life? Consider your parents, teachers, coaches, siblings, colleagues, friends, and mentors. Explore losses and health crises, highs and lows in your career. Reflect on key decisions and turning points.

To help you capture these key events or key periods of time, go to CashmanLeadership. com and click on StoryLine. Complete the chronological exercise and the accompanying reflection designed to help you capture key learnings, values, and insights. I strongly urge you to do this transformative exercise. The StoryLine takes the typical concept of self-awareness—as merely being an understanding of our strengths and development areas—and elevates it to the breakthrough perspective of *"Where do my strengths and development areas come from? How did I acquire these strengths? Where did I form these values? Why are certain challenges particularly difficult for me?"*

Take a pause, and deepen your self-awareness by seeing and connecting the dots to your life stories. In her book *The Gifts of Imperfection,* Brené Brown, well-known speaker, researcher, and author, said, "Owning our story can be hard but not nearly as difficult as spending our lives running from it. Embracing our vulnerabilities is risky but not nearly as dangerous as giving up on love and belonging and joy—the experiences that make us the most vulnerable. Only when we are brave enough to explore the darkness will we discover the infinite power of our light."

Set the book down and explore the StoryLine now. Many insights are waiting for you in this crucial exercise.

When you have completed your StoryLine, take this potentially transformative exercise to another level. Fully write the short stories for two or three of the most impactful stories from your StoryLine. Flesh them out as best you can. Naming these experiences and reflecting on them brings a certain amount of insight and emotion, but writing the full story brings them fully to life and brings their deep significance to light.

SIX PRACTICES FOR INSPIRING STORIES

Story Mastery requires a continual process of acquiring, collecting, refining, and expressing narratives that move you and others to greater aspiration. Consider these practices as you work on this transformative skill:

- *Story Mastery Practice One: Dig Deep*

  Stories elevate souls by shaking off the dust of daily living and revealing the interwoven fabric of traumas, values, privileges, losses, and learnings. Like an archaeologist exploring our personal and professional pasts, we need to excavate and discover our most formative, impactful, value-creating stories. The StoryLine Reflection Exercise available at CashmanLeadership.com is designed precisely for this purpose. It is one of the most important exercises in this entire book because it helps us connect to our whole selves: to our courage and our achievements; to our humility and our failures; to our most important opportunities for learning and our greatest influences; and to our vulnerabilities and our heartfelt values.

- *Story Mastery Practice Two: Create a Collection of Stories*

  As a leader, if you say something is important or valued, then what are your stories that illustrate, demonstrate, and inspire people in that direction? An important leadership development practice is to begin to archive your stories that correlate with your most deeply held beliefs, values, and leadership principles. Having a large collection of stories will allow you to easily access the most relevant in a given situation. *Become the curator of your ever-expanding story collection.*

- *Story Mastery Practice Three: Practice Your Stories*

  Knowing your story well and understanding its compelling meaning takes practice. Write your stories down. Practice them aloud. Feel the emotional impact as you share them. Have the courage to let your emotion surface as you speak, instead of pushing it down. If you get a little "shaky," that is a positive sign. You are exercising your emotional muscles. *The journey to inspiring others begins with the practice of self-inspiration.*

- *Story Mastery Practice Four: Find the Stories around You*

  Start to notice when a story moves you. It may come to you from a movie, book, news report, friend, colleague, situation that you witness, or innumerable other sources. Here is the key: do not let the inspiration pass without a moment of reflection. Ask yourself: Why is this story moving me? What stories, challenges, gifts, influences, or mentors is this story reminding me of? What is this story telling me about what is absent from my life? Pause and capture your story to strengthen your self-awareness and authenticity. Then ask yourself: Can this story serve others? Do I have the courage to share it? In what circumstances might I share it to illustrate deeper learning, challenges, or values? *Stories are all around us and within us.*

- **Story Mastery Practice Five: Remember Relevance**
Always keep in mind that the stories are for the purpose of inspiring others. They are not about you; they are about the deeper human challenges, struggles, and blessings that we all share. Stories are about aligning and experiencing important, compelling topics together. They are not about you and your performance. *Stories are the language of leadership: authentic and courageous influence that creates enduring value.*

- **Story Mastery Practice Six: Observe and Learn from the Vulnerability in Great Stories**
Notice how stories inspire you. What was it about the delivery that contributed to the relevance to you? What was the learning or message that touched you? How might you authentically model this? Our vulnerability is usually not so easy to confront or share. Brené Brown explains it this way: "The difficult thing is that vulnerability is the first thing I look for in you and the last thing I'm willing to show you. In you it's courage and daring. In me it's weakness." But as writer Chris Jami beautifully expressed, "To share your weakness is to make yourself vulnerable; to make yourself vulnerable is to show your strength."

Like with all new skills, you may feel a bit clumsy at first in your storytelling. However, even stumbling a little can deepen the authenticity and draw people closer. Your initial awkwardness reveals a vulnerability that is very compelling and attractive to others, as counterintuitive as this may feel to you. Listeners see your humanness and make an empathic connection. *When we can point out the places we have stumbled along the way, we demonstrate legs made strong by the stress of authentic living.*

FIVE SHADOWS OF DESTRUCTIVE STORIES

Storyteller beware! Stories can also cast a negative shadow on the leader, team, or organization. Because of their immense influencing power, stories can be used for harmful purposes or destructive ends. Derek Thompson, author of *Hit Makers* and senior editor for *Atlantic* magazine, says, "Stories are weapons for good or ill." Here are some of the signs to watch out for in yourself and others:

- **Destructive Story One: Stories That Exclude**

  Throughout history, there have been stories that diminish, demonize, or discount people as individuals and as entire groups. This type of storytelling can serve the leader and activate pride and exclusivity for the individual listener and a specific audience in the short term. However, we all know the long-term damage this creates for the excluded groups, as well as for the group that uses these stories to leverage negative, self-interested, fear-based power. It is a type of "authenticity" that does not create enduring value. These stories are dangerous because they work and because, in the long run, they threaten us all.

  > *Free yourself from the inauthenticity and disempowerment of your story.*
  > —Steve Maraboli

- **Destructive Story Two: Stories That Tell One Way of Being, Behaving, or Seeing the World**

  Stories that reinforce the idea that "we have the answer, the one right answer, and they do not," tend to create artificial boundaries and attempt to limit our heritage as a learning, evolving, and innovating species. Some of our traditional stories are wonderful reminders of the life-enriching values that we want to sustain. However, our emerging stories may be the most compelling and significant. These stories capture the nuances of life's complexities and possibilities. Be wary of stories that claim to hold "THE ONLY ANSWER." Under the guise of inspiration, they are often master manipulations.

- **Destructive Story Three: Stories Designed to Make Us Look Good**

  We have all experienced a story whose intention is to make the teller look good in the eyes of others. This person wants to be seen as the hero at the center of the story. This narcissistic use of stories may benefit the image of the leader in the short run, but more often it diminishes credibility and followership for both the short term and the long term. *Stories designed to impress are typically not very impressive.*

In general, stories in which you, the teller, are central are best if they are stories about learning or stories about overcoming tough circumstances. They may be challenging or self-deprecating stories that illustrate how others helped you. Stories crafted with you as the learner and someone else as the hero tend to be the most engaging and relevant to others. Remember, oxytocin flows when we share stories of character or overcoming difficulties.

- *Destructive Story Four: Stories That Are Emotionally Detached*
When stories move us, they often move others. Stories that are told with emotional detachment separate us from the audience, and rightfully so, because they call into question our authenticity and motives. If you cannot feel the passion, feel the message, and feel the learning, do not tell the story, because it will cast a shadow on you and the audience. People will doubt your authenticity, because you are not present emotionally. A very wise CEO shared with me that "People have an instinctive, uncanny ability to sense real emotion and authenticity. Therefore, it is up to us to lead—to go first into vulnerability and genuine openness."

- *Destructive Story Five: Stories That Misrepresent*
Research shows that all humans lie. It's part of our humanness. One of the first steps to authenticity is to admit our lack of it from time to time, especially with loved ones, team members, and customers. Being courageous enough to admit this lack of authenticity may be extremely painful and trust breaking, but if genuine, it can rebuild connections and even deepen them in the long run. Self-awareness is critical here. Stories that misrepresent may have some immediate gain or avoid pain in the short run, but they can create massive harm in the long run.
Nearly all of us share painful stories of losing trust through misrepresentation. It is one of the most traumatic lessons on both sides of the exchange. There are few things that I know for sure, but deep pain has taught me that these stories are never worth it in the long run. "If you want to be successful, you must respect one rule: Never lie to yourself," reflects Brazilian writer Paul Coelho. *The journey to authenticity begins by turning away from the lies we tell others and culminates with an even tougher climb to character, which involves the cessation of lies we tell to ourselves.*

Powerful stories can either create or destroy tremendous value; make sure that your stories inspire at the intersection of self-awareness and service.

STORIES FROM THE INSIDE OUT

Stories shape our identity, values, beliefs, behaviors, and how we influence others. Sometimes we are aware of the influence our stories have on us, and sometimes we are not. Fortunately, stories have a process and a structure. We can become aware of our stories, allowing us to study, practice, and refine them. We can understand them in the same way that we understand where our blue eyes, black hair, and personality originated. Research in epigenetics suggests that traumatic experiences from one generation can be passed on, through unique DNA expression, to the next generation. In this way, you could say that stories are even part of our physiological makeup. They are an intrinsic part of the fabric of our lives, part of the intimate dynamics that have formed us at our core. The more we access and comprehend our own stories, the more we can use them to accelerate the growth and inspiration of others.

> *Stories are the single most important tool in a leader's toolkit.*
> —Howard Gardner

Story Mastery includes a five-step process for developing this skill.

Step One: Know Your Story. The journey to self-awareness and greater leadership impact begins here. Without this first reflective step, there is no point in going further.

Step Two: Reframe Your Story by examining whether your interpretation or internalization of the story still serves you and others. Ask yourself if this narrative and belief system, which was appropriate in the past, is still relevant today. Does it need to be reframed to serve you and others in new, meaningful ways? Is the story a lie that needs to be discarded? *The story we tell ourselves about our life experiences reveals the essential patterns we must bring to self-awareness in order to move from personal mythology to personal authenticity.* This is the journey through our belief systems.

Step Three: Be Your Story. This is the journey to authenticity. Knowing your story is great, but if you do not embody the story, or at least attempt to be it, your voice will be superficial.

Step Four: Express Your Story. This is the journey to inspiration, when you work on powerful, relevant ways to share your stories.

Step Five: Discover the Plot. This is the journey to purpose, in which we surface the meaningful themes that have been running through our life.

The following diagram illustrates the critical process of generating stories from the inside out:

Stories from the Inside Out

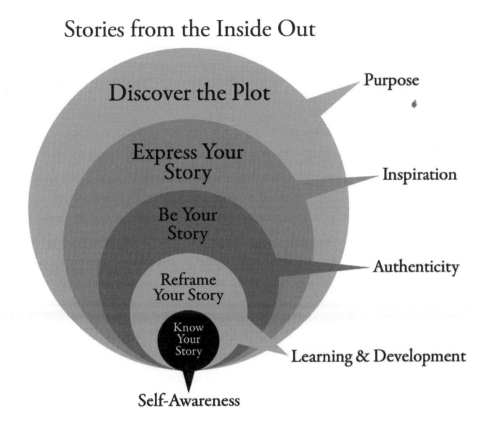

FOUR PRINCIPLES OF STORY MASTERY

Keep these principles in mind as you begin to master this new vocabulary for leadership activation:

*1. **Know Your Story:*** Your most potent, energizing, and engaging stories reside in your life story. In a conversation with John Maxwell, speaker and author of *Intentional Living* and many other books, he shared the story of a precious gift his executive assistant gave him many years ago. It was a book entitled *The Greatest Story Ever Told*. She waited and watched while John opened the book and paged through it, only to find that every page was blank. When he looked up at her with a confused look, she told him, "You write it. Be the author of your own incredible story." That was the inspiration for his first book.

Dedicate yourself to knowing your story, understanding the ups and downs that formed you, and creating a masterpiece of living and leading. As Joseph Campbell counseled, "If you are going to have a story, have a big story or none at all."

2. Practice Stories: When learning a language, knowing the vocabulary and grammar is not enough. We have to practice it aloud, speak it at every opportunity. Stories are the same. They become more powerful and impactful the more we actually tell them. Start practicing by reciting your stories to yourself. Ensure that you feel the story and see yourself in it, but not as the central focus. Make sure it is not about you but about the challenges, learning, and values that were revealed. In personal or family environs, practice your stories as memories that everyone can relate to. In a business or team situation, practice telling stories of appreciation for your colleagues and the value that they bring. At larger gatherings, see if you can reveal aspects of yourself that illustrate your real challenges, values, learnings, influences, or passions. Opportunities to practice are everywhere. Build your story muscle with small, private repetitions, and over time, build to even stronger, weightier inspiration.

> *I think that good story-telling of any kind does promote a humility in that it encourages you to see the world the way that other people see it.*
>
> —Jonathan Dee

3. Find the Intersection of Authenticity and Relevance: At this sweet spot, you—the storyteller—and your listeners experience the lessons, emotions, and connective energy all at the same time. It is a moment of elevation and fullness, when time seems to stand still, and we share the resonance. In certain keynote speeches, I can feel an audience hold its collective breath and get deeply still and quiet because the experience is so completely shared. No distractions break the silence. Aspire for this fulfilling intersection of authenticity and relevance to hopefully generate experiences of shared inspiration.

4. Find Purpose: Invest the time to discover the deeper themes of your life stories. Ask yourself: *What are the key learnings? What values do I know for sure? What gifts do I seem to bring in most situations? What are the gifts that others have inspired in me?*

Our lives are like well-crafted novels, rich with traumas, blessings, surprises, and significance. However, rarely do we pause to discover the plot. The story of our life is not merely a recounting of what has happened to us but rather a deep distillation of the most meaningful themes connecting the highs and lows of our life. Continually examining our life story gets us ever closer to our reason for being and contribution, which is the subject of our next chapter: Purpose Mastery.

LEADERSHIP GROWTH PLAN

STORY MASTERY

Take some time to invest in knowing and expressing your stories. Consider how much energy, power, and influence you could activate through your leadership voice with stories. Reflect on: *How could I better use stories to inspire and to serve?*

1. Areas for Building Awareness:

   - _____
   - _____
   - _____

2. New Commitments to Make:

   - _____
   - _____
   - _____

3. New Practices to Begin:

   - _____
   - _____
   - _____

4. Potential Obstacles:

   - _____
   - _____
   - _____

5. Timeline and Measures of Success:

   - _____
   - _____
   - _____

CHAPTER THREE

PURPOSE MASTERY

Leading On-Purpose

Purpose powers performance. It elevates leaders and teams to move from short-term success to long-term significance. It engages and energizes workforces, customers, vendors, distributors, communities and stakeholders around a common mission, something bigger than products and larger than profit. It is the foundational meaning that unleashes latent energy and motivation as it generates enduring value. Purpose seeks to answer the essential question: *Why is it so important that we exist?*

TO LEVER OR TO UNILEVER?

As leaders we have a responsibility to address this significant question: "Why is it so important that we exist?" With this question, we courageously face *who we are* and *how we are* in the world. As we reflect on it and the battle that rages for the soul of capitalism, we also may want to consider the following: How do we view capitalism and the role of business? Will we define business solely in terms of transactional financial levers, designed to accumulate capital, or will we apply our vision to shape business as a more universal lever that serves a higher, more sustainable purpose? Will the top 2 percent serve the 98 percent, or will the top 2 percent dominate, control, and be served by the 98 percent?

Unilever takes the purpose-driven lever and seeks to serve 100 percent. Their Core Values are much more than aspirational concepts. Their purpose statement is more than a slogan. Yes, they struggle to live it at times, but the constant struggle to serve is a worthy aspiration. As purpose-driven leaders remind themselves over and over again, purpose is not perfection but the pursuit of service-fueled value.

Dedicating themselves to the Core Values of "*integrity, responsibility, respect, and pioneering,*" Unilever's Core Purpose keeps them focused on succeeding "with the highest standards of corporate behavior towards everyone we work with, the communities we touch, and the environment on which we have an impact." There is no company-centric charge to be "number one based on financial metrics" or claim that "winning is all that matters" in their purpose statement. Their considerable success is driven by their conviction to serve.

Perhaps you are skeptical. You are thinking: "Sure, I've heard this before. Another company with a beautiful list of spoken values and a purpose statement, but so totally caught up in its relentless performance drive that its intention and spirit is rarely lived." Paul Polman, CEO of Unilever, expressed his genuine belief and conviction in purpose-driven leadership and the power of service in this statement for a *Huffington Post* article, "Doing Well by Doing Good": "The power of purpose, passion, and positive attitude drive great long-term business results. Above all, the moment you realize that it's not about yourself but about working for the common good, or helping others, that's when you unlock the true leader in yourself." When purpose becomes personal, it becomes real and powerful.

Recently, Unilever recruited another purpose-driven leader, Marijn Dekkers, to be Chairman of its board. Like Polman has done through his leadership, Dekkers created significant, enduring value during his tenure as CEO of Bayer. His leadership brought vitality and relevance to Bayer's purpose, to their culture, to their leadership growth, and to their market value. Commenting on this purpose-driven value creation, Dekkers shared this with me: "It is relatively easy to pull financial levers to generate short-term profit. Many people can do that. What is challenging, and the real skill of leadership, is to inspire sustainable growth by relentlessly serving *all* stakeholders, not just shareholders but employees, customers, vendors, communities, and the planet. When purpose becomes the generator of profit, then long-term success, service, and sustainability have a chance to be realized."

> *Man can face any "what" if he has a big enough "why."*
> —Friederick Nietzsche

In the end, we have to challenge ourselves with a very tough question: As individual leaders, as organizations, and as participants in a more conscious capitalism, do we see ourselves as being in service to all those we touch, or do we see ourselves as being served by them? *Service is the soul of purpose-driven leadership and sustainable capitalism.*

HAS PERFORMANCE BECOME YOUR PURPOSE?

A while ago I was working with the CEO of a global food company. She was well known for her decisive, performance-oriented style. Unlike some hyper-driven leaders, she was also highly effective in coaching her key people and bonding with her senior team. However, a compelling purpose was missing. She had never made it clear to people why they should drive so hard.

At one point in our engagement, I asked, "Has performance become your purpose?" Liking the idea, she quickly responded, "Yes. That's it. We are here to perform." Pausing for a moment to let what she had said sink in, I then asked, "Are you sure? Is this really why people choose to be here? Is this why your customers choose your products? Is it why it is important that your company exists?" Reflecting more carefully, she hesitantly responded, "I guess, when you put it that way, I've always thought deep down that our company exists at its most fundamental level to nourish the world, one person at a time."

Her awareness almost surprised her, and it sparked a newfound openness. She sat up more attentively, pleased with her insight. I dug a little deeper. "What would it look like if instead of performance being your purpose, 'nourishing people' was your purpose?" You could see the purpose/performance reframe sorting through her mind and her whole being. She shared, "People could really relate to that purpose. We could likely marshal all sorts of energy and engagement if everyone felt that what they were really doing in their jobs was nourishing people. It might even be our distinguishing difference."

As she embedded this new purpose into her work with her senior team, they witnessed her enthusiasm. Slowly, over time, people began to see that her drive and team skills were more meaningful and authentic, because they were supported by this more compelling reason to perform. She had begun a critical leadership reframe: moving from performance being their purpose to purpose elevating their performance to new heights.

Core Purpose operates at the high-performing intersection where our Core Talents and Core Values come together. It is the value-creating, catalytic moment when our gifts make a meaningful, enduring difference. When we split off our values from our talents, or vice versa, we compromise purpose and sustained performance.

About a year ago, Benton came to us for coaching. While he was highly valued by his company for his results and intellect, he was so entrenched in non-listening and aggressive behavior that I questioned if it would be worthwhile to invest the resources to develop him. At first it was a struggle, but eventually Benton surprised us and genuinely engaged in the process. We helped him see that his Core Talents—his intellect, drive for results, and ability to get things done—were coming through consistently at work.

> *If you want to identify me, ask me not where I live, or what I like to eat, or how I comb my hair, but ask me what I am living for, in detail, ask me what I think is keeping me from living fully for the thing I want to live for.*
>
> —Thomas Merton

However, at times his Core Values—compassion and connection—were not. Interestingly, when working with his own team, Benton's Core Talents and Core Values were present and operating in sync. The same was true at home. Benton was a popular coach of his daughter's soccer teams. He was present and involved with his wife and other members of his family. But when interacting with his peers and higher-level leaders, Benton introverted his Core Values. He split them off from his Core Talents. In these situations, he was competitive, closed, and defensive. His talents became liabilities. A big shadow was cast, because his values were hidden from certain groups.

Benton surprised us. Once he realized what he was doing, he found the awareness and new behaviors energizing. He wanted to change. His HR person called us and said, "This is incredible. Rarely in my career have we seen such a remarkable transformation." Now, the feedback from Benton's peers and high-level managers is that he is listening and is improving significantly in building trust. Occasionally, he will slip, but more often than not, he catches himself and steps forward with both his talents and his values. Once Benton got the whole picture and saw the consequences of splitting off his values from his talents, he was committed to leading on-purpose.

PURPOSE: THE BIG WHY

I've lost track of the number of times a frustrated CEO has approached me wondering, "Why aren't our people more engaged with the new strategy? What we need to do and how to get there are crystal clear. But the more I push, the less motivated people seem to be. What's missing?"

There are three big realities that we, as leaders, have to clarify and place in meaningful relationship for our organizations to thrive:

- The Big What Question (Vision): *What is possible for us to become?*
- The Big How Question (Strategy): *How will we get there?*
- The Big Why Question (Purpose): *Why is it so important that we exist in the world?*

Unfortunately, too often we deal with these three realities in the wrong sequence. We largely over-focus on the What and the How and under-focus on the Why. While it may be counterintuitive to many leaders, the most strategic and energizing place to begin is *Purpose*: the Big Why. Through the lens of purpose, we focus on a compelling reason for being and can then envision a future worthy of our collective talents, energies, and resources. By focusing on purpose—an aspiration that lifts us and infuses significant meaning in our day-to-day work—and putting it first, we catalyze our courage and authentic influence to create enduring value.

Our commitment to purpose compels us to ask additional, profound, Big What questions: What will we become in five to ten years if we live our purpose? What larger difference will we serve through our efforts and the enterprise? What is possible through purpose? Purpose brings energy and motivation to fuel the vision and the strategy. *Managers tend to focus on the What and How, wondering Why anything else is important; leaders awaken the wonder of Why to envision a more expanded, compelling What and How.*

Focusing on the Why, and clearing the way for others to do so as well, takes courage. In a conversation with Aaron Hurst, entrepreneur and author of *The Purpose Economy*, he shared, "We need to find ways to help people build courage instead of fear, and we need to clear the path for more authentic, creative expression." Leading with Why embodies and fosters courageous self-expression.

PURPOSE POWERS PERFORMANCE

The growing attention that purpose is getting with business leaders is not merely because of its honorable intentions but also because it is demonstrating the tangible value of enterprises that "do well by doing good."

Bob Eichinger and Michael Lombardo, cofounders of Lominger, tell us "much research has shown that organizations with sound and inspiring missions and visions do better in the marketplace. Sound missions and visions motivate and guide people on how to allot their time and how to make choices."

In *Good to Great*, Jim Collins writes about the preservation of what he calls "core legacy," the combination of Core Values and Core Purpose, as a feature of enduring companies that went from "good to great to built to last." Collins explains that there are not necessarily any "right" or "wrong" values, but there is the necessity to have them and live them, because they provide a "reason for being beyond making money. Enduring great companies preserve their core values and purpose while their business strategies and operating practices endlessly adapt to a changing world."

> *Purpose enables hundreds of employees to make thousands of decisions in unison.*
>
> —Gary Burnison

However, if any company, especially a fast-paced, growth company, is going to be able to hold true to its rock-solid values and purpose, its leader must be able to comprehend and articulate on a moment's notice his or her own Core Purpose. Howard Schultz, Chairman of Starbucks, warns us:

> Whatever your culture, your values, your guiding principles, you have to take steps to inculcate them in the organization early in its life so that they can guide every decision, every hire, every strategic objective you set. Whether you are the CEO or a lower level employee, the single most important thing you do at work each day is communicate your values to others.

More enterprises are doing just that: putting their purpose at the forefront of their reason for performance. In a new study, "People on a Mission," consultants Elaine Dinos, Janet Feldman, and Rick Lash studied purpose-driven companies in the consumer sector and interviewed thirty founders, CEOs, and senior executives of companies that had "a clear, visible, authentic purpose, engaged employees, customer-oriented cultures, and strong financial results." They found that companies focused on purpose and values reported annual growth rates of 9.85 percent, compared to 2.4 percent for the entire S&P 500 consumer sector—more than four times the growth rate. "Imbuing an organization with a core purpose can be hard work, requiring a deep, abiding commitment from the top," said Feldman. The study concluded that leaders need to back up their commitment to purpose with key practices:

- Hire people who connect with the purpose.
- Be transparent in leadership actions aligned to purpose.
- Offer incentive plans based on an employee's holistic contributions.

Some of the top companies who participated in the study were Chobani, TOMS, Etsy, Warby Parker, KIND Snacks, and West Elm. There were four conditions that fueled their success:

- The CEO led with purpose.
- People were clearly the top priority.
- Culture encouraged community and bringing best selves to work.
- Enabling practices and systems aligned with purpose.

Dinos said, "When an organization has a clear purpose, it unleashes the power and drive of the entire workforce, harnessing and focusing that combined effort in one aligned direction."

David Lubetzky, founder and CEO of KIND Snacks, is a great example of a leader whose vision and strategy for creating enterprises has been driven by compelling values and purpose. He is also inspired by his personal experience and his worldview. Lubetzky, the son of a Holocaust survivor, grew up hearing stories of his father's survival in Dachau concentration camp during World War II. In one story, Lubetzky's father told him that a guard tossed him a potato when no one was looking. In his mind, it was this guard's simple act of kindness that made it possible for him to know that he could survive. Despite the horror and harshness of his experience, he could get through it because he knew that kindness still existed. The power of this simple act of kindness gave him hope. This story always stuck with David, and it is the core reason behind KIND. Lubetzky is a staunch believer that we can create a culture of kindness and empathy and that business enterprises can be a force both for good and for profit.

Lubetzky embodies the KIND brand and purpose while also nurturing its profitability and success. The company employs 600 people and sells its products in more than 150,000 stores. In the last five years, they have generated 111 percent compound annual growth rate, and since its inception in 2004, the company has sold more than one billion KIND bars. Lubetzky's employees see him as a humanitarian "who happens to be a great businessperson."

The results of the study show that "people want to do good and serve something better at the same time." Purpose-driven leadership fulfills the Big Why question and gives all stakeholders a worthy, compelling reason to be engaged.

What happens when there is no clear aspirational purpose, or it gets lost or sacrificed? A 2016 *Financial Times* article posits that when purpose is missing, there is "a subtle alchemical shift, the metrics fill the vacuum, muscling out any wider purpose with the imperative of hitting the numbers. This transposition of ends and means is often disastrous because methods, now geared to meeting the metric, are detached from customer purpose—so banks sell payment protection insurance to people who do not need it, or VW managers manipulate emissions readings to meet targets." The article, entitled "Companies with a purpose beyond profit tend to make more money," goes on to explain that metrics are important to make the outcomes of purpose tangible. However, leaders must always remember to put meaning first and metrics second.

DISCOVERING THE CORE

The high-performance nucleus of purpose-driven leadership is where our Core Talents are in service to our Core Values. This is the value-creating state of authentic leadership, where the whole person is present and making a tangible difference. Clarifying this dynamic intersection, where our talents and values meet, is the important goal of Purpose Mastery: optimizing our gifts in service to the greater difference we aspire to make with others.

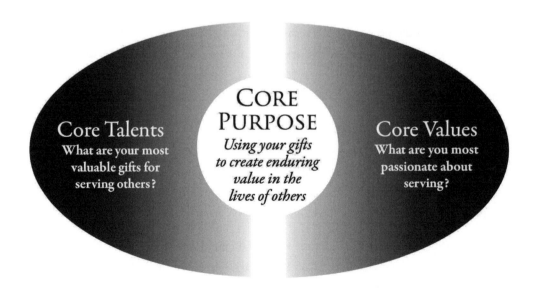

Core Talents
What are your most valuable gifts for serving others?

CORE PURPOSE
Using your gifts to create enduring value in the lives of others

Core Values
What are you most passionate about serving?

IDENTIFYING CORE TALENTS

All of us have particular skills, talents, or gifts in which we excel. Some come to us almost naturally; others evolve through study and experience. Regardless of their origin and path of development, Core Talents are those that make us and others feel energized or in "flow," as scientist Mihaly Csikszentmihalyi would call it. Csikszentmihalyi, well known for his research and writings on "flow," or "optimal experience," explains that among other things, when in "flow" we are absorbed in the task at hand. We may lose track of time, not even realizing how long and hard we have been applying our unique talents. The experience is so enjoyable that we would do it even if we didn't have to. At the end of the day, although we may be tired, we don't feel drained. Instead we feel a strong sense of fulfillment, and we look forward to the next day with eager anticipation.

> *The secret of success is constancy of purpose.*
> —Benjamin Disraeli

Dr. Martin Seligman, in his work on "learned optimism," calls Core Talents "signature strengths." He says that when we use "signature strengths" in our work, we increase our opportunities for more happiness in our lives. Turning our work-life into our "life's work" may be one of the most critical growth areas for moving from management transaction to leadership transformation. *In the end, the true measure of our lives will likely be less about our accomplishments and more about how our gifts have made an enduring, purpose-driven difference in the lives of people.*

REFLECTION

CORE TALENTS

Think back over your career and your life. Recall those times when you felt most energized giving your gifts to others. You might have been engaged in something more personal or seemingly inconsequential, such as coaching a golf partner or walking with a friend. Or you might have been involved in something bigger, more visible or dramatic, such as envisioning a new product or an innovative strategy. Think about those times when you were at your best, when you and others were most energized and engaged. Capture some of those experiences by writing them down. Ask yourself and respond to the following questions and statements:

1. What gifts can people count on me for? _____

2. When I am making a difference/creating value, my talents that "show up" are _____
   _____

3. Other people consistently tell me I make a difference by_____

4. When I am working with others, and we are most energized and engaged, I am contributing _____

5. I am passionate about contributing_____

6. In summary, my Core Talents, the gifts that make a difference, are:

RECOGNIZING CORE VALUES

The late Warren Bennis contended that the purpose of leadership is to "remind people what is important." Reminding others what is important certainly penetrates the essence of leadership, doesn't it? However, before we can remind others what is important, we first need to know what is important to us. Sounds easy? Often, it is not. We all like to think we know what we stand for, but knowing our authentic values—the guiding principles rooted deep in our hearts and guts—is one of the most challenging aspects of self-discovery. Although many individuals prefer to take the easier route and avoid it, the work of identifying real values is worth the effort on many fronts.

In *Purpose: The Starting Point of Great Companies*, Nikos Mourkogiannis cites a survey of leading corporate executives, conducted by the Aspen Institute and Booz Allen Hamilton. This survey confirmed a connection between financial performance and values, "showing that financial leaders were more likely to make 'values' explicit by codifying or articulating them."

When we asked one client what was important to him, he responded by rattling off the typical list: family, work ethic, making a difference, serving others. Like our client, many

of us would automatically recite, "My family is the most important thing in my life. Contributing to the welfare of the less fortunate is crucial. Mentoring my employees is a high priority." Well, those all sound good, and they are all values worthy of high regard. But are they really your most important values? Is this where you really invest your time and energy? Or have you blindly adopted them from your environment? Although we would be reluctant to admit it, our spoken values are often a reflection of what our family believes, what our organization says is important, or what

> *People with a sense of purpose have learned to let life question them and have moved the focus of their attention and concern away from themselves to others.*
>
> —Richard Leider

our latest reading tells us. However, our authentic values and sense of meaning are deeper than this. *Authentic values are forged in the traumas and privileges of our unique life story.*

While coaching Michael, a highly effective leader, I learned that on the surface he was a great communicator. He was articulate, direct, and concise. If anything, he was a bit too polished. To his surprise, he received feedback that people didn't trust him. This information came from not just a couple of people but several key colleagues and staff members—people crucial to his success. The news was a complete shock to him. Reeling from the feedback, he said, "I work hard on my communication skills and tell it like it is. My intentions are good. What's wrong?"

To help Michael discover the answer, we began examining how people perceived him and how he perceived himself. Eventually, it was clear. Under stress or crisis, Michael didn't inspire and move people. The more a crisis heated up, the more polished and detached his communication became. People couldn't connect with him. They couldn't sense where he was coming from, what he considered important and compelling. As a result, people didn't trust him. They felt that he was smooth, slick, clear, and calm, but he wasn't real. He wasn't drawing from anything truly meaningful from within.

Michael realized that he couldn't be a more authentic and inspiring leader by further refining his presentation skills; he had to look deeply and honestly at what was important to him. After some intensive work unearthing his most relevant and profound learning experiences in his career and life, he began to connect to his deeper values. He started sharing his most authentic, values-infused stories to communicate his core. Under crisis, he shared a story about his first career failure and what he had learned about overcoming obstacles. While relating his father's sage advice about running the family business, he unexpectedly choked up in the middle of the anecdote. He gave depth, dimension, and texture to his previously smooth leadership style. Slowly but surely, Michael rebuilt trust brick by brick, value by value, and story by story.

REFLECTION

CORE VALUES

Remind yourself what is important by reflecting on key life experiences and lessons learned. Consider the questions and statements below to help you consider what you stand for as a leader. Reflect on them and on your earlier StoryLine exercise. Capture your responses by writing them down.

1. What has your life taught you about what is precious and valuable?

2. What have the traumas and losses in your life taught you about what is most important?

3. What have the privileges of your life taught you about what is of value?

4. What is worth risking your life for?

5. _____ gives me the greatest meaning in life or work.

6. In summary, my Core Values, the principles I stand for, are:

REVEALING CORE PURPOSE

We also helped Michael uncover his Core Purpose—how his gifts served the needs of others. At first, this was a foreign idea. "I just do my job and get results!" he insisted. "But how do you bring your whole self forward as you are getting results?" I pressed. "What is your unique, meaningful contribution?" To help him access deeper patterns, I asked him to project, without any limitations, the five lives he would most like to live. Then, over a couple of sessions, we found the aspirational themes contained in these projections, which illuminated and clarified his Core Purpose: *Applying insight and vision to realize new possibilities.* When he made his

Core Purpose conscious, his realization was stunning. We could feel it in the room—a deep, reverent clarity about who he really was. With this heightened awareness, we then looked at each part of his life—family, career, community, himself—and analyzed how aligned or misaligned his Core Purpose was with each of these.

To Michael's surprise, his Core Purpose had the lowest alignment to himself. So the real work was to strengthen his own connection to his Core Purpose so that he could bring forward more insight and vision to realize new possibilities for himself. How could he be even more courageous in realizing more possibilities? How could he be more insightful and visionary in developing himself? How could he realize new possibilities in the ways he showed up in his own life? As he did this personal alignment work, a foundation was built to bring his Core Purpose into all facets of his life. Later, he commented in a coaching session, "Core Purpose is like my compass. It helps to point all my energy, behaviors, and decisions in the right direction."

Paul Van Oyen, CEO of Etex, a $3 billion building materials firm based in Brussels, shared this potent purpose perspective: "Purpose only serves you when it guides you. When purpose guides your decisions as a person, as a leader, as a team member, and in your life, then its real power is apparent and unleashed."

A while ago, I learned a valuable lesson about purpose in an unexpected setting. In our building, our offices and restrooms were cleaned daily by a young woman. A recent immigrant from Somalia, she was always gloriously dressed in colorful fabrics. I was always struck by the delight with which she approached her seemingly mundane duties. One evening, she was joyously singing a beautiful song as she worked. Approaching her in the hallway, I commented, "You really love your work, don't you?" Her demeanor stiffened, and she became very serious. She set down her mop, looked piercingly into me, and with a penetrating, instructive tone said, "Sir, I do not love to clean bathrooms." Then with a soft, warm heart, she added, "I love *while* I clean bathrooms!"

I felt blessed to be mentored by such a wise woman, and her advice reminded me of a wonderful story. There once was a leader of a major monastery in China who was known for his purposeful teaching. However, instead of lecturing people on his teaching and getting lost in theory and concept, he would demonstrate his purposefulness by sweeping the steps of the monastery with all his being. People would come to the entry inquiring about the leader of the monastery, and the "sweeper" would say, "The teacher is teaching now." Because most of the aspirants were looking for something external—for their preconceived idea of a spiritual teacher—they rarely recognized that the entire teaching and meaning were present in how the wise teacher approached all of his life's work.

Purpose is not a goal to be set. It is not something we create. It is not some "great idea" we come up with. It is something we discover. Purpose is there all the time, and it's waiting for us. It is our value-creating contribution in life; it is what we

> *The purpose of life is to discover your gift.*
> *The work of life is to develop it.*
> *The meaning of life is to give your gift away.*
> —David Viscott

have been prepared to express. In *Synchronicity—The Inner Path of Leadership*, Joseph Jaworski writes, "[Purpose] is the call to service, giving our life over to something larger than ourselves, the call to become what we were meant to become—the call to achieve our vital design." If we ignore this calling, no amount of external success can make us feel complete.

CORE PURPOSE AND CORE DEVELOPMENT

Paul Laudicina, Chairman of the Global Business Policy Council and former Chairman and CEO of A.T. Kearney, engaged us for a combination *Chief Executive Institute* and *LifePlan Institute* to culminate his last two years as CEO and to transition to the next phase of his life's work. In the course of our work together, his Core Purpose became abundantly clear. When Paul was at his best, creating optimal value in all arenas of his life, three key gifts came together: *Insight, Intelligence*, and *Influence*. Whether he was consulting with a world leader, guiding his organization, or connecting with his family at home, his "**I³**", as he calls it, was operating. But there was also a flip side, a shadow to Paul's purpose. When he was not living his "**I³**", or when he was living only parts of it, his Core Development challenges might surface. To remind himself

> *Ever more, people today have the means to live, but not the meaning to live for.*
> —Victor Frankl

of his development plan, he came up with his "**A³**": *Action, Acknowledgment*, and *Ambition*. Paul learned how to monitor when too much personal action or ambition and too little acknowledgment of others were overshadowing his purpose. He also became aware that when his Core Purpose burned bright enough, there were no development shadows.

Paul reflected, "Real self-awareness involves comprehending our gifts and gaffs in the heat of performance. Clarifying my I^3—Core Purpose—and my A^3—Core Development—has been transformative to my life and leadership. It continues to 'live with me' years later." *Transactive managers examine others through the lens of performance; purpose-driven leaders examine themselves to clarify the performance impact of their light and their shadows.*

"MOVING UPSTAIRS" TO OUR PURPOSE

Jack Hawley writes, in *Reawakening the Spirit in Work*, "Our life direction is about moving into the vacant upstairs flat." Purpose is that home within, that place where our talents, values, and service-drive reside. It's there all the time, waiting for our arrival. We may have been too busy "living our life downstairs" to even notice.

A few years ago, I worked with an executive who had recently realized that she had been "living downstairs." She entered my office in a down mood, and after very little chitchat, she blurted out, "Cake mixes don't give any meaning to my life!" Caught off guard, I started laughing. She wasn't amused, and said, "I'm serious. I used to love my job, but it just doesn't seem important to me anymore." After I worked with her for a while, she began to explore the contents of her "upstairs flat." Her discovery centered on "using her innovative and conceptual gifts to enrich and to nourish people's lives." She had been "living downstairs" for so long that she actually thought that cake mixes were supposed to give meaning to her life! Her purpose became overshadowed by her day-to-day focus. When she finally uncovered her purpose—*to enrich and to nourish others through innovation*—her attitude about her job changed, her creativity returned, and her performance soared. Her life wasn't about cake mixes; it was about being a creative force to enhance people's lives. This realization permeated her entire life situation, and nearly everyone in her life sensed her renewal.

> *I slept and dreamt that life was joy,*
> *I awoke and saw that life was service,*
> *I acted and behold,*
> *Service was joy.*
>
> — Rabindranath Tagore

PURPOSE IS BIGGER AND DEEPER THAN OUR GOALS

How often have you heard someone say about extraordinary people, "He was born to do this. She was born to do that." It is as if the "thing" was their only goal, their only reason for being.

What happens when the "thing" is done or the career is over? Does that mean the person no longer has a purpose? Are these people then expendable from life? *Purpose is the natural flow of our gifts as they serve those we touch.* Sometimes we may inhibit or ignore this flow, but it is always there, seeking expression. How it manifests depends on our ability to open up to it and the particular circumstances we may be facing at the time. Purpose is constant; the manifestation of purpose is always changing to serve the situation.

I once had a client who asked me, "How can I tell the difference between obsessively driven behavior and purposefully driven behavior? It is difficult to tell them apart sometimes." Purpose releases energy. The higher the purpose, the greater the energy. Purpose also frees us. The more profound the purpose, the greater the sense of freedom. Purpose opens up possibilities. Obsession drains our energy and binds us to the activity itself. Less joy, less energy, and less freedom are the results. When observing the passionate, focused behavior of people, it can sometimes be difficult to know if they were being passionately obsessive or passionately purposeful. If the behavior is adding energy, joy, and fulfillment to them and others, then it is probably coming from a purposeful place. In Mihaly Csikszentimihalyi's words:

> Flow lifts the course of life to a different level. Alienation gives way to involvement, enjoyment replaces boredom, helplessness turns into a feeling of control, and psychic energy works to reinforce the sense of self, instead of being lost in the service of external goals. When experience is intrinsically rewarding, life is justified in the present, instead of being held hostage to a hypothetical future gain.

BRIDGING INDIVIDUAL AND ORGANIZATIONAL PURPOSE

In 2014, Baxter decided to spin off its BioScience division into a new public company. They called it Baxalta, and Ludwig Hantson, now CEO of Alexion, was Baxalta's CEO at the time. Ludwig was determined to rapidly develop innovative products supported by an innovative culture. This was no easy task. Fortunately, Ludwig thoroughly understood the huge downside of allowing performance to be the purpose of the organization. He partnered with Korn Ferry and me to foster "Purpose-Driven Leadership" for the top 200 leaders at Baxalta.

Commenting on this purpose accelerator, Ludwig asserted, "Baxalta's purpose-driven performance was a key driver in significantly increasing market cap by $10 billion in a twelve-month period. Helping people to tackle their leadership challenges with substantially enhanced self-awareness, shared purpose, and shared inspiration was invaluable in supporting our strategic and cultural transformation." *Purpose powers performance.*

Anne-Marie Law, CHRO of Baxalta at the time and now CHRO of Alexion, added this perspective: "Rarely in my career have I seen so many people so deeply touched and committed to contributing to shared meaning and purpose. Helping people connect to their individual and collective purpose multiplies cultural and financial value. Being involved in this process was clearly one of the most impactful in my career. It produced tangible financial value through inspired performance."

> *If you don't know Why,*
> *you can't know How.*
> —Simon Sinek

A while ago, I had the great fortune to be invited to NASA to give a keynote speech. Honestly, I was particularly excited because their offer included a personal tour of the Goddard Space Flight Center, where components of the new Webb telescope, a successor to the Hubble Space Telescope, were being assembled. The tour and the experience of being there was amazing. But to my surprise, I was most inspired by the interviews I conducted with many of the scientists and leaders at NASA in preparation for the keynote. I wanted to get a sense of their world and their meaning mindset. At the end of each interview, I asked everyone the same question: "What is the purpose of your work?" Person after person responded with generally the same purpose-inspired vision: "We explore the universe to improve lives on our planet." It was both astonishing and uplifting to hear the precise alignment of their skill, capabilities, and values encapsulated in this passionate, larger-than-us-all aspiration. Their clarity of purpose inspires a pause to reflect: how can each of us better contribute our talents to serve a larger purpose?

INFUSING LIFE WITH PURPOSE

It's not so surprising to see people come to their feet to applaud the retirement of a senior executive. Half may be sad to see that person leaving, and the other half may be happy, so everyone stands. More unusual is a standing ovation triggered by the announcement of a new person stepping into a leadership role.

Novartis Consumer was struggling with manufacturing issues. The business was in steep decline, and there had been three leaders in a three-year period. They wanted to find the right leader to bring together and optimize its leadership talent and business model. Novartis decided to place their trust in one of their own, Brian McNamara. As a General Manager running a key region, Brian had established a clear leadership brand, and he was loved for it. He had spent his career and his life building relationships, teams, and cultures. He knew how to do turnarounds by engaging people first and then inspiring them to exceed expectations. Upon the announcement of Brian's new role as Divisional CEO, there was a spontaneous, collective release, a feeling of "It's about time our guy was selected!" This pent-up feeling exploded into a rollicking, screaming, whistling standing ovation. It was stunning!

> *The Purpose Economy is where movements and markets come together.*
>
> —Aaron Hurst

So why do people feel such respect and appreciation for Brian and his leadership? Simple: Brian cares, and he gets results. Everyone knows it. He cares about you, and he cares about making a difference together. He builds trust by connecting genuinely with humor and empathy, and he inspires a deep confidence that emboldens people to take on tough challenges. Brian takes extra moments to be present and coach people.

In working with Brian, who is now CEO of GSK Consumer—a joint venture with Novartis—we did some deep exploration of his Core Purpose. Examining the peaks and valleys of his life, we found an overarching theme present when Brian is at his best: *infusing life in people*. Brian is utterly committed to infusing life in his family, friends, teams, customers, products, and his own health and fitness. Commenting on his purpose, Brian reflected, "As long as I am 'all-in' . . . infusing life, my life is good and meaningful. Shared energy is high, and contributions are optimal. Infusing life is the one thing that I have to do; everything else is secondary."

ORBITING AROUND CORE PURPOSE

You may think I have this "purpose thing" all figured out. Actually, the only thing I know for sure is that it is a critically important, endless journey of exploration. While the core may be a constant, ever-present reality throughout life, our clarity increases over time as we heighten our awareness and dedicate ourselves to discovering it. It is a bit like orbiting around a hazy planet and slowly focusing the image.

This focusing process is expedited by engaging in a journey to answer two critical questions:

- What is so important to me that I am endlessly fascinated by it?
- When I am at my best and creating value for others, what am I bringing to make this happen?

In my case, I have always held a compelling interest in human growth—how it happens, why it happens, the psychology of it, the history of it, and the future of it. I think of this fascination with human growth as the gravitational core that I revolve around. To me, it is vitally important and endlessly engaging. It is my Core Value, the thing I am willing to dedicate my life to.

> *This world of ours has been constructed like a superbly written novel; we pursue the tale with avidity, hoping to discover the plot.*
>
> —Sir Arthur Keith

Over time, I have been fortunate to develop some Core Talents to serve this Core Value of human growth. When these Core Talents are showing up and serving transformative growth, good things happen. When I am at my best, these Core Talents are *creativity* and *inspiration*.

When we dedicate ourselves to clarifying our Core Purpose, it will slowly emerge. Sometimes, in a quiet moment, an insight will come. Other times, on a walk with a friend, you will feel its presence. Its energetic vitality might be revealed while you are working or involved in a special interest. Glimpses will come at home or maybe while on vacation. Sometimes, the most powerful moments will break through when we least expect it. But when that clear insight comes, it is like a ball of yarn that gets thrown across our life, and the thread connects all our significant life experiences.

When it came into focus for me, I realized that whether I was seeking my education in psychology, teaching people to meditate, being an executive coach, building our consulting practice, writing books, giving keynote speeches, or being in family life, it was really only about one thing for me: *bringing forth creativity and inspiration to foster transcendent growth.* That was it—my reason for being, how my gifts could serve and touch others.

SIX THOUSAND DAYS

While leading a team-building session in Europe to help foster a more purpose-driven culture in a global company, the CEO had arranged for the group to visit a nearby Tibetan Buddhist monastery. The group was a bit reluctant, but the monk was very gracious. He greeted us, seated us in the meditation hall, and immediately engaged us in a provocative conversation. Although I've been fortunate to learn from many great teachers, I was unprepared when he singled me out at the very beginning of the discourse and asked me, "Tell me, how many days do you have left to live?"

I was stunned by the profound question, but surprisingly the answer flashed in my mind. "Six thousand days," I responded.

The monk reflected, and slowly replied, "That sounds about right. So, if you have six thousand days, do you want to waste any of them? Do you want to waste any of those days in frustration, anger, or not living your purpose?" The power, depth, and personal relevance of his existential question simultaneously disturbed me and inspired me into a reflective state of mind. He "forced" me to wrestle with it. It reminded me how one powerful question can change our lives . . . and how precious and purpose-filled every moment of life is.

Alex Gorsky, Chairman and CEO of Johnson & Johnson, shared with me his own insightful story about the significance of using our time for greatest impact. As a young cadet at West Point, Alex sat in the audience with his classmates during their orientation while the Dean of Academic Affairs addressed the entire corps. He told the first-year cadets, "Some of you will succeed. Some will fail. What will make the difference is how you use your 'scraps of time.'"

By reminding ourselves of the limited amount of time we really have, a positive tension arises and urges us to do something significant, something grounded in service. The monk's challenging question followed me for days and circulates within me still, as does the dean's admonition. Both remind me not to waste a day . . . on-purpose.

Take a little time now to ask yourself the same question the wise monk asked me: "How many days do you have left to live?" Really calculate it—come up with a number. Now, ask yourself, "Knowing the limited number of days I have, what do I want to do? How do I want to be?" What is your purpose-fueled vision for how you are going to lead and live those days?

> *We rise by lifting others.*
> *If service is below you,*
> *leadership is beyond you.*
> —Robert G. Ingersol

Purpose Mastery frames all our life and career experiences as part of a meaningful whole. When we understand purpose, all the challenging experiences of our lives serve to forge

...cter, and meaning. Although life may be challenging, every experience becomes ...very challenge an opportunity through which we learn and live more pur-... en we lack purpose, immediate circumstances dominate our awareness and overshadow our reason for being; life tends to lose connection with its true nature. Teilhard de Chardin wrote, "We are not human beings having a spiritual experience. We are spiritual beings having a human experience." *Purpose is spirit seeking expression; awareness of it allows us to see our lives more clearly from the inside out.*

You may be thinking that all this seems a bit esoteric. However, Core Purpose may be one of the most practical, useful ways to lead and live transformatively. It converts average-performing organizations, teams, families, and relationships into highly spirited, effective ones. It transforms employees, team members, spouses, or friends into partners. With purpose, managers become leaders. With purpose, we not only become leaders of organizations, we become leaders of life.

EIGHT PRINCIPLES OF PURPOSE MASTERY

Keep the following principles in mind as you begin to master leading on-purpose:

1. Get in Touch with What Is Important to You: Understanding our values, what gives meaning to our lives, gives us the "GPS coordinates" of our purpose.

If you have trouble identifying what is really important to you, pay attention to what energizes and excites you, what expands your boundaries and brings you happiness. At various points in your life, you will face a vague sense that there must be something more, some deeper meaning. You may want to dive deep into your experiences during these times to uncover your purpose-seeking expression. At these moments, your purpose may be calling, but your lack of listening creates the vagueness.

2. Act "On-Purpose": Most people have an intuitive feeling about their purpose in life. Turning this hazy intuition into a clear, tangible commitment helps turn a dream into a reality. David Prosser, retired Chairman of RTW, shared with me, "When your commitments are aligned with your purpose, then great things will happen." Committing yourself to pursuing your purpose will marshal energies and potentialities within that you did not know you had. David Whyte shares, "Take any step toward our destiny through creative action . . . the universe turns toward us, realizing we are there, alive and about to make our mark."

3. Find Team Core Purpose: While personal purpose is transformative for leaders, team purpose is powerful for the entire enterprise. Once you get clear on how your gifts make a difference, consider engaging your team around a similar exercise. When a team's purpose supports the organization's mission and strategy, great things happen. What is your team's Core Purpose? What are the distinguishing differences your group has? What is the big impact, big service, or big difference that you are going to collectively achieve? Why does this team exist? Imagine a team of leaders clear on both their individual purpose and their

> *The Purpose Effect results in a higher calling, where individuals and organizations seek to improve society to benefit all stakeholders.*
>
> —Dan Pontefract

collective purpose. Sound like a great place to be? This could be your team. Connect your individual purpose to the broader mission, and tremendous energy and engagement will be unleashed.

Stuart Parker, CEO of USAA, found a way to make the intersection of personal and organizational purpose very clear. Stuart had personal challenge coins made, similar to those used by military leaders to recognize excellence in members of their command. One side is engraved with Stuart's personal purpose—*"Mission, Trust, Freedom"*—along with pilot wings he wore during his career in the United States Air Force. On the flip side are the USAA eagle and the company's values: "Service, Loyalty, Honesty, Integrity." He wanted to convey a powerful reflection: How can your purpose serve our collective mission? Find pragmatic ways to make personal and team purpose tangible and at the forefront of daily work.

4. Do Not Mistake the Path for the Goal: Be careful not to simply adopt other people's views of your purpose. Too often, people internalize the latest personal development trend, spiritual teaching, or management guru theory into a dogmatic, inflexible, restrictive practice. This is mistaking the path for the goal. Finding your purpose is finding how your gifts can serve, not just adopting someone else's value systems. Personal development programs, religious systems, and great teachers are the guides, the techniques—not the goal. Be careful with programs or systems that impose beliefs onto you, thereby creating dependency and externalization of the real you. If the process values your uniqueness, individuality, and personal path, it may be helpful. Always remind yourself that the program or practice, no matter how stimulating or fulfilling, is the methodology—not the goal. The essence of Purpose Mastery is the very personal process of discovering how your gifts can serve something bigger.

5. Focus on Service: Purpose is not purposeful without serving others. It is not self-expression for its own sake; it is self-expression that creates value for those around you. Therefore, key into your gifts, but don't stop there. Focus on expressing your gifts to improve the lives of everyone and everything you touch.

6. Be Purposeful in All Domains: Too often we might be purposeful in one domain of our life but not in another. We may be purposeful at work and not so much at home, or we may be purposeful in personal relationships but not in our work. Once you clarify how your gifts can make a difference, examine the degree to which you are being purposeful in all parts of your life. Seeing these purpose gaps can reveal our real growth challenges. Too many leaders have lost their sense of purpose because they were not using their gifts in their personal lives or were not fully expressing their deepest personal values in their work. Congruence of purpose in all domains of our life is the aspiration of Purpose Mastery.

7. Learn from "Failure": Failure is a subjective label we apply to unintended or unexpected experiences. Usually, we are unwilling or unable to integrate these experiences into a meaningful context. From the vantage point of Purpose Mastery, failure does not exist. It is life attempting to teach us some new lessons or trying to point us toward some new directions. As Warren Bennis wrote in *On Becoming a Leader*, "Everywhere you trip is where the treasure lies." But we have to be open as we "trip." The next time you are experiencing something you didn't intend or expect, ask yourself, "What can I learn from this?" When we are living life on-purpose, every life experience helps us decode the hieroglyphics of meaning. In the words of Emerson, "The world becomes a glass dictionary."

8. Be Flexible: Genuine insight into our purpose can take the form of a recurring theme that connects divergent spheres of our lives. Like an orchestra interpreting a symphony, the expression of our purpose will change. For instance, someone's real purpose in life may be to guide and nurture others. At different stages of the life cycle, this will be expressed very differently—as a student, parent, professional, and retiree. We need to be flexible, open to the process of expressing our internal sense of purpose in many different roles and life circumstances. *Transactive managers follow set procedures in a consistent, predictable manner; transformative leaders flex to a myriad of conditions, gracefully dancing around a purpose-filled core.*

LEADERSHIP GROWTH PLAN

PURPOSE MASTERY

It's time to take a deep breath and capture some insights and commitments that can make a genuine difference in your life and in your leadership. As you do this, keep asking yourself: *What are my gifts, and what value do they create when they serve others?*

1. Areas for Building Awareness:

  - _____
  - _____
  - _____

2. New Commitments to Make:

  - _____
  - _____
  - _____

3. New Practices to Begin:

  - _____
  - _____
  - _____

4. Potential Obstacles:

  - _____
  - _____
  - _____

5. Timeline and Measures of Success:

  - _____
  - _____
  - _____

CHAPTER FOUR

INTERPERSONAL MASTERY

Leading through Synergy and Service

Martin was an incredibly gifted executive; his talent and intelligence were apparent in everything he did. At early stages of his career, his cognitive skills helped him excel in many challenging assignments. As his achievements advanced, Martin started to believe "his press" and internalized the belief that "he was the person who made things happen at this organization." He began to lose touch with the synergy that was supporting his accomplishments. He thought he was the prime mover, and in reality his teams were the ones creating and supporting his achievements. Gradually his relationships and team dynamics became strained, and he couldn't understand why.

To help Martin break through his self-limiting view, we asked him to outline each key event in his life over the past few years, focusing on the people who made each event possible. It didn't take him long to recognize the web of interdependence that was supporting his success. He became aware of initiatives for which he had taken credit and for which he now needed to acknowledge others. He was beginning to bridge personal power with synergy power to enhance broader contribution.

Marijn Dekkers, Chairman of Unilever, shared this wise counsel with me on developing highly driven leaders: "If you think that you are the primary reason for your company's success, think again. If after this second consideration, you still think you are the hero in this story, then get a coach."

Studies validate precisely what we've seen while assessing and developing leaders over the past thirty years—leaders must expand their competencies from simply getting results to adding value through collaboration. The Hay Group's research on engagement has demonstrated

...oteworthy results. Companies with highly engaged employees have 2.5 times the revenue growth of organizations with moderate to low engagement.

> *The true worth of a man is not to be found in man himself, but in the colors and textures that come alive in others because of him.*
> —Albert Schweitzer

In their book, *The Extraordinary Leader*, John Zenger and Joseph Folkman reported research findings, based on 400,000 360° assessments, which show that the most successful leaders possess multiple strengths, or "powerful combinations" of competencies. They found that of those leaders with elevated competencies in both Results Drive and Interpersonal Connection, 67 percent were in the ninetieth percentile for leadership effectiveness. However, in the group of leaders who had only high Results Drive, only 13 percent were in the ninetieth percentile for leadership effectiveness. These dramatic statistics point us to the following equation: *results competencies plus interpersonal competencies equals top leadership performance.*

TWO PRINCIPAL STREAMS OF LEADERSHIP DEVELOPMENT

The mounting research illustrates what we find in the trenches with our clients. There appear to be two main streams of development in leadership. Both approaches can get results. One of these leadership approaches is extremely hard-driving and forceful, with a strong sense of personal power—in short, an "I" leader who gets results. These leaders have no problem asserting their power of voice, even at the expense of morale, at times. This heroic type of leader needs to become more collaborative and relational to bring results to the next level. At times, this kind of hard-driving leadership takes its toll on others. Employees become worn out and drained. They question their purpose and whether or not the money is worth it. This type of leader needs to be more receptive and to develop more authentic connections and greater performance.

The other leadership approach is more interpersonally connected. These leaders are strongly collaborative and synergistic, and their power of connection ("We") is so strong that they may not appropriately put forth enough of their own power of voice ("I") when required. These leaders need to become more forceful and courageous in expressing their authentic influence to create heightened engagement.

In organizations, there is an underground debate, or what might be called a cultural battle, going on between proponents of one stream of leadership and the other. Some say that we need more hard-edged "I" leaders, who assert their power of voice to get more results. On the other side of the debate, people assert that we need more of the team-oriented "We" leaders to foster performance. They say we would be better off if the hard-edged, driving leaders would just step back and connect more.

Based on research and on what we see with our clients, there is really no basis for this debate. If we aspire to genuine, world-class leadership, we need to develop both streams: power of voice, "I"; and power of connection, "We." What do you need to do more of, less of, or differently regarding these streams of development? Do you need to develop more "I" or more "We"?

Interpersonal Mastery is about balancing our courageous influence—our voice—with human connection. This is not easy. As a matter of fact, it is one of the most difficult leadership challenges. When we have two powerful elements—our power of voice and our power of connection—coming together, we experience one of our most significant leadership moments. But it is much more challenging than simply bringing forward our "Authentic I" and our "Connected We." The following story, which really happened to a friend of David Whyte and is similar to Dr. Jerry Harvey's "Abilene Paradox," illustrates the challenges even very senior leaders face when it comes to speaking up with a more powerful voice.

David's friend, an executive and member of a senior team, was getting ready to retire from a successful corporate career. His reputation was intact. Financially, he was in great shape. By all measures, he was set. His CEO had a pet project that was important to him, but the CEO was frustrated by his senior team, because they didn't seem to support it. The truth was they didn't think the project had value, and they hoped, if they kept avoiding it, the CEO would forget about it. He didn't. Instead, one day the CEO called his senior team into the conference room and said, "Okay. I want to hear from each of you about this project. On a scale of one to ten, ten meaning you are fully behind this strategy and one meaning you are against it." He turned to the first person on his right and said, "Okay. What do you think?"

David's friend thought to himself, "Wow! Now the CEO is going to get some real feedback." But to his surprise and disappointment, the first team member said, "Ten, Bob." The next said, "Ten, Bob." The next "brave" soul said, "Nine and a half, Bob." When the CEO got all the way around the table to David's friend, despite the fact that he had nothing to lose, in a meek, mouse-like voice, he registered his "Ten, Bob."

All of us do "Ten, Bobs." But there are also times when we dare to take a different stance. These are the moments of real leadership, when we courageously step forward instead of cautiously stepping away. When we step forward, we align our voice, our values, and our experience in a manner that is solid and value-creating. How can you be more courageous, authentic, and aligned when doing so is not popular? What have been your "Ten, Bob" moments? What are the situations that most inhibit your authentic voice?

> *Collaboration is vital to sustain what we call profound or really deep change, because without it, organizations are just overwhelmed by the forces of the status quo.*
>
> —Peter Senge

Culture—both corporate and societal—influences us powerfully from the outside in, toward the "I" or the "We" leadership approaches. Both approaches have an upside and a downside. Just as the tough, results-dominated culture has its downside or shadow consequences, so does the culture that supports too much niceness and politeness. These companies are pleasant, wonderful places to work. But the shadow is that people may be overly nice or passive-aggressive. Often, they avoid the tough conversations and constructive conflict. Authentic influence may be sacrificed on the altar of niceness. As a result, individual points of view may not come forward, and innovation may be compromised. World-class leadership is catalyzed by a courageous mixture of personal authenticity and interpersonal connection.

BUILDING RELATIONSHIP BRIDGES

Relationships are the bridges that connect authenticity to influence and value creation. Leadership is not influence for its own sake; it is influence that makes a difference and enriches the lives of others. Leadership does not exist in a vacuum. It always operates in context, in relationship. *While leaders may lead by virtue of who they are, leaders also create value by virtue of their relationships.* As the chairman of a global technology services firm shared with me, "Leadership is not about sitting in your office and dreaming up strategy; it is about touching the organization through personal presence and relationship."

As crucial as relationships are to leadership success, many of us have a difficult time breaking out of the self-limiting illusion that we are "the ones that make things happen." All too often, successful, achievement-oriented people mistakenly believe they are the principal source of accomplishments in their groups or organizations. Most leaders would not admit to this, but often their behavior clearly demonstrates this belief.

Research by the Saratoga Institute makes a startling case for the consequences of poor interpersonal skills. The Institute interviewed 19,700 people—exiting employees and their bosses. The results indicated that 85 percent of bosses said that their former employees left for more compensation and opportunity. On the other hand, 80 percent of the exiting employees said that they left because of poor relationships, poor development, and poor coaching from the boss.

Unfortunately, many driven leaders fail to comprehend that nothing is accomplished without engaging in relationships and appreciating the unique contributions of many, many people. Some leaders even feel slowed down or frustrated by the teaming or synergy process. Larry Perlman, former Chairman and CEO of Ceridian over a twenty-two-year tenure, sees it differently: "Leadership will not add enough value if it only comes from the top; it needs to come from the very guts of the business itself to make a meaningful and enduring difference."

Jim Collins has described leaders with the combination of humility and fierce resolve as "tofu leaders: leaders who are somewhat bland, mix really well with everything around them, and provide lots of sustenance and value." These leaders tend to take less credit for themselves and make certain that others receive it. Perhaps a more heroic, take-no-prisoners approach is needed in some business environments, but today, sustaining leaders must be able to blend people effectiveness with affinity for results.

Bob Eichinger, cofounder of Lominger International, adds that interpersonal skills are what separate high-performing leaders from the rest of the pack. "The key difference between good leaders and legacy leaders is not only about results; it's about their people competencies. Legacy leaders are the orchestra conductors. They get the right people in the right chairs. They make it happen by bringing it all together."

Roger Lacey, board member of Johnsonville Foods and former head of Corporate Strategy at 3M Company, shared this perspective on team leadership: "Ultimately, strategy, leadership, and teaming have to find their high-performing intersection. When companies leverage world-class strategy with world-class leadership and teaming, enduring momentum is possible."

> ...d at
> ...understood; be
> disturbed rather at not
> being understanding.
>
> —Chinese proverb

In addition to not seeing ourselves as the key driver of our organizations, as leaders we must also admit that very little of what we know can be said to be truly our own. Our language, culture, education, and beliefs have all come to us through others. We have acquired them through relationships. James Flaherty, author of *Coaching: Evoking Excellence in Others*, has personally taught me this key principle: Those who say they are truly "self-made leaders" are ignoring many generations of people before them, and they often lack the confidence and character to learn from and give credit to others.

BALANCING PERSONAL POWER WITH SYNERGY POWER AND CONTRIBUTION POWER

One of the crucial development challenges for most leaders is learning how to authentically influence in a manner that also creates lasting value. This is not to say that leaders are not getting results; they usually are. Too often, though, they lack results that sustain value and contribution at the same time. How often do leaders get results but leave a wake of bodies in the process? How often do businesses get results but leave people or the environment damaged? This is getting results without making an enduring contribution.

A while ago, I had the good fortune to sit down and talk with John Dalla Costa, author of *The Ethical Imperative*. While I shared my perspective about leadership, I was dying to ask John, "What the heck is ethics?" At the appropriate moment, I sprang the question. To my surprise, John's answer was succinct: "Ethics is others." I thought, "That's it? Twenty-five years of research and the answer is three small words?" Later, as I let John's concentrated wisdom sink in, the profound simplicity and complexity of his definition hit me. Leaders face ethical dilemmas every day, and they usually boil down to *people*—managing constant stakeholder-related trade-offs and serving one constituency better or more than another.

Ken Melrose, Toro Chairman and CEO for twenty-two years, shared with me one of the company's ethical dilemmas, which centered around a lawnmower product that had become a new commercial market standard. The product is unique because it turns on a dime but also has a very low center of gravity. Consequently, it is very hard to overturn. But in the rare instance that it does overturn, it flips over 180° and can seriously injure the operator. While the mower met compliance standards, Toro decided to add a roll bar behind the seat as an added safety precaution, and they did so without raising the price on newly manufactured units.

As the company further considered the needs of others, Toro faced another tough decision. What about existing units? Don't they deserve the same ethical treatment? The initial, Pollyanna answer was yes, but the strict financial answer was *no*. So, what was the right thing to do? Were old customers as valuable as new ones, and were they as important as shareholders, who may have invested much more of themselves in the company? Melrose's company installed the roll bars on all machines, new and old, at their own cost. They reasoned that although the decision was immediately costly for shareholders, the value-creating decision

> *One need ask only one question. "What for? What am I to unify my being for?" The reply is: Not for my own sake.*
>
> —Martin Buber

served both the customers and investors in the long haul. Seeing the longer-term consequences to all constituents, to all the "others," Toro made a tough, ethical leadership decision.

In their discussion of "intentional work" in *Presence: An Exploration of Profound Change in People, Organizations, and Society*, Peter Senge and his coauthors—C. Otto Scharmer, Joseph Jaworski, and Betty Sue Flowers—say, "When people in leadership positions begin to serve a vision infused with a larger purpose, their work shifts naturally from producing results to encouraging the growth of people who produce results." Too many organizations today take a very mechanistic approach to this model. Many companies tend to focus on results at all costs and drive the organization and people to support these goals.

This mechanistic approach prizes results over synergy and synergy over the individual. It's an outside-in view of organizations and people. This approach to leading organizations leaves people feeling devalued and wondering, "Where do I fit in? Why am I here?" It's an approach to leadership that misses the power of human engagement. As opposed to a mechanistic business, an organic one sees people as the source of creativity and dynamism. In this type of organization, personal power supports synergy power, which in turn contributes something of value to multiple constituencies. This inside-out model of organizations creates a purposeful culture where people are constantly thinking, "How can I make more of a contribution? How can I bring my gifts to others to make a difference?" It's a purposeful, dynamic approach to organizational leadership that values and leverages the power of human aspiration.

Unfortunately, many leaders are limiting their effectiveness by using only their personal power to drive results. In the process, they have adopted a tough, get-it-done persona, devoid of much emotional intelligence or sustained performance. Winning at all costs rules the day, and relationships are seen as a means to get results. Unknowingly, long-term, sustainable results are being compromised because the collaborative power of the organization is suboptimal.

Peter Block, in his book *Stewardship*, wrote, "We are reluctant to let go of the belief that 'if I am to care for something, I must control it.'" A while ago I spoke to a CEO who had started to build his bridge from personal power to relational power. After a long struggle "to set his organization right," he finally had to change his approach and value the power of synergy. Describing his experience, he told me, "My rules just weren't working anymore. The more I tried to assert my will, the worse things got. Not only was I attempting to take total responsibility for the turnaround, I also was taking the total blame for any problems. I was amazingly self-centered. I believed the fate of the entire business was mine alone. Letting go of that belief freed me to really lead us to a new future."

> *How much larger your life would be if your self could become smaller in it.*
> —G. K. Chesterton

Paul Walsh, Chairman and CEO of Diageo for twelve years, described it to me this way: "As managers, we are trained as cops, who are supposed to keep things under control. As leaders, we need to shift from control to trust." Giving an apt description of balancing personal power with synergy power, he went on to say, "I don't care who you are or how great you are, no one person can totally claim the victory or totally abstain from the defeat." Learning to move our belief from thinking, "I have all the answers," to "together, we have all the answers," is the first crucial step to Interpersonal Mastery.

The late David McClelland, Harvard professor, author of *The Achieving Society*, and foundational thought leader with our Hay Group, pioneered breakthrough research that clarified eighty overall motives and three principle leadership motive categories: achievement, affiliation, and power. Interestingly, within the power motive, he differentiated two types of power: Personalized Power and Socialized Power. Rick Lash, a Hay Group colleague, explains this critical leadership dynamic: "While we all use Personalized Power to some degree to achieve our goals, when Personalized Power is all about serving the self or ego, it can create d at least limit sustained value creation. Socialized Power is about going beyond self to others and includes acting for a larger purpose. In an increasingly complex and diverse Socialized Power becomes critical to enduring leadership success."

The constant reconciliation of Personalized Power and Socialized Power—the "I" motive and the "We" motive—is the real work of leadership development. This brings us to the ultimate questions of Interpersonal Mastery: Is the "I" mainly serving the "I"? Or is the "I" mainly in service to the "We" and the broader, more purposeful enterprise achievement? The answer to these foundational questions will determine the fate of your leaders, teams, organizations, and quite possibly our planet.

REDUCING THE INTENTION-PERCEPTION GAP

The second step for leaders is to realize that we often lack full awareness of our impact on others. We assume, to an amazing degree, that other people clearly and fully receive our intended communication. It's a *huge* leap of faith that does not hold up under close examination. Have you ever had a great laugh with a group of people and then asked each person what they thought was so funny? Probably, you were surprised to discover the unique perspective from which each person interprets the world.

All of us have been communicating our intentions since we delivered our first kick in our mother's womb. Since then, our rich, well-practiced, internal conversations have evolved considerably, and we take for granted that others are receiving precisely our intended meaning. We express ourselves, and then we are shocked when our messages are misunderstood. Emerson wrote: "Men imagine that they communicate their virtue or vice only by overt actions, and do not see that virtue or vice emit a breath every moment."

Becoming skilled at receiving feedback *from* others is crucial to ensuring that our influence is beneficial *to* others. Effective leadership requires us to constantly reduce the gap between intended and perceived communication. As one CEO likes to remind me, "I always start with API—Assumption of Positive Intent. Ninety-five percent of the leaders I know want to do well for themselves and others." Although most leaders have good intentions, the way those intentions show up can be quite diverse. Ambrose Bierce wrote with great insight and humor, "In each human heart are a tiger, an ass and a nightingale. Diversity of character is due to their unequal activity."

BEYOND 360° FEEDBACK TO 720° DEVELOPMENT

The tool most organizations use to help leaders deal with the intention-perception gap is 360° feedback. With such programs, leaders are given feedback from multiple sources on their behavior, skills, and leadership competencies.

Unfortunately, 360° feedback does not reveal the whole person. From a developmental perspective, it reveals only a portion of the person, rather than the total picture. This is particularly true when 360° feedback is the sole source of input given to the leader. If a development process is modeled primarily around 360° feedback, executives only learn how to create themselves in the image of others. As a result, they learn how to act instead of how to be—a direct route to following, not leading. In a provocative way, I tell most of my client organizations, "You don't need 360° feedback. What you need for leaders is *720° development*." After they give me a polite, somewhat confused stare, I elaborate that 360° feedback in the absence of new self-knowledge often has two limitations:

1. It can create a defensive reaction, in which case no growth takes place.

2. It encourages people to simply deliver the desired behaviors without giving them the personal insight and motivation to grow—a formula destined to limit authentic influence by creating actors, not leaders.

> *If you are irritated by every rub, how will your mirror be polished?*
>
> —Rumi

But 720° Development is different. It begins with an Inside-Out 360°—a deep, broad, valid, integrated assessment of our personality traits, motives, and competencies as well as our current and desired stages of development. This first stage ensures that we begin to master a more authentic understanding of ourselves. Then, an Outside-In 360° is completed to give broad feedback on how people above, across from, and below us perceive our strengths and areas of development. With 720° Development, leaders now have a more complete context to reconcile their inner and outer realities.

For instance, I worked with a vice president of a consumer products company who received 360° feedback from his company prior to our coaching. He was perceived as too aggressive and untrustworthy. He was devastated by the feedback, because he lacked the self-awareness to meaningfully interpret the harsh input. He had no idea what to do. Should he pull back on his relationships and be less aggressive? If he did that, wouldn't it further erode his sense of trust with people? Because he didn't know himself at a deep enough level, he was unable to assimilate the feedback and was developmentally paralyzed.

After completing our *Executive to Leader Institute* and getting an integrated, 720° view of himself, this executive had

> *People will forget what you said, people will forget what you did, but people will never forget how you made them feel.*
>
> —Maya Angelou

much more clarity of his entire situation. For the first time, he became objectively aware that he was extremely aggressive and dominant. He'd had no idea his interpersonal style was so far beyond the norm for leaders. Suddenly he had a context in which to understand the value of the feedback, and he was motivated to show up in a manner more consistent with his real intentions. Regarding the trustworthiness factor, we found in the Inside-Out 360° that he was a very honest person of high integrity. However, his somewhat introverted, aloof approach with people was creating a perception that he held things back. Knowing this, the challenge was of a different order. He needed to spend more time with peer relationships to let people get to know him. Once he got the complete 720° Development, he was able to engage actively in a development plan to move forward.

INTIMATE CONNECTION OF PERSONAL MASTERY AND INTERPERSONAL MASTERY

As we discussed earlier in the book, mastery of *Leadership from the Inside Out* is about consciously making a difference by fully applying our talents. This does not mean that we lead only from the inside out. On the contrary, we lead just as much from the outside in. Leadership is a constant dynamic between the inner and the outer and vice versa. We are in a continuing flow, a dynamic relationship with ourselves, our customers, our employees, and our personal relationships. Ultimately, we want a balance of leading from the inside out and from the outside in. Our decisions and actions are in a dynamic loop from us to others and back again. To practice leadership at the highest level of value creation, we need to consciously reconcile inside-out and outside-in dynamics:

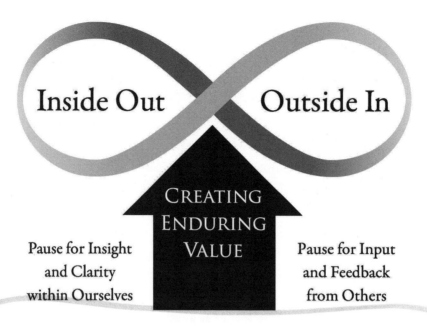

Therefore, in addition to using 720° Development as a best practice, it is also important to get feedback in real time. As you are interacting with others, are you watching for discomfort, misunderstanding, inappropriate silence, or energy shifts in people? Ask people for their feedback on your views and how you are coming across. Even if you are quite sure people are listening, ask them what they think. Encourage people to challenge you. Ask people if there are other ways to view the topic at hand. Make sure they have received your intentions. If not, ask them what they heard, and then take the time to clarify until you are satisfied your intentions have been received. This will serve a threefold purpose:

1. Your influence will be even more authentic and create more value.
2. You will learn more about how you are being perceived.
3. You will develop more effective ways to communicate.

In *100 Things You Need to Know: Best People Practices for Managers & HR*, Eichinger, Lombardo, and Ulrich report results of a study showing that "although it might seem mildly counterintuitive, high potentials, and especially executives, get less feedback. They are more likely to be told how wonderfully they are doing; specific feedback or even formal performance appraisals can be rare." Don't let yourself fall into this trap. Make 720° Development and real-time feedback a way to accelerate your self-awareness and interpersonal awareness.

THE INCLUSION PARADOX CREATES VALUE

The relationship between self-awareness and awareness of others is at the foundation of activating talent and collaboration in an inclusive, multicultural workforce. Andrés Tapia is an expert in workplace solutions, diversity, and inclusion. In his compelling book *The Inclusion Paradox*, Tapia asserts that if leaders want to attract and retain top talent, they have to foster work environments in which a wide diversity of people thrive. To do this, leaders must understand the distinction between diversity and inclusion.

"Diversity is the mix; inclusion is making the mix work." To make the mix work, leaders must become culturally agile. At the heart of cultural agility is awareness—self-awareness and awareness of others. "It is not enough," Tapia clarifies in our conversations, "to embrace and celebrate difference. Leaders need to understand in a deep, visceral, business-grounded way how to activate diversity." Tapia passionately explains, "Each of us, even the white male, has his own individual biography that defines and influences why he walks and talks the way he does, why he thinks, believes, and acts the way he does."

Politely ignoring and not talking about our differences is a liability. "Calling out differences unleashes the true creative contributions of diverse perspectives that play off each other and lead to better work relationships, greater innovation, and profitability that benefit individuals, teams, and organizations," Tapia concludes. Authentic inclusion never makes people choose between their core identity and adding value at work. This is the Inclusion Paradox: incorporating our differences in our daily work, policies, structures, and strategies makes us stronger as individuals, teams, organizations, communities, and societies. *Transactive managers seek control through conformity with the past, while transformative leaders discover new frontiers by being open, inclusive, and innovative.*

OPENING UP POSSIBILITIES

I was driving around a city lake in Minneapolis on a brilliant spring day. As you may know, spring in Minneapolis is dramatic. From the depths of winter, everything explodes into life. Seemingly all at once, the trees bloom and the birds return. As I was driving along, appreciating all of this renewal, a big fat robin flew into the front grille of my car and was killed immediately. I pulled over to check it out, and there was nothing I could do. As I drove away, I thought about this beautiful bird who just a moment ago had been enjoying her life, tending

ıg her purpose. In a flash, I came along and unintentionally shut all
n do we do that in our relationships? How often, as leaders, do we
our organizations and shut others down?

> *...ees*
> *...e;*
> *courage is also w... it takes*
> *to sit down and listen.*
> —Winston Churchill

Practicing Interpersonal Mastery isn't easy, and it takes time. We don't always feel we have the time to pause and listen. When I return from lengthy business trips, I want to head into my office to "get things done." My first internal reaction to colleagues walking in is, "Yeah, what do you want?" But the important interpersonal discipline is to move away from my keyboard and my "busyness" and be present with them for a few minutes. The results-oriented part of me feels like I just slowed down, but this is eventually counterbalanced by the people-oriented part of me that knows I just gave someone else fuel to go faster.

Marilyn Carlson Nelson, one of *Fortune* magazine's "50 Most Powerful Women in Business" and CEO for seventeen years of Carlson Companies, one of the largest privately held corporations in the United States, expressed this perspective: "Employees who feel that their management cares about them as a person, in return care about the organization in which they work. And isn't that the key to a successful enterprise?"

MOVING FROM LEADER TO OPENER

One of the most crucial qualities in a leader is courageous openness—openness to new possibilities in the marketplace, openness to new learnings and innovation, openness to relationships, openness to new ways of doing things, openness to encouraging people to pursue possibilities. Openness is so important to leadership that maybe we should stop calling people "leaders" and rename the most effective ones "openers." *Leaders open up or shut down opportunities in direct proportion to how open or shut down they are to themselves and to others.*

We worked with a senior executive a while ago who sincerely believed in openness. What he didn't realize was that his way of being direct and frank with people was actually shutting them down. He believed in openness and authenticity, but his approach was creating the opposite effect. It was a total mystery to him. He even rationalized it by saying that other people in his organization just weren't as open as he was. What was missing was openness to himself. He could be open and direct when it came to driving people to results or expressing criticism, but he could not be open about his fears, limitations, inadequacies, or vulnerabilities. As a result, his embodiment of "openness" was very limited.

Once he gained the inner strength and confidence to be more open about his real concerns and feelings, it came as a great surprise to him how other people opened up to him. He told me, "It was startling to me that people opened up and supported me as I opened up and shared my vulnerabilities. I built my career by being invulnerable. I was very open about the work, but very fearful about revealing myself. I didn't understand that I was distancing people in the process. I now understand that more openness in the organization begins with me."

Anne Morrow Lindbergh wrote, "When one is a stranger to oneself, then one is estranged from others, too. If one is out of touch with oneself, then one cannot touch others." As a world-class, international consultant, Suzanne really touched her clients. When asked why her clients had such outstanding regard for her, she quickly replied, "I treat each one with the respect and service of an honored guest. I feel privileged to be associated with them and want them to feel served. I can't fully explain it; I just treat them like a guest in my home."

Unfortunately, Suzanne's coworkers reported that they did not feel like guests. They felt that Suzanne only cared about "looking special" in her clients' eyes and cared very little about them. Suzanne was not aware of her excessive need to "be special." This need was generated by her Shadow Belief: "I'm not good enough as I am." As a result, Suzanne was driven to validate her uniqueness from the outside. Once she understood this dynamic and comprehended emotionally how mistreated her coworkers felt, she was very motivated to treat everyone in her life as "guests." She worked on her limiting beliefs and changed her relationship paradigm from self-service to service-to-others.

TRUSTING AND ENGAGING IN CONSTRUCTIVE CONFLICT

In helping senior teams elevate their game to the next level, we consistently find that two crucial areas are in need of development: trust and constructive conflict. Teams that can authentically face these two interpersonal challenges can accelerate performance greatly.

Following the merger of two major consumer products firms, a newly forming team came face-to-face with these two critical issues. While they acted very friendly and cordial to each other on the surface, the truth was the two groups' members really did not trust each other.

Consequently, they did not have the courage and the relationship to engage openly and honestly or to have constructive conflict. As a result, they generated no new innovative strategies, and they relied on a series of fast executions. The business pace became sluggish, falling directly in step with the low level of trust and engagement holding back the senior team. As is common with most senior teams, team members retreated to the comforts of their function or business unit to do their "real work."

We were engaged to create a forum for these people to build relationships, get to know each other, forge a purpose bigger than their concern for themselves, gain the tools to have positive conflict, and eventually build trust. An undertaking like this is much more than an off-site event. We worked through this process, individually and collectively, over several months. Slowly our meetings warmed up. With respect and understanding, leaders began to challenge each other. Individual leaders committed to coaching sessions to get ready to show up in new ways. The CEO embodied new behaviors and "walked the talk" of the new values and purpose expressed by the team. After nine months, our measures of trust increased by 60 percent, and over twelve months they increased by 76 percent. Dealing with conflict constructively improved significantly. The team had internalized Interpersonal Mastery at a new and rewarding level.

> *Holding on to anger is like grasping a hot coal with the intent of throwing it at someone else: you are the one who gets burned.*
>
> —Buddha

On the value of team development from the inside out, Brad Hewitt, CEO of Thrivent Financial, commented: "In today's fast-paced world, it is critical to elevate team and personal development to a new level. Team and self-awareness are essential for excellence. Integrating in-depth, inside-out processes for key team members with in-depth, outside-in perspectives from the marketplace is crucial to keep pace. Taking this more holistic approach does impact personal, team, and strategic growth." Real team development involves integrating Personal Mastery, Interpersonal Mastery, and Strategic Mastery—all in one process.

REFLECTION

BUILDING RELATIONSHIPS

Take some time to reflect on the following questions to help develop and build relationships:

1. Under what conditions do you shut down communication?

2. What beliefs are causing you to shut down under those conditions?

3. How can you be more open in future situations?

4. Do you need to strengthen your "I" or your "We" to build even more authentic relationships?

5. How can you more effectively build your relationship bridges?

6. How can you bring your team trust and team effectiveness to a new level?

SIX PRINCIPLES OF AUTHENTIC INTERPERSONAL MASTERY

Authenticity is the core of relationships around which synergy and trust grow. Imagine a relationship without authenticity. Can it survive? Certainly not long term. Authenticity is the life force of relationships; it is the true voice of the leader as it touches other people's hearts. From observing the most effective leaders, I would suggest there are Six Principles for Authentic Interpersonal Mastery, that bridge genuine influence to value creation.

1. Know Yourself Authentically: Variations of the phrase *nosce te ipsum*, "know thyself," appear throughout the ages, in the writings of Ovid, Cicero, and Socrates, in the sayings of the Seven Sages of Greece, on the entrance to the temple of Apollo, in Christian writings, and in Eastern texts. One scholar says it was part of Shakespeare's "regular moral and religious diet."

ads its way through history as the preeminent precept in life.

"Full wise is he that can himself know."

...g: "Trust is within ourselves."

Pope: "And all our knowledge is, ourselves to know."

Montaigne: "If a man does not know himself, how should he know his functions and his powers?"

Saint-Exupéry: "Each man must look to himself to teach him the meaning of life."

Lao Tzu: "Knowledge of self is the source of our abilities."

More contemporary thinkers, from Ralph Waldo Emerson to Abraham Maslow and Warren Bennis, have carried on the tradition. Emerson wrote, "The purpose of life seems to be to acquaint man with himself." Bennis wrote: "Letting the self emerge is the essential task of leaders." If we want to be more effective with others, we first need to become more effective with ourselves. Instead of focusing on finding the right partner (in business or friendships), seek to *be* the right partner. Commit to the journey of self-awareness through Personal Mastery. To connect with others, we first must connect with ourselves.

2. Listen Authentically: How often are we truly present with someone? How often do we pause, set aside all our concerns—past, present, and future—and completely "be there" for

> *The most important thing in communication is to hear what isn't being said.*
>
> —Peter Drucker

someone else? How often do we really hear what the other person is saying and feeling without filtering it heavily through our own immediate concerns and time pressures? Authentic listening is not easy. We hear the words, but rarely do we really listen. We hear the words, but do we also "hear" the emotions, fears, beliefs, and underlying concerns?

Authentic listening is not a technique. It involves deep care for the other person that goes beyond our self-centered needs. It is about standing in their shoes or seeing through their eyes. It is about empathy. Listening authentically is centered on the principle of psychological reciprocity: to influence others, we must first be open to their influence. Authentic listening is the attempt to place the other person's self-expression as primary at that moment.

Listening is not the same as waiting for the other person to finish speaking. I find it amusing to observe leaders who think that not speaking is the same as really listening. Fidgeting in their chairs and doing several things at once, many leaders give numerous, simultaneous cues that they are anywhere but present with people. One successful senior executive I was about to coach was so agitated while I was talking to him that he actually threw his pen across the room. His impatience and inner distress were so strong, he couldn't even listen to me for a minute without his "dis-ease" bursting through his body and making him fling his Montblanc across my office! It was a very embarrassing moment for him to see precisely what other people witnessed in his behavior.

Try practicing authentic listening. Be with people, and have the goal to fully understand the thoughts and feelings they are trying to express. Use your questions and comments to draw them out, to open them up, and to clarify what is said rather than expressing your view, closing them down, and saying only what you want. Not only will this help you understand what value and contribution the other person has, it will also create a new openness in the relationship that will allow you to express yourself more authentically.

> *If A is success in life, then A equals x plus y plus z. Work is x, y is play, and z is keeping your mouth shut.*
>
> —Albert Einstein

Authentic listening creates the platform for openness, trust, and team effectiveness. Being open to valuing and attending to different perspectives from diverse sources results in a more complete understanding of issues and more innovative solutions. Research has clearly identified communication skills as core to leadership effectiveness, and listening skills are the core of communication. *Authentic listening is the soul of synergy.*

3. Influence Authentically: Authentic influence is a delicate subject for many leaders. I have yet to meet a leader who would admit readily that he or she lacks some degree of integrity. I also have yet to meet a leader who has complete integrity in all parts of his or her life.

Integrity goes far beyond telling the truth. Integrity means total congruence between who we are and what we do. It is a formidable goal, worthy of spending a lifetime getting there. How often have we held back something that we feel is important because we are fearful of expressing it? How often have we expressed something in a slightly more favorable light to avoid hurting someone's feelings? How often have we protected someone from what we consider a tough message? How often have we feigned modesty for something we were really proud of?

Authentic influence is the true voice of the leader. We speak it from our character, and it creates trust, synergy, and connection with everyone around us. Authentic influence is not

...ng our presentation style—it's deeper than that. Some of the most authentic ...ow stumble around a bit in their delivery, but the words come right from their hearts and experiences. You can feel it. You feel their conviction and the integral connection of who they are and what they say. Benjamin Franklin wrote, "Think innocently and justly, and if you speak, speak accordingly."

Authentic influence is about straight talk that creates value. It's not about hurting people with bluntness or insensitivity. Expressing yourself authentically is sharing your real thoughts and feelings in a manner that opens up possibilities. It's not about delivering only positive messages and avoiding the negatives—sometimes the most difficult messages can open up the most possibilities if shared in a thoughtful, compassionate manner.

> *Effective leaders put words to the formless longings and deeply felt needs of others.*
>
> —Warren Bennis

Influencing authentically is what one CEO I know calls "caring confrontation"—the unique blending of straight talk with a genuine concern for people. Like many leaders, my CEO friend had been uncomfortable with such interaction for years. As his career progressed, he realized, "Real caring involves giving people the tough feedback they need to grow." Another very self-aware CEO put it this way: "A leader's ability to be appropriately tough is directly proportional to the depth and quality of his or her relationships." Carl Jung said it this way: "To confront a person in his shadow is to show him his light."

Start observing how authentically you are expressing yourself. Fernando Flores, communications expert and founder of Business Design Associates and Pluralistic Networks, boiled down his powerful communication paradigm to this: "A human society operates through the expression of requests and promises." Are you authentically expressing your requests? Are you authentically fulfilling your promises? Are you authentically reiterating a request or a promise when needed? Use this model as a guide to authentic influence; it is very transformative.

4. Appreciate Authentically: As leaders, we do too much and appreciate too little. Has anyone ever appreciated you too much? It would probably be safe to say that human beings have an infinite capacity to be appreciated. Lenny Bruce wrote, "There are never enough 'I love yous.'" A mentor of mine once told me, "Love is an extreme case of appreciation."

However, as leaders we don't appreciate enough, much less love enough. In fact, we have banned the "L" word from business. In spite of the fact that the "L" word is the substance that unifies teams, builds cultures, fosters commitment, and bonds people to an organization, it is not socially acceptable even to say the "L" word in a business context. We can say we hate someone with no repercus-

Appreciation is a wonderful thing. It makes what is excellent in others belong to us as well.

—Voltaire

sions, but if we say we love someone, we may be banished for life! In lieu of this cultural taboo, let's insert the word "appreciation." Appreciation is one type of influence that creates value. It energizes people and makes them want to exceed their goals and perceived limits.

Criticism is one type of influence that often does not add value. What it typically adds is fear and insecurity. Criticism may get some short-term results, but a constant dosage tends to be toxic. Judging others critically doesn't define *them*, anyway; it defines *us*. An Islamic aphorism suggests that "a thankful person is thankful under all circumstances. A complaining soul complains even if he lives in paradise."

As leaders, we need to follow the advice of William Penn: "If there is any kindness I can show, or any good thing I can do to any fellow being, let me do it now, and not deter or neglect it, as I shall not pass this way again." What would an organization or team be like if people willingly expressed this type of appreciation for one another?

Studies done by John Gottmann, and described in his book *Why Marriages Succeed or Fail*, found that relationships that had a five-to-one ratio of appreciation to criticism were thriving, healthy, and productive. However, relationships that were at a one-to-one ratio of appreciation to criticism were doomed to failure. Divorces were the inevitable result of falling to a one-to-one ratio or lower.

Discipline yourself to practice authentic appreciation. Look for what is going well—point it out and have some fun celebrating good things as they come up. Shift your analysis of situations from finding fault to finding the value being added. Move from critic to coach. As Thomas Ebeling, CEO of ProSieben Media, shared, "Moving from critic to coach may be one of the most powerful tools we have as leaders to generate energy, engagement, enthusiasm, and results in an organization. It is very challenging to practice, but it is at the core of transformational leadership."

Acknowledge effort and intention even if the results are occasionally lacking. Trust that your appreciation will energize people. Commit to a culture of acknowledgment and appreciation; have team members commit to being a source of acknowledgment and appreciation to one another. Appreciation transmits energy, and as Emerson wrote, "The world belongs to the energetic." Multiply your leadership energy through the practice of genuine appreciation.

5. Share Stories Authentically: As we have discussed and illustrated, stories are the language of leadership. They separate a boring, detached, closed manager from an inspiring, connected, open leader. Real power emanates from our ability to connect with those around us.

> *Authentic conversations have a distinct character. They value inclusion over exclusion, curiosity over prejudice, commonality over difference, and inquiry over domination.*
> —Mickey Connolly

That is the power and universality of classics: stories that, regardless of their time or their place, connect us emotionally to themes, characters, and conflicts that are still relevant today. Your real-life personal or career stories are inspiring tools for building relationship bridges. "To communicate is not just a matter of pushing information at another person," Daniel Goleman said. "It's creating an experience to engage their emotional gut, and that's an emotional craft." Craft authentic stories to bring your values to life and to build deeper emotional connection with your people.

6. Serve Authentically: As a very wise, eighty-five-year-old CEO shared with me, "I think one of the key questions every leader must ask himself or herself is, 'How do I want to be of service to others?'" Ultimately, a leader is not judged so much by how well he or she leads but by how well he or she serves. All value and contribution are achieved through service. Do we have any other purpose in life but to serve? Leadership is a continuum of service. We serve our organization, our people, our customers, our marketplace, our community, and our family. We serve all our relationships while also serving our deepest values and our purpose. At the heart of service is the principle of interdependence: relationships are effective when mutual benefits are served.

> *The truth will not necessarily set you free, but truthfulness will.*
> —Ken Wilber

In *Stewardship*, Peter Block captures the essence of serving authentically: "There is pride in leadership; it evokes images of direction. There is humility in stewardship; it evokes images of service. Service is central to the idea of stewardship."

As leaders, when we move from control to service, we acknowledge that we are not the origin of achievement. This shift is an emotional and spiritual breakthrough. Several years ago, I had the privilege of speaking at a Greenleaf Servant Leadership Conference, where Dee Hock also was a keynote speaker. As you may know, Dee Hock, CEO of Visa and author of *Birth of the Chaordic Age*, was named one of the eight people who most changed the world through business in the last fifty years. Including himself in a reflection about leadership, Dee said, "When we as leaders get in the bad habit of thinking that other people are there to support our success, we're actually not leaders, we're tyrants. Only when we go through the emotional, psychological, and spiritual transformation to realize our role is to serve others, do we deserve to be called a leader." This is a powerful reframing of the way we typically perceive leadership, isn't it?

As we advance through leadership roles, it is easy to get caught up in the "bad habits" of thinking that others are there principally to serve our needs. But once we are conscious of this more powerful perspective, it is easier to move from leadership that is self-serving and short term to leadership that is constituency-serving and sustainable. As Winston Churchill said in often-quoted words, "We make a living by what we get. We make a life by what we give." *We are measured as a manager by what we produce; we are judged as a leader by what we give.*

Practice serving authentically. Start by appreciating the bigger forces around and beyond you that are guiding the whole process. Understand that you are fortunate to have this particular role. Appreciate it; then let your talents and gifts come forth. Bryant Hinckley summed it up well in *Hours with Our Leaders*:

> Service is the virtue that distinguished the great of all times and which they will be remembered by. It places a mark of nobility upon its disciples. It is the dividing line which separates the two great groups of the world—those who help and those who hinder, those who lift and those who lean, those who contribute and those who only consume. How much better it is to give than to receive. Service in any form is comely and beautiful. To give encouragement, to impart sympathy, to show interest, to banish fear, to build self-confidence and awaken hope in the hearts of others, in short—to love them and to show it—is to render the most precious service.

LEADERSHIP GROWTH PLAN

INTERPERSONAL MASTERY

Reflect on the learnings that have surfaced as you read this chapter. Consider some new areas of Awareness, Commitment, and Practice, as well as potential obstacles, resources, and signs or measures of success. Reflect on the question: *How could I serve and connect more as a leader?*

1. Areas for Building Awareness:

   - _____
   - _____
   - _____

2. New Commitments to Make:

   - _____
   - _____
   - _____

3. New Practices to Begin:

   - _____
   - _____
   - _____

4. Potential Obstacles:

   - _____
   - _____
   - _____

5. Timeline and Measures of Success:

   - _____
   - _____
   - _____

CHAPTER FIVE

CHANGE MASTERY

Leading with Agility

The north shore of Lake Superior is really an awesome sight. The lake is an inland sea—by surface area, the largest body of fresh water in the world. Cool, fresh pine scents the air. Black, rocky cliffs form an imposing backdrop as they disappear into the water's edge. Waterfalls tumble down, and rivers rush to their destinations. As calming and refreshing as Superior is, she also is dangerously unpredictable. At a moment's notice, her calm temperament can become a raging force, swallowing huge ships whenever she pleases. Remember Gordon Lightfoot's song about the *Edmund Fitzgerald*? The *Edmund Fitzgerald* was one of Superior's victims.

Growing up in Minnesota, from a young age I received serious warnings about the Great Lake from my elders: "You can only survive the cold water of Superior for four or five minutes." Despite all the warnings, in an adventurous spirit, I decided to swim the lake.

Donning my wet suit (I'm not completely crazy), I entered the water. As I dove in, the cold water overwhelmed me. It felt breathtakingly, bone-achingly cold. In the first couple of minutes, I believed all the advice of my upbringing. I was sure I could not handle the cold. Then the water in my wet suit started to warm up, and everything changed. I became intensely aware of being the only human in this huge, watery mass. As I swam near the shore, I closely watched the spears of light passing through the gentle waves. When I swam further into its depths, the blackness of unbelievably deep drop-offs appeared and revealed the lake's immensity. After a short distance, new underwater cliffs and rock formations came into view. Swimming from point to point, I met with an odd mix of feelings. Ecstatic one moment and fearful the next, I sensed that all my emotions were possible and heightened as I explored this first-time experience.

The cold water kept my heart rate so slow I could go on and on without difficulty. As I progressed, I had the distinct sensation that the lake was choosing to be cooperative with me. Yet I was aware of the tentativeness of the welcome. If she tired of my adventure, I would be history. I was immersed in the body of the lake, and she was accepting my presence, for the moment.

After about three quarters of a mile down the coast, I decided not to overstay my welcome, and I turned back. As I feared, the lake grew impatient. Her waves, which moments ago swelled gently, now rolled harshly and threateningly. Because of the steep cliffs along the shoreline, there was no exit. An enjoyable swim was becoming a dangerous dilemma. All I could do was stay relaxed, tolerate the turbulent, changing waters, and keep my destination in sight.

Fortunately, I reached the shore minutes before the lake decided to "wake up." Exhilarated and thankful, I walked up the cliffs. Passing an old-timer along the way, I noticed him staring at me in disbelief. Irritated, he snarled, "You know, a fella could get killed doing that!" He looked astonished as I responded, "I know. But isn't it wonderful to be alive?"

UNCOVERING THE LEARNING AND GROWTH CONTAINED IN CHANGE

Our lives are much like swimming in Superior. We dive into the water, and we never really know what is going to happen next. We operate under the illusion that life remains constant, but in reality everything is always changing. From breath to breath, we exchange so many atoms that we change the makeup of our physiology in a moment. In the course of one year, 98 percent of all our atoms are exchanged for new ones; we are literally new people each year. Our lives are an endless flow of change.

Although it may be true that we can't "step into the same river twice," as Heraclitus said, once we step in, we are part of that river's flow. Since birth, we have been swept up in a raging, constantly changing, never-ending flow of experience. Sometimes we love the flow of life; sometimes we hate it and resist it. But because the flow of the river is constant, we have no choice in the matter. We have to change. It is part of the price of admission to life. Every moment, our cells are changing; our thoughts are changing; our emotions are changing; our relationships, our marketplace, our finances are changing. Change is endless and relentless.

We have no choice in the matter except for one aspect—mastering our *ability to adapt and to learn*. Most leadership research illustrates that as we go up the executive ladder, we need to become increasingly comfortable with uncertainty and sudden change. As leaders, we must have the

> *People don't resist change.*
> *They resist being changed.*
> - Peter Senge

"integrative ability" to weave together and make sense of apparently disjointed pieces, crafting novel and innovative solutions. At the same time, we need to have the self-confidence to make decisions on the spot, even in the absence of compelling, complete data. The qualities needed at the top—courage, openness, authentic listening, adaptability—also indicate that leaders need to be comfortable with and able to embrace the "grayness" that comes from multiple points of view coming at us at once. In other words, we have to master our adaptability mentally, emotionally, strategically, and impersonally.

Dr. Daniel Vasella, Chairman and CEO of Novartis for seventeen years, was named "the most influential European business leader of the last 25 years" in a poll of *Financial Times* readers and one of *Time* magazine's 100 most influential people in the world. He told the graduates at Mumbai's Indian School of Business, "Be comfortable with seemingly contradictory situations, feelings, and actions. You will of course encounter many people who cannot deal with ambiguity, people who always want simplicity and clarity. So, you as leaders will have to create the clear direction for them."

Based on a multiyear study by the Center for Creative Leadership (CCL), the number-one issue facing senior leadership is "Dealing with Complex Challenges." This finding has many connections to our own research findings that the most important competency in shortest supply today is "Dealing with Ambiguity." CCL defines complex challenges as problems with these characteristics:

- Lack a clearly defined solution
- Remain beyond an individual's or single group's ability to overcome
- Have significant strategic, cultural, environmental, and marketplace impact
- Create a paradox of reflection and action
- Render traditional solutions ineffective
- Demand flexibility and agility as challenges shift seemingly overnight

...dership skills are required to navigate complex challenges:

- Collaboration rather than heroics
- Building and mending relationships
- Participative management
- Change management and adaptability
- Risk taking

Learning to be open to the potential lessons contained in all change is no small task. Quite often we are dragged "kicking and screaming" to every lesson. As my colleague Janet Feldman likes to say, "People change more often because they feel the heat than because they *see the light.*"

> *Surprise is the greatest gift which life can give us.*
> —Boris Pasternak

Glenn, a senior executive in a fast-growth, medium-size company, was about to feel the heat. He was extremely bright, with a Ph.D. in a technical discipline. His intellectual prowess was exceptional, but his emotional and interpersonal skills were not as highly developed. As he advanced through the growing organization, these liabilities became more prominent. Unfortunately, Glenn never really comprehended the importance of developing agility in these areas. Despite honest feedback, professional assessment, and coaching, he just wasn't ready to grow. Because he didn't see the light, the heat overcame him, and he was terminated.

Glenn had never "failed" at anything in his life; the shock of this change was dramatic. For the first time, he was truly vulnerable. As William Bridges would have described it in his insightful writing on change, Glenn was "between the ending and the new beginning." He was in the "journey through the wilderness." He was finally ready to learn about his style and personality. For the first time, he committed to an action plan to transform his leadership approaches. Within months, he purchased his own business and created a new life. He succeeded because he was open to the purposeful learning contained in the change process.

Learning Agility is a key to unlocking our Change Mastery. In fact, research studies by CCL, Mike Lombardo and Bob Eichinger of Lominger, Robert Sternberg and his colleagues at Yale University, and Daniel Goleman all point to Learning Agility as being more predictive of long-term potential than raw IQ. Learning Agility is a complex set of skills that allows us to learn something in one situation and apply it in a completely different situation. It is about gathering patterns from one context and using those patterns in a completely new context. Learning Agility is the ability to make sense and success of something we have never seen or done before. In short, Learning Agility is Change Mastery—*the ability to learn, adapt, and apply ourselves in constantly changing, first-time conditions.*

With the Korn Ferry Assessment of Leadership Potential (KFALP), it is possible to measure Learning Agility across five dimensions: Mental Agility, People Agility, Results Agility, Change Agility, and Self-Awareness. While results vary between different groups, quite often the Core Development needs fall into two areas: People Agility and Change Agility. The core skill needed for People Agility? Listening. The Core Development need in Change Agility? Bringing clarity to ambiguity. Another study yielded similar results, correlating high engagement with the combination of Learning Agility, empathy, tolerance for ambiguity, and a social leadership style. Executives with this combination of traits were more likely to be engaged than those with other combinations. As my colleague Bob Eichinger likes to say with his characteristic wit and wisdom, "There are 'just' two problems left to solve in business: PEOPLE and CHANGE!"

Jim was a tough, crusty executive from the "old school." He was extremely bright and got exceptional results, but he also "bored holes" right through people in his drive for excellence. If someone didn't meet Jim's expectations, he would rant and rave. Fewer and fewer people wanted to work with him. His lack of People Agility and Change Agility was starting to limit career progression.

When Jim was referred to us for executive coaching, I wasn't hopeful. I knew his reputation and doubted he was open to change. After several sessions at our *Executive to Leader Institute*, he was rapidly peeling away layers of self-understanding. To my surprise, he was eagerly open to growth. He didn't intend to impact people negatively; he just didn't know how to get results differently. Years of parental modeling combined with a history of patterning himself after an extremely demanding, insecure boss had set his conditioning in place. Underneath the surface was a caring, sensitive, character-driven person. His family life and personal life were clear evidence of his inner being. Once he found congruence between his inner life and outer life, he engaged in his change journey in a much more authentic and passionate way.

BREAKING OLD PATTERNS AND OPENING UP TO CHANGE

Positive change requires letting go of old patterns and taking a fresh approach. It demands going beyond our preconceived ideas. A story about the relationship of a teacher and student illustrates this principle. A student who thought he had it all figured out would visit his teacher each day for private lessons about life. Despite the teacher's attempts to share her life experience, the student always resisted.

One day the teacher took a different approach. When her student arrived, the teacher asked him if he would like some tea. The teacher then proceeded to set the tea table and brought in a huge pot of piping-hot tea. She filled the student's cup, but once the cup was full, she continued to pour. Tea overflowed. Covering the table and streaming onto the beautiful carpet, the hot tea ruined everything. The student was shocked. He jumped from his chair and started screaming at the teacher, "Stop! You must be crazy! You're ruining everything! Can't you see what you are doing?" The teacher continued her pouring as if the student wasn't present until the entire teapot was empty. Only then did she look calmly at the student and respond, "If you want to receive my tea, you must keep *your* cup empty."

Like a wise student, we can gain insight only if we are open to change. How often have you taken a detour in traffic and discovered a new, better route? Perhaps you have lost a job or relationship, only to connect with a better situation later. How many times has your once-favorite restaurant closed, and you discovered a wonderful, new restaurant to replace it? How many difficult or unpleasant experiences end up being the most instructive? Change is always our teacher, pointing in new directions, suggesting new options, and testing our potentialities. *Change challenges our current reality by forcing a new reality to rush in.* If we're open to it—if our cup is empty—new possibilities flow into our lives. If we're not open to change, we respond to it like an enemy we have to fend off.

> *When you're finished changing, you're finished.*
> —Benjamin Franklin

Unfortunately, resistance is a losing battle because change is a relentless opponent. When we resist change, what is the hidden dynamic? We are usually attempting to defend ourselves from the fear of loss. We fear that we will not survive the change without something familiar being lost. This is an accurate perception. We will lose something. However, we will also gain something. It may be something better, if we are open to the purposeful learning present.

One of the most lucid descriptions of how the change process feels comes from Danaan Parry in *Warriors of the Heart*:

Sometimes I feel that my life is a series of trapeze swings. I'm either hanging on to a trapeze bar swinging along or, for a few moments in my life, I'm hurtling across space in between bars.

Most of the time, I spend my life hanging on for dear life to my trapeze-bar-of-the-moment. It carries me along at a certain steady rate of swing, and I have the feeling that I'm in control of my life. I know most of the right questions and even some of the right answers. But once in a while, as I'm merrily (or not-so-merrily) swinging along, I look out ahead of me into the distance, and what do I see? I see another trapeze bar swing toward me. It's empty, and I know, in that place in me that knows, that this new trapeze bar has my name on it. It is my next step, my growth, my aliveness coming to get me. In my heart-of-hearts, I know that for me to grow, I must release my grip on this present, well-known bar to move to the new one.

> *Things do not change; we change.*
> —Henry David Thoreau

Every time it happens to me, I hope that I won't have to grab the new bar. But in my knowing place I know that I must totally release my grasp on my old bar, and for some moment in time, I must hurdle across space before I can grab onto the new bar. Each time I am filled with terror. It doesn't matter that in all my previous hurdles across the void of unknowing, I have always made it. Each time I am afraid that I will miss, that I will be crushed on unseen rocks in the bottomless chasm between the bars. But I do it anyway. Perhaps this is the essence of what the mystics call the faith experience. No guarantees, no net, no insurance policies, but you do it anyway because somehow, to keep hanging on to the old bar is no longer on the list of alternatives. And so for an eternity that can last a microsecond or a thousand lifetimes, I soar across the dark void of "the past is gone; the future is not yet here." It's called transition. I

> *Change is the timeless interplay of the forces of creation and destruction.*
> —Janet Feldman

have come to believe that is the only place that real change occurs. I mean real change, not the pseudo-change that only lasts until the next time my old buttons get punched.

So, if change is so great, why do we fear it? We fear it because change always involves both creation and destruction. As something new is created, something old is destroyed. The bud is destroyed as the flower blooms. The chrysalis is destroyed as the butterfly ascends. Our hesitation comes as we face the prospect of replacing the familiar with the unknown. An existing product fails, and a new one is conceived. A job is lost, and a new career begins. At the junction of those two realities, most of us retreat. Usually, it is only after change is thrust upon us that we accept it, because only then do we realize our life may actually be better.

DEVELOPING PRESENT-MOMENT AWARENESS TO DEAL WITH CHANGE EFFECTIVELY

Even though the only "place" we can handle change is in the present, most of us live our lives in the past or the future. Until we learn to live our lives in the flow of the present, we can never really deal with change effectively. At the most fundamental level of our lives, there is only the present moment. When we worry about keeping things like they were in the past and avoiding some new, unknown future, we limit our ability to influence our success in the present. If our awareness is cluttered by the static of the past and future, we can never truly focus on the now. As a result, we can never perform to the height of our abilities, particularly in the midst of dynamic change.

We need to become focused on the now, like a professional athlete with single-minded devotion to a task in the midst of dynamic competition. As we build our focus in the present, we begin to gain confidence that we can handle and learn from whatever comes our way. It's an inner confidence that we can deal with real change—unexpected change—not just the run-of-the-mill type of anticipated change. In *Head, Heart and Guts: How the World's Best Companies Develop Complete Leaders*, David Dotlich, Peter Cairo, and Stephen Rhinesmith quote Bill Weldon, past Chairman and CEO of Johnson & Johnson: "Sometimes a leader must be able to endure chaos and appreciate it in order to discover the right thing to do."

Learning to cultivate this centered, present-moment awareness takes practice on a day-to-day level. We can begin with mundane levels of change and then build our change capacity to higher more dynamic levels, much like an athlete does in training. Several months ago, I was returning from a conference in New York City. Like most conferences, it was a combination of learning, inspiration, good and bad speakers, not enough sleep, and uninspired hotel food. Needless to say, I was ready to return home. My flight back to Minneapolis went smoothly. I arrived at the gate fifteen minutes early, and my baggage was the first off the plane. Everything went like clockwork. I had "found time" on my hands. My colleague and I had agreed that she would pick me up at the airport after her appointment at a client's offices nearby. We would have lunch and catch up with each other and the business. So I went to the curb and waited. What was I going to do with this newfound time in my life?

As I waited near the passenger pick-up area, I could still feel the buzz of New York City in my head, and I could sense the same on-edge energy around me. Every person who was waiting seemed to be in an irritable mood. One guy repeatedly pounded his fist on the trunk of an arriving car so his spouse would open the trunk latch. Another, with his smartphone plastered to his cheek, hurled his bags into the back seat and began shouting orders at his companion. As I was observing the scene, I said to myself, "This is no way to live. I'm going to make sure my colleague feels appreciated when she gets here. I'm going to wait patiently."

Maintaining this patient attitude was fairly easy for the first half hour; after all, I had arrived early and had gained a half hour in my life. But when the second half hour began, I was starting to feel those primordial "time is of the essence" rumblings. Catching myself regressing toward the early stages of behavioral evolution demonstrated by my "curb mates," I affirmed, "I don't care it if takes an hour. I'm going to be kind, and in the meantime I'm going to extract whatever learning I can from the present moment." As an entrepreneur and creative type of person, I frequently live my life in the future. I am thinking of the next new program we'll design, the next keynote I'll make, or the next client I'll meet.

However, standing there in the midst of this curbside scene with anxiously waiting people and a crush of cars jockeying for position, I truly became aware of what it was like to be in the present. My commitment was so complete that it changed my perception of the situation. Letting go of my rigid time focus and my tendency to focus on the future, I started to notice things in the present. The air was fresh, crisp, clear. I noticed how excited the children and dogs in the approaching cars were as they came to pick up moms and dads, grandmas and grandpas, aunts and uncles. Even though the people they were picking

> *In order to be utterly happy, the only thing necessary is to refrain from comparing this moment with other moments in the past, which I often did not fully enjoy because I was comparing them with other moments of the future.*
>
> —André Gide

e sometimes grumpy, it didn't matter to the kids or animals; they were in the joy of the
nt. I started to feel good. I was unwinding and relaxing. I was dealing with change on
an everyday level.

Eventually my colleague phoned. Her client meeting had run slightly long, midday traffic
was a bit snarly, and she regretted the delay. When she did arrive, in keeping with my commitment, I approached her car smiling and buoyant, gave her a warm greeting, and said,
"Thanks," before she had the chance to apologize for running late. As we headed to a nearby
restaurant for lunch, she asked me how the flight was. I said with all sincerity, "The flight
was fine, but the last hour of waiting was really terrific. I got some great insights about being
present." Her eyes widened as she glanced quickly from the merging traffic and with her
sharp, tongue-in-cheek wit, said, "We really need to get you back to the office. You've been
away too long!"

How often does our inability to master those everyday situations cause unnecessary stress, tension, loss of productivity, and ineffective relationships? The ability to cope with large and small
changes not only improves the quality of our lives; it also greatly enhances our effectiveness.

BRIDGING THE PARADOX OF IMMEDIATE FOCUS
AND BROAD AWARENESS FOR LEADING DURING
TURBULENT TIMES

The most effective people we have coached over the years have been able to straddle an
important paradox. They could sustain a sharp, localized focus in the present moment while
also maintaining a broad, visionary context. Being able to maintain a sharp focus and broad
comprehension simultaneously is one of the most important qualities for both leadership
effectiveness and dealing with change. It reminds me of how I felt in Lake Superior as the
waves were kicking up. In order to cope, I had to relax and focus on the quality of my swim
stroke while at the same time keeping the goal clearly in mind. Too much attention on one
or the other, and the results could have been disastrous. Effective people can bridge these two
realities as they navigate through change. Admittedly, doing so can be a real challenge when
dramatic, unexpected change brings us to our knees.

Walter was a highly successful CHRO for a global financial services company. His career had
been a steady progression through the organization. He wasn't flashy. He was solid, reliable,

and responsible, and he got results. He had been loyal to
the organization and was totally dedicated to it. When
the organizational dynamics rapidly shifted, he didn't fit
anymore. He was totally shocked and devastated. Walter
conducted a long, tough job search, which took its toll on
him and his finances.

> *Experience is not what*
> *happens to a man; it is*
> *what a man does with*
> *what happens to him.*
>
> —Aldous Huxley

Eventually he found a new job and sat down with me to celebrate. To my surprise, he couldn't
say a word; all he could do was sob deeply and gasp for air. I knew he was happy, but this was
extreme. Once composed, he said, "Kevin, I probably should have told you this before, but I
was so ashamed. I almost took my life two months ago. I went into my garage, sealed off all
the doors and cracks, and turned on my car. As I sat there intending to end it all, a mentor's
wise advice flashed through my mind: when times are really tough, focus on what's important
to you, where you want to end up, and on the people you love. I thought of my daughter and
everything I still wanted to do with my life. I flew out of the car and got into the fresh air just
in time. I'm so emotional today because I didn't just get a job; I got my life."

I am always inspired by these reminders of how our purpose, values, and loved ones are the
rudders that help us navigate the raging whitewater of change.

LEARNING TO TRUST OURSELVES AMID DYNAMIC CHANGE

Sometimes even our purpose and values aren't enough to get us through change. At times,
things are moving so rapidly that all we can do is trust. Some years ago, I was driving about
fifty miles per hour in a rainstorm on an interstate highway. As I drove through this blinding
rain, I was listening to an audiotape about trusting yourself during tough times. Little did I
know how relevant the tape's message was going to be. A moment later, I heard something hit
my roof and realized the fancy, long windshield wiper—my one and only wiper blade—on
my fancy new car had flown right over the top of my vehicle. I could not see a thing.

Naturally, I started to panic. Then I heard this reassuring voice on the tape encouraging me
to trust myself. So I did. I trusted my intuition and navigated my way off the freeway. I'm
still amazed that I didn't crash. When I got back to the office, I told a colleague about what
had happened and my amazing "trust experience." She advised, "Trust me and get rid of that

stupid car!" In times of rapid change, trusting ourselves and our intuition may be our only guide. If that doesn't work, at least buy a car with two wiper blades.

In the business world, maintaining trust through turbulent times can be very challenging, particularly when coming face-to-face with failure. At Toro, trust is the bridge to a "freedom-to-fail" environment. Ken Melrose, former CEO of Toro, shared with me a real-life story of a Toro team that failed in its attempt to save the company time and money by making a new metal hood for a riding lawn mower. Unfortunately, after considerable investment, the project failed.

> *Trust is our trail guide through the wilderness of change.*
> —Bill McCarthy

A short time later, Ken called the team to his office. As they gathered outside, they feared the worst. However, when they entered Ken's office, they were completely surprised to be greeted by a celebration, with balloons and refreshments. Ken shared with them, "Most innovative ideas don't work out. We need to keep trusting, creating, risking, and celebrating the good 'tries,' particularly when things don't work out." Rooted in the CEO's authentic embodiment of trust and Change Mastery, this "Go for it" attitude spread throughout the company, infusing everyone with energy, confidence, and the genuine permission to innovate.

LEADERSHIP DEVELOPMENT AS MEASURED BY OUR ABILITY TO ADAPT

Adaptability may be the most crucial quality for effectively dealing with change. I'm sure it's not an exaggeration to say that our personal and professional effectiveness is in direct proportion to our ability to adapt to change. Even the evolution of our species can be measured by its resilient ability to adapt. In *The Guardian*, Buckminster Fuller wrote, "Everyone is too specialized now. We couldn't be getting ourselves into worse trouble since we know that biological species become extinct because they overspecialize and fail to adapt. Society is all tied up with specialization. If nature had wanted you to be a specialist, she'd have had you born with one eye and with a microscope attached to it."

Many people live like they are observing life through the fixed gaze of a microscope. The most fatal obstacle to an effective life is a fixed, unyielding point of view. If we view life in a single-dimensional manner, we will always be disappointed and frustrated. With such a rigid, fixed view, life will never "live up" to our limited definitions. Our lives will be shattered at the first unexpected experience. Because life is growth and motion, a fixed, inflexible view is the greatest threat to effective leading and living. As Arnold Toynbee said in *Cities on the Move*, "The quality in human nature on which we must pin our hopes is its proven adaptability." If we hope to be more effective leaders, we must pin our hopes on our ability to deal with all life throws at us by changing, adapting, and growing.

BECOMING THE CEO OF CHANGE

Change is usually seen as something happening "out there": the world changes, products change, competition changes, systems and processes change, and technology changes. While I was coaching a CEO on a major change initiative, he hesitantly said to me, "Let me get this straight: You mean to say that I'm going to have to change?" *All significant change begins with us.* As Peter Block writes in *Stewardship*, "If there is no transformation inside each of us, all the structural change in the world will have no impact on our institution."

Korn Ferry Institute researchers James Lewis and Stu Crandell reported findings from a study of 267 C-suite executives, who were evaluated to determine which competencies were most prevalent among highly engaged executives, as compared to their less engaged peers. Two differentiated competencies (out of thirty-eight) emerged and appeared in all five of the industry sectors studied. "Manages ambiguity" and "being resilient" were the two critical competencies exhibited by the most highly engaged executives. In short, the most change-agile leaders tended to be the ones who were most engaged in our volatile, unpredictable, complex, and ambiguous world.

A powerful societal shift is happening around the globe and supporting this change-agile paradigm. The "BNP Paribas Global Entrepreneur Report 2016" cited a study led by Scorpio Partners and referred to this trend as "The Emergence of the 'Millennipreneur.'" The generation born between 1980 and 1985 is creating companies in the new economy and in traditional sectors at a rate more than 200 percent faster than the baby boomers did at a similar age." Change Agility and the ability to navigate ambiguity are increas-

> *Intelligence is the ability to adapt to change.*
> —Stephen Hawking

ingly becoming the preferred traits in leaders. *A new generation of transformative leaders is converting ambiguity to agility, complexity to clarity, resistance to resilience, chaos to creativity, and employment to entrepreneurship.* From the vantage point of Change Mastery, we all are on a journey to become the "CEO of Change" in our lives, our careers, and our organizations.

CHANGE YOURSELF . . . CHANGE THE WORLD

David Prosser, retired Chairman of RTW, shared with me how he went through his own change process and reinvented himself:

> Twenty years ago, I was sixty years old, and by all external measures I was very successful. While standing outside my lake home in suburban Minneapolis, I looked around me, and I noticed, as if for the first time, my huge home with my expensive Mercedes parked in front. In a moment, it dawned on me that despite all this external stuff and success, I wasn't happy.
>
> I knew then and there that I needed to transform myself to transform my life. Over the next few years, I committed myself to personal growth. My personal work culminated in the realization that I wanted to serve people by making a difference in the world. This reinvention of myself eventually led me to found RTW, which is committed to transforming workers' compensation systems in the United States. If you want to change the world, start by changing yourself. Then go out and change the world.

> *A change in heart is the essence of all other change, and it is brought about by the re-education of the mind.*
>
> —Emmeline Pethick-Lawrence

Terry Neill said, "Change is a door that can only be opened from the inside." Yet I know many leaders who, despite enormous competencies and skills, do not make the connection between their own growth and transformation and that of their organization. Transformation is not an event but an ongoing process of knowing who we are, maintaining a clear vision of what we want to create, and then going for it. The same holds true for organizations. *Change yourself; change your organization; change the world.*

CHANGE INITIATIVES RARELY SUCCEED

Most research on personal or organizational change is not pretty. Indeed, most initiatives—between 50 percent and 75 percent—do not succeed. Just look at these arguments for failure: A.T. Kearney found that 58 percent of all mergers fail to reach their goals, and 77 percent add no value. Vantage Partners found that 70 percent of all strategic alliances fail, and Arthur D.

Little found that 67 percent of Fortune 500 quality initiatives yielded no significant quality improvements. According to the Hoover Institute, 66 percent of venture capital start-ups failed to return the original investment.

The picture doesn't get any brighter on the individual level, where research shows that 50–75 percent of smoking cessation or weight-loss programs don't succeed either. The conclusion? Change is tough. The critical follow-up question: Why do more than 25 percent work?

As we have seen, Learning Agility is a core factor. In addition, the underlying architecture of agility—our neurophysiology—is fundamental. David Rock, management consultant and author of *Quiet Leadership*, and Jeffrey Schwartz, research scientist and author of *The Mind and the Brain*, coauthored an article, "The Neuroscience of Leadership," published in *strategy+business* magazine. The article sharply connects the latest research on the brain with leadership imperatives, especially for effecting successful change initiatives. In fact, Rock and Schwartz go so far as to say, "Managers who understand the recent breakthroughs in cognitive science can lead and influence mindful change: organizational transformation that takes into account the physiological nature of the brain and the ways in which it predisposes people to resist some forms of leadership and accept others." The authors identify three reasons change initiatives fail:

1. Change resistance is real; it makes people physiologically uncomfortable and "amplifies stress."

2. Typical, outside-in behavior models don't work for the long term, because they rely on external rather than internal drivers.

3. Trying to persuade people to embrace change through outside-in communication initiatives or presentations is not compelling and engaging enough for people.

Based on neuroscience, the authors identify four key imperatives for successful change:

1. Focus people's attention on the new idea, and help them map a clear vision of what their world will look like from the inside out.

2. Create an environment in which talking about and sharing this vision is part of the everyday experience.

3. Give people space for reflection and insight to digest the change possibilities from the inside out.

4. Keep reminding people what is important; leave problems in the past and focus on identifying and creating new behaviors and solutions.

Rock and Schwartz maintain that our brain is not hardwired. It changes. We physically change our brain, make new neurons and connections. This contention is validated by the work of other scientists, including Jon Kabat-Zinn, research scientist and creator of the Mindfulness-Based Stress Reduction (MBSR) program; Richard Davidson, neuroscientist at the University of Wisconsin, who has studied mindfulness and regulation of attention; and Daniel Goleman, whose recent work has been on the critical capability of leaders to direct attention by learning first to focus their own attention and to develop three important types of awareness—self-awareness, awareness of others, and awareness of the broader world. This body of work demonstrates that as leaders we can increase—physiologically—our adaptability to change, and as a result stay more open and engaged as we focus and navigate the change that we want to bring about.

> *Sometimes you win, sometimes you learn.*
>
> —John Maxwell

Through thirty years of helping leaders, teams, and organizations navigate change, we have codified seven Change Mastery shifts on which we can focus our attention to increase our Change Agility:

SEVEN CHANGE MASTERY SHIFTS

- *Change Mastery Shift 1: From Problem Focus to Opportunity Focus*
Transformative leaders tend to perceive and pursue the opportunities inherent in change.

- *Change Mastery Shift 2: From Short-Term Focus to Long-Term Focus*
Transformative leaders don't lose sight of their long-term vision in the midst of change.

- *Change Mastery Shift 3: From Circumstance Focus to Purpose Focus*
Transformative leaders maintain a clear sense of purpose, value, and meaning to rise above immediate circumstances.

- *Change Mastery Shift 4: From Control Focus to Agility Focus*
Transformative leaders understand that control is a management principle that yields a certain degree of results. However, agility, flexibility, and innovation are leadership principles that sustain results over the long haul.

- *Change Mastery Shift 5: From Self-Focus to Service Focus*
Transformative leaders buffer their teams and organizations from the stress of change by managing, neutralizing, and/or transcending their own stress to serve the team's needs more effectively.

- *Change Mastery Shift 6: From Expertise Focus to Listening Focus*
Transformative leaders stay open and practice authentic listening to stay connected to others and to consider multiple, innovative solutions.

- *Change Mastery Shift 7: From Doubt Focus to Trust Focus*
Transformative leaders are more secure in themselves; they possess a sense that they can handle whatever may come their way; their self-awareness and self-trust are stronger than the potential threats of change.

REFLECTION

DEALING WITH CHANGE

Let's take some time to bring this closer to home. Use the following questions to reflect on how you deal with change in your life:

1. Think about the times you faced major crises or challenges. What qualities or potentialities arose? What qualities would you like to develop further during those times of crisis? What were the key things you learned during those times?

2. When presented with a new experience, what is your first reaction?

3. How do you react when you have invested significant work and effort into something and it doesn't work out? What do you fear most?

4. The next time you face a potential loss, how will you address it?

5. Reflect on how well you manage the following:
   - Focus on Opportunities vs. Problems
   - Focus on Long Term vs. Short Term
   - Focus on Purpose vs. Circumstance
   - Focus on Adaptability vs. Control
   - Focus on Service vs. Self
   - Focus on Listening vs. Expertise

6. What are your biggest challenges when it comes to learning from first-time situations?

MEASURING OUR ABILITY TO DEAL WITH CHANGE

Managing change is a hot topic today. Leaders at all levels of the organization are being challenged to perform like no other time in business history. How well do we prepare our talent to be up to the task? Certainly, most training in change management and process improvement is valuable. But are we really preparing leaders and all employees to thrive in change? Are we helping people develop the inner resilience required, or are we throwing them into the lion's den of change and hoping they will somehow survive?

With the rapid changes in our digital age, the old-world "survival of the fittest" mentality is becoming obsolete. The whole idea of "fittest" needs to be redefined. No longer a measure of physical prowess or power, it needs to be reconsidered in terms of survival of the most aware, the most willing to learn, or the most flexible—mentally, emotionally, and spiritually. The emerging paradigm for success in the coming years will shift from the concept of external exertion to one of internal mastery. Survival of the most aware and most adaptable is becoming the true underlying foundation for lasting effectiveness. Are we gaining mastery from the inside out to withstand the tumult of change, or are we reacting and defending ourselves against every change that comes our way?

> *Nearly all men can stand adversity, but if you want to test a man's character, give him power.*
>
> —Abraham Lincoln

If our fear of loss exceeds our personal coping strategies, we will be overwhelmed and therefore ineffective in dealing with change. It all boils down to accessing the Learning Agility within us. Imagine how bold and wonderful our lives would be if our purpose, vision, and resilience were so strong that fear did not have a hold over us. Outstanding leaders, like Franklin Delano Roosevelt, understand this dynamic: "We have nothing to fear but fear itself." These words are spoken from a place of true character—a place of unshakable inner conviction, strength, and awareness. They are not merely a cleverly crafted phrase but an expression of a deep, character-driven leader. Imagine your life totally free of fear. You would harbor no financial fear, no fear of failure, no fear of loss—no fear whatsoever. How would you live? How would you change? If you could not fail, what would you do?

SEVEN PRINCIPLES OF CHANGE MASTERY

1. Be Open to Learning: When we resist change, all our energy is bound up in the effort to maintain the status quo. In this restricted state of awareness, we miss the lessons within and around us. There's no need to deny the challenges you are experiencing. Encourage yourself to open up consciously to the learning hidden in changing circumstances. Grow with the flow . . . and grow within the creative tension of change.

2. Practice Present-Moment Awareness: In the midst of change, we often cope by escaping mentally and emotionally to the past or future. As a result, we rarely live in the present. Imagine an athlete preoccupied with the last play or the next competition instead of the play at hand. Would he or she be successful? Developing focus on the present moment allows us to begin to "connect up" a series of present-moment successes into a lifetime of effectiveness. Think about it: Isn't the present moment our only shot at success?

3. Integrate Immediate Focus and Broad Awareness: Paradoxically, highly effective people have learned to integrate a localized focus with a comprehensive awareness. They zero in on the present moment without losing the broader sense of their vision and purpose. Being deeply focused yet simultaneously aware of the meaningful context of our lives is one of the keys to enduring success. Many successful people describe their broad, purposeful awareness as being like a screen on which all the focused, localized events of their lives are connected in a meaningful way.

4. Trust Yourself: Sometimes the "G-forces" of change are so intense that all we can do is sit back, hold on, and trust that everything will work out. Developing our inner ability to trust is crucial as we hurl through the air between the potent forces of creation and destruction. As André Gide wrote, "One does not discover new lands without consenting to lose sight of the shore for a very long time." *The essence of Change Mastery is self-trust that serves others.*

5. Develop Resilience through Mental/Emotional Stretching: Our current state of development or personal evolution can be measured directly by our ability to adapt. Our life shrinks and expands in proportion to our personal flexibility. To "limber up," start stretching yourself in the mundane, everyday events of life. How are you adapting to the slow traffic? How are you reacting to being late for an important presentation or being open to someone else's "unusual" style or background? What is your response to trying something new?

Gradually increase your emotional/mental/spiritual flexibility to make yourself more agile for life's major events. Follow the same principles used for physical training: stretch, don't strain—nanometers of daily progress are sufficient. As we regularly practice this type of training, our elasticity may be experienced as a calm and centered sense of self in the midst of unpredictable events. Follow the advice of Benjamin Franklin: "Be not disturbed at trifles or at accidents, common or unavoidable."

6. Remember That All Significant Change Begins with Self-Change: Recently, a CEO of a global organization asked us to both facilitate leadership development for his top people and help them get a deeper, more intimate sense of their highest-potential talent. We have a program called *LeaderSuccession* that intimately involves the CEO, CHRO, and a small group of six people, who experience profound leadership development from the inside out and the outside in. When this CEO asked if he should be there to "kick it off," we said, "Absolutely not. You need to be there for the *entire* three days." While he hesitated to invest the time, he was extremely glad that he did.

> *We may not transform reality, but we may transform ourselves. And if we transform ourselves, we might just change the world a little bit.*
>
> —Gary Snyder

During this experience, the top talent built new self-awareness, learned teaming skills, mastered coaching others, got insights into their own leadership challenges, and understood the powerful balance of personal power and relational power. Also, the CEO got to intimately know some of his key talent for succession preciseness. But the biggest, most unexpected benefit was the CEO's own growth and development. Presumably, he was there to "observe." To his credit, he shifted from observation to co-learning, and he was the most surprised to find that he accelerated his own progression. Additionally, he modeled the open, developmental behavior he wanted to see in others. *If you want to develop your people, be the development you want to see.*

7. Take the Leap: Accept the fact that you will naturally feel some hesitation and anxiety when facing the trapeze bar of change. Learning to see beyond the fear of loss and into a more purposeful vision gives us the courage to take the leap. When faced with going to "a new edge," think of the bold inner confidence expressed in this Zen poem:

> *Ride your horse along the edge of the sword,*
> *Hide yourself in the middle of the flames,*
> *Blossoms of the fruit tree bloom in the fire,*
> *The sun rises in the evening.*

LEADERSHIP GROWTH PLAN

CHANGE MASTERY

Reflect on the learnings that have surfaced as you read this chapter. Reflect on the question: *How can I enhance my agility and learning during times of challenging change?*

1. Areas for Building Awareness:

   - _____
   - _____
   - _____

2. New Commitments to Make:

   - _____
   - _____
   - _____

3. New Practices to Begin:

   - _____
   - _____
   - _____

4. Potential Obstacles:

   - _____
   - _____

5. Timeline and Measures of Success:

   - _____
   - _____
   - _____

CHAPTER SIX

RESILIENCE MASTERY

Leading with Energy

While researching and writing this book, we interviewed more than 100 CEOs. The purpose of these meetings was to solicit their views on leadership and to have them challenge our viewpoints. Additionally, we conducted a survey to discover which areas of mastery leaders perceived as most relevant and which areas they viewed as the most challenging. The results of our interviews were very clear-cut: 74 percent of the CEOs saw Personal Mastery as the most relevant to their leadership effectiveness, while 67 percent saw Interpersonal Mastery as the second most relevant. However, 92 percent of them selected Resilience Mastery as the most challenging personally.

For most leaders I meet, balancing work and home life still is a lofty, rarely achieved goal. Yet the more I encounter the time-oriented, mechanistic formula of work/life balance (i.e., working a certain number of hours, exercising four times a week, spending a certain number of evenings a week with family), the less useful and relevant I find it. Although each day brings nearly impossible demands on our time, with too many meetings, obligations, and 24/7 connectivity in a global marketplace, it is our resilience and energy, not the clock, that are stressed daily. Most days begin like a sprint and then turn into a triathlon of meetings, e-mails, and presentations.

Let's face it, time is a finite resource. We get twenty-four hours, no matter how we carve them up. However, shifting our focus from *time management* to *energy leadership* can allow us to discover our own unique formula for *sustained energy and resilience* to serve our most important constituencies.

When I met for the first time with Tim, a CEO succession candidate in a global industrial products company, I sensed a few cracks in his macho, results-oriented armor. I asked how he was doing, and his quick response was, "Fine, but traveling lots." I asked how many weekends he had been home over the last six months, and he had to stop and think. "Well . . . let me see . . . four . . . or maybe five. It's fine. Really. Just part of the job." Tim's ambition-fueled denial was getting harder and harder to dismiss. While he was racking up diamonds on his frequent flyer status, Tim was missing countless school and social events. Interestingly, his mind seemed to be handling it, but his body, spirit, and family weren't fairing so well. It was cause for great concern because mental acuity can be very misleading, while energy and resilience levels tend to be quite telling.

Ariel, a marketing executive and mother of three children under the age of seven, told me that she handles "normal" days of work and family just fine. The worst thing for her is when she has to be on the phone at night, for hours, with customers in Asia. She doesn't get enough sleep, and that throws everything else off kilter the next day. She is worn out, more anxious, and "loses it" easily with people at work and with the kids at home.

David, the CFO of a mid-size company and another extreme traveler, shared his wake-up call with me. Returning from a two-week business trip, he was lifting his luggage out of the trunk of his car when his four-year-old son walked into the garage from the house. Surprised by the unfamiliar sight of a man in his garage, the child ran back into the house screaming. His son actually mistook him for an intruder! In that moment, David knew it was time to reenter all parts of his life. That's the essence of our challenge as leaders: finding enough energy, resilience, and connection to serve all our important life priorities without any one of them, or us, "running out" in a panic.

> *Managers control resources;*
> *leaders multiply energy.*
> —Anne Tessien

RESILIENCE IS A CONSTANT CHALLENGE

I'm no exception. My life has been a whirlwind since December 2006, when Korn Ferry acquired my firm, LeaderSource. Now, ten years into our integration, we are delighted with all the synergies and new opportunities we have been fortunate to create. We have more than 130 offices in sixty countries, more than 7,000 associates, and an unparalleled ability to expand the reach of our talent management programs around the world. Like Tim and David, I often travel the globe. The demands of life definitely challenge my mental, physical, emotional, and spiritual well-being. The sudden changes of this extraordinary period of growth definitely present constant challenges to my own mastery of resilience. Fortunately, my life experience—learning from previous growth spurts and the foundation of my practices—has helped me manage my energy through this expansion.

However, seventeen years ago, I naively thought that I had this work/life balance thing pretty well figured out. On some levels I did, as long as my life didn't change beyond expectations. However, our leadership development and executive coaching practice took a sudden leap forward, doubling in size over a very short period. With this sudden growth spurt, my life was wonderfully out of balance. I say "wonderfully" because I loved the work. My problem was that it was too much of a good thing. I felt as if I was sitting at an incredible feast, and I was not able to push away from the table. The "indigestion" of too much work was causing harmful symptoms: strain in relationships, reduced energy level, diminished passion, and physical stress.

All this culminated in serious but manageable health issues. Unfortunately, the intensity of these symptoms had to become sufficiently painful before I paid attention. I needed to shift my focus from a time-oriented balancing act to an energy and resilience-rich process. It took a few months of focused attention to take my life back. Over time, I was able to lay an even strong foundation for dealing with future growth challenges, and it has paid off for me during this current one.

Although I feel somewhat more confident in Resilience Mastery now, I would agree with my CEO colleagues that balance or Resilience Mastery is a constant challenge. A slightly revised version of a witty and insightful E. B. White quote gives me perspective: "I arise in the morning torn between a desire to *save the world* and a desire to *savor the world*. This makes it hard to plan the day." How often do you feel the tension between your desire to serve and your need to savor? It's not always easy to choose, because both are so important.

RESILIENCE TRENDS AT THE TOP

Barry Posner, leadership professor at Santa Clara University Leavey School of Business, has observed an emerging trend in keeping with my own observations regarding CEOs today. We are both hard-pressed to name a single Fortune 500 CEO who is terribly overweight. Recent research at the Center for Creative Leadership (CCL) that followed 757 executives over a five-year period identified a similar trend. Top executives were healthier than the average American. They drank less alcohol, smoked less, and were much more likely to exercise regularly. CCL also found that the fitness of an executive influenced the perception of their energy level, self-discipline, and competence.

The era of the "Martini Mad Men" is gone. The superhuman demands of business require it. Arianna Huffington thought that she had it all: money and power. She learned the hard way that money and power are no substitute for something as foundational as sleep and healthy lifestyle. In 2007, working eighteen-hour days, Huffington passed out in her office and woke up in a pool of blood from a broken cheekbone and cuts over one eye. After an extensive medical examination, she was told that she was suffering from exhaustion.

> *In the midst of winter, I finally learned there was in me an invincible summer.*
> —Albert Camus

Since then, Huffington has been dedicated to getting enough restful sleep. She has been on a crusade to promote a healthier work culture and lifestyle and to redefine success. Through her books, *Thrive* and *The Sleep Revolution*, as well as her website, ThriveGlobal.com, she makes her case. She argues for cutting back on working hours, as well as de-stressing and supporting well-being. She promotes the science around why we need restful sleep and ways to ensure high-quality sleep, starting with not bringing our smartphones into the bedroom. While Huffington wants us to slow down, take better care of ourselves, and get enough sleep, she also wants us to consider her metrics for success beyond money and power: "well-being, wisdom, a capacity for wonder, and giving."

Most of the CEOs I advise have some type of energy-building, fitness, and lifestyle-support routine. These range from daily swims, Pilates, yoga, and triathlon or marathon training to meditation, massage, and preventive medicine. Most have created routines that are a combination of practices that suit them.

Brian Cornell, CEO of Target, a $70 billion retailer with 341,000 employees, is a great example of this emerging trend of fit executives. Looking at Brian, anyone can see that he is just that—fit, energetic, and ready to take on the world. Jonathan Dahl and Tierney Remick interviewed Brian recently for Korn Ferry's *Briefings* magazine and asked him about his resilience-building practices and how they support his vitality:

> Well, there are a few, and all have to do with energy management, much like an athlete who is preparing for competition. When I'm getting ready for a big meeting, I make sure that I get the right combination of rest and preparation time. If someone on my team

tells me, "Brian, I was up until 2:00 a.m. working on this presentation and came back to the office at 7:00 a.m.," that tells me that they might be prepared, but do I want this person to lead a big meeting or make an important decision when they are completely fatigued?

Our culture has sent a message that operating with a sleep deficit is some kind of badge of honor. I don't agree. Also, I like to only take forty-five minutes for one-hour meetings. Why? We all need mental and personal breathers in our day. Maybe you can use that time to call home, take a short walk to recharge, or have a healthy snack. Optimal resilience and energy require small but crucial behaviors to ensure that we all are prepared to perform.

While physical fitness is an important part of resilience, Arianna Huffington and Brian Cornell make an excellent point about sleep. Studies in neuroscience show that sleep is not just rest for the body. It is during sleep, or even quiet times, that an essential process for the brain takes place. It is a sort of cleansing process, when new neurons and new synapses may develop.

When we, as leaders, authentically model fitness and resilience, we have a chance to embed it into our culture. Moving ourselves and those around us from the efficiency of time management to the more life-supporting, transformative potential of energy leadership is crucial to fueling sustained success.

MOVING FROM TIME MANAGEMENT TO ENERGY LEADERSHIP

Each new "convenience" that makes our smartphones smarter, our connections swifter, and information more accessible simultaneously delivers some convenience and ten new things to do. Is it possible that doing more and more is not the answer?

Particularly in career settings, the potential for feeling overwhelmed is great. High-performing people naturally want to achieve more and more. High-performing organizations exhibit an insatiable desire to pile more and more responsibility on key people. On top of this, many companies, thinking they need to operate leaner and leaner, require fewer people to carry out more work. At precisely the time when people need to draw on greater resources of energy and drive, their reserves may be depleted. Finding ways to refresh and to revitalize ourselves has never been more crucial to our productivity and personal sustainability.

> *It's not only the scenery you miss by going too fast—you also miss the sense of where you're going and why.*
>
> —Eddie Cantor

Research reported by Tony Schwartz and Catherine McCarthy in a *Harvard Business Review* article, "Manage Your Energy, Not Your Time," addresses this issue. "The core problem with working longer hours is that time is a finite resource. Energy is a different story. Defined in physics as the capacity to work, energy comes from four main wellsprings in human beings: the body, emotions, mind and spirit." This is a salient issue for individuals, teams, and the organizations we lead. Schwartz and McCarthy continue, "To effectively reenergize their workforces, organizations need to shift from getting more out of people to investing more in them, so they are motivated—and able—to bring more of themselves to work every day. To recharge themselves, individuals need to recognize the costs of energy-depleting behaviors and then take responsibility for changing them, regardless of the circumstances they're facing."

The research Schwartz and McCarthy described in the article has received attention because it reported the impressive, tangible results of a group of employees, called the "pilot energy management group," over the performance of a control group. "The participants outperformed the controls on a series of financial metrics. . . . They also reported substantial improvements in their customer relationships, their engagement with work, and their personal satisfaction." Take a moment to pause on the following time versus energy reflection.

REFLECTION

TIME MANAGEMENT VS. ENERGY LEADERSHIP

Study the lists below. Then reflect on the questions that follow.

TIME MANAGEMENT	VS.	ENERGY LEADERSHIP
Efficient		Effective
Managing Resources		Multiplying Energy
Clock-Focused		Contribution-Focused
Performance-Driven		Purpose-Driven
Time-Starved		Time-Expanded
Energy-Spending		Energy-Renewing
Organized		Original

- How can you move from Time Management to Energy Leadership more often?

- What will you need to do more of, less of, or differently to practice Energy Leadership more often?

Have you ever noticed how differently you feel about doing something at the end of the day that you really like and want to do—say, going for a dance lesson, attending a sporting event, working in the garden, or having a quiet dinner with friends? Contrast this with doing something that you really dislike and don't want to do but feel obliged to do—working on a financial line-item report, attending a committee meeting, or cleaning out the garage. Let's stop for a moment and remember how we feel in those situations. When we have to force ourselves to do something, we feel deflated, tired, bored, and anxious to find a way to put it off until the next day, when we might have more energy. But when we are faced with doing something we really enjoy, our energy is abundant.

That energy is the key—the instrument to joy, purpose, resilience, and sustained success. Let's step out on this ledge a little further. What if we had so much of what we wanted in our life, we didn't have time for what we didn't want? Step back for a moment and imagine how energizing that would be.

A results-oriented yet unassuming man, Rick had a long list of achievements. However, Rick had ignored two very important constituents for quite some time: himself and his health. As a new executive in a global firm, he came to our *Executive to Leader Institute* program with the same determination he brought to all of his challenges. We learned that Rick really loved to be outdoors and longed for this rejuvenation. Feedback told us that people around him did not feel connected to him, and some lacked trust in him as a result. They had contact with him only at formal events, and they didn't know him very well. Rick also told us that his doctor recommended that he lose some weight. We challenged Rick to come up with a daily practice that would build energy, health, and relationships all at once.

At first he struggled to come up with something. Then, he came to us with his commitment: he would take daily, short walks. Three times weekly he would invite employees and colleagues to join him, for no other reason than to get to know each other. Rick found that he really looked forward to the walks in all seasons. He was energized by them, and his energy was evident to all the people around him. He returned happier and more energetic. In fact, he felt buoyant. He lost weight, increased his own energy, and multiplied it with others. Leaders must access and expand energy in every way possible to sustain success.

Unfortunately, some leaders still minimize the value of resilience in enhancing leadership performance. A while ago, I met with a senior executive in a major corporation who was keenly interested in our coaching and development programs. He was extremely engaged by how we integrated Personal Mastery, Interpersonal Mastery, and Purpose Mastery in our *Executive to Leader Institute*. However, he was totally against including Resilience Mastery as part of his program. He strongly objected to the relevance of it. "What does having a more resilient life have to do with my leadership performance anyway?"

> *What is without periods of rest will not endure.*
>
> —Ovid

Because I knew this person's reputation for blowing up at people for insignificant things, I knew he needed more resilience, and I needed to press the point. However, even after a lengthy discussion on how being more resilient directly affects how we lead, as well as our ability to cope with the endless demands of highly responsible positions, he was still resistant. Rather than press him further, I gave him some materials and suggested we get together in a few days.

The meeting never happened. The forty-two-year-old executive died of a massive heart attack two days later. Incorporating resilience practices into our lifestyle is not a luxury; it is a necessity. As leaders, resilience allows us first to survive and second to thrive.

WHAT HEALTHY, PRODUCTIVE 100-YEAR-OLDS CAN TEACH LEADERS

A five-year study, completed by Dr. Leonard Poon of the University of Georgia, revealed some interesting principles affecting resilience. In his study of ninety-seven active, productive people over 100 years of age, he found that they had mastered four common characteristics:

1. *Optimism:* They tended to have a positive view of the past and future. They were not dominated by worry or negativity.
2. *Engagement:* They were actively involved in life. They were not passive observers, allowing life to pass them by.
3. *Mobility:* They stayed active physically. One person was an aerobics instructor. Most walked or gardened daily.
4. *Adaptability to Loss:* They had an extraordinary ability to stay balanced by adapting to and accepting change and loss. Even though most of them had lost their families and friends, they still had a zest for learning and living.

What was their secret to healthy lifestyle? They were happy, involved, active, resilient people. They had become leaders of life.

RESILIENCE IS A DYNAMIC PROCESS

Resilience Mastery is not a static, rigid process; it is a type of centered fluidity that lets us go in any direction with ease and agility. Being resilient means we can recover our balance even in the midst of action. Separating our career, personal, family, emotional, and spiritual lives into distinct pieces and then trying to balance the parts on a scale is impossible. Managing the entire dynamic is the key. We need to identify the dynamics that run through all the pieces and then influence our resilience at that level.

Mastery of Resilience is about practicing inner and outer behaviors that keep us grounded and centered so we can deal with all the dynamics outside. As we build more resilience, we can do more with ease. Actually, when we are resilient, we can shoulder more weight with less effort, because we are strong at our very core. We have a strong foundation to handle unforeseen crises, instead of the anxiety and constant fear that one more unexpected problem will take us down. Finding ways to build that resilient foundation from the inside out is the key to Resilience Mastery.

Charlotte was hesitant and fearful about taking on another executive position. She had left her previous company and position because she was completely burned out. But because Charlotte's husband was fully supportive of her returning to her professional career, and her teenage children were increasingly independent, she decided to get back in the game—but this time, she would be supported by coaching.

> *The world breaks everyone, and afterward, some are strong at the broken places.*
> —Ernest Hemingway

Charlotte is action-oriented, so it was important to find new behaviors that she could implement easily and that would yield results quickly. We helped her formulate a plan that addressed the four domains of resilience: physical, mental, emotional, and spiritual. Because Charlotte carried some extra weight, we suggested a regular routine of weight training, cardiovascular exercise, and conscious food choices, which would help her attain a healthier weight and more physical energy. She noticed an increase in her stamina, even on more sedentary days of meetings, and her stamina increased dramatically after she lost twenty pounds.

An important aspect of Charlotte's Resilience Mastery plan was her lake cabin and boat, as well as her orientation toward inspiring visuals. Even when Charlotte couldn't actually be at the lake for renewal, accessible photos and mental images of the lake during the various seasons were extremely helpful to her. Time with family and friends, stretches of quiet time, short breaks for walks, visualizations, and breathing practices have helped Charlotte reenter her professional life in a new, more sustainable way.

What is your plan to maintain and restore your energy to a new level? Are you aware that your Resilience Mastery needs more support? Are you seeing and feeling the signs but ignoring them? Take a few minutes to review the following: Ten Signs of Lack of Resilience Mastery and Ten Signs of Resilience Mastery. Be honest with yourself as you read them. These are a great place to begin reformulating your own energy restoration plan.

TEN SIGNS OF LACK OF RESILIENCE

- Nervous, Manic Energy
- Wandering, Unfocused Mind
- Externally Driven Motivation
- Negativity
- Strain in Relationships

- Dullness, Lack of Inspiration
- Depression and Fatigue
- Achievement via Strain and Effort
- Less than Optimal Productivity
- Feeling "Overwhelmed" by Situations

TEN SIGNS OF RESILIENCE MASTERY

- Smooth, Abundant Energy
- Ability to Focus Deeply
- Internally Driven Motivation
- Optimism
- Fulfilling, Intimate Relationships

- Creativity and Innovation
- Vitality and Enthusiasm
- Achievement with Ease
- Optimal Productivity
- Feeling "on Top of" Situations

NATURE'S RESILIENCE: REST AND ACTIVITY

How do we go about finding more resilience in our lives? The best model for resilience exists in nature. All resilience in nature comes about through alternate cycles of rest and activity. The cycles of day and night and the seasonal cycles constantly balance a rest phase with an active phase. Nature expresses its vitality in the active phase and reconnects with its vitality in the rest phase. Each phase interacts in just the right combination to achieve dynamic balance. Our lives are similar, with one major difference: We get to choose the quantity and quality of activity, as well as the quantity and quality of rest. When we choose inappropriately, our life is out of whack. When we choose well, we experience vitality. Nature lets us choose freely, but she also gives us immediate feedback on how well we have chosen. As we learn to listen better, our energy and resilience increase.

Jack Groppel and Bob Andelman, authors of *The Corporate Athlete: How to Achieve Maximal Performance in Business and Life*, rocked the corporate world when they applied the principles of stress and recovery used in coaching world-class athletes to working with corporate leaders, teams, and organizations.

In another article on the same topic, "Stress & Recovery: Important Keys to Engagement," James Loehr and Jack Groppel echo what we see in nature and apply it to the "corporate athlete": "Stress is the stimulus for growth; recovery is when growth occurs. If you have no recovery, you have no growth." To illustrate their point in athletic terms, they describe the four levels of recovery—physical, mental, emotional, and spiritual—that a professional tennis player has to shift into for recovery within seconds between points. The authors assert, "Everything they do can be accomplished by business people." Pressing us further, they suggest asking ourselves the question, "How valuable would it be for my people to learn to recapture energy in small time intervals during their workday?" The result, they say, is "more productivity at work and ample reserves left over for home. As a result performance goes up and loyalty improves."

> *Stress is in the eye of the beholder; it can inspire a purposeful vision, or it can cast a dark shadow.*
>
> —Dina Rauker

Most imbalances in our society come from two major sources: We tend to overdo our activity, and we tend to underdo our recovery. The formula for fostering more resilience in our lives usually involves two things:

1. Improve the quality of activity and reduce the quantity somewhat.
2. Improve the quality and quantity of our rest and recovery.

TEN PRINCIPLES OF RESILIENCE MASTERY

What are some ways to satisfy both of the two above requirements? Although there could be many others, here are several ways to center our lives in an integrated, holistic way:

1. Be On-Purpose, but Be Aware: Of all the points of resilience, discovering our purpose is one of the most important. It is our centered position of strength. When we are on-purpose, it is difficult for others or for circumstances to knock us off balance. While we are caught up in the activity of our lives, we seldom ask ourselves, "Why?" As Thoreau reflected, "It is not enough to be busy; so are the ants. The question is, what are we busy about?" Rather than simply amassing a great pile of achievements or experiences, our lives can be about burning a passionate fire that illuminates our way. But we have to be careful. As our passionate purpose burns strongly, our devotion to it can also drain our energy. If we become so single-minded about our mission, we can begin to ignore the rest required to sustain our purpose.

2. Fostering Your Energy vs. Managing Time: Time management is a function of the clock. It is outside of us. It is the domain of management. Energy management is the domain of leadership. It comes from within and has the capacity to increase and help us optimize our potential. Therefore, doing everything possible to keep our energy level higher and more abundant than the challenges we face is the key to resilience. When energy is low, life and leadership are a drain. When our energy is strong, we can face tremendous pressure and challenge, and we can thrive despite them. If "the world belongs to the energetic," as Emerson said, then let's find all the practices necessary to enhance our energy levels.

What practices have you abandoned that were your energy boosters? What people in your life generate energy? What people deplete your energy? What fitness, fun, or spiritual practices give you the greatest lift? Put together an energy plan; include only the practices that you really love. These are your sustainable energy enhancers.

3. Learning to Exercise with Ease: You may be surprised to hear this from someone who formerly competed in triathlons for years, but we are killing ourselves with our unenlightened approaches to exercise. Unknowingly, most people don't exercise; they punish themselves. The "no pain, no gain" mentality usually creates more fatigue, stress, and risk for injury than any real type of fitness. We really need to rethink exercise as a lifelong, sustainable practice.

> *Fitness has to be fun. If it is not play, there will be no fitness. Play, you see, is the process. Fitness is merely the product.*
>
> —George Sheehan

We need to go to a deeper level and ask ourselves, "What is the *purpose* of exercise?" Certainly losing weight, looking good, or setting a new personal record are some superficial purposes, but they're not the most profound, compelling ones. If you are a professional athlete, the purpose may be to express your spirit in the physical realm as no one else has done before.

Isn't it about rejuvenating ourselves, about bringing more vitality, energy, and joy of movement into our lives? For me, the purpose of exercise is to strengthen our vehicle so it can more effectively support our overall life purpose. It's about being present and in joy, "enjoying" the movement of body and spirit. A pretty heady framework for push-ups, dumbbells, and sweaty runs, isn't it?

Activities you tend to enjoy bring energy and resilience. Activities you dislike create energy drain and imbalance. The joy of the activity itself is as health-giving as the aerobic effect. Besides, if you don't enjoy it, but you force yourself to do it, you will either "succeed" in becoming disciplined and rigid, or you will quit eventually anyway. We stay with what we love. Find ways that you love to move your physical being to generate renewed energy.

If you are having trouble finding time to keep active, remember, Thomas Jefferson believed in getting two hours of exercise every day. If someone who wrote the U.S. Declaration of Independence, became president, and was secretary of state could find two hours a day, you can find twenty or thirty minutes a few times a week! Try two twenty-minute walks per day. Use them as your breaks. Or, like the new breed of executive, take outdoor walking meetings sometimes, as opposed to feeling that you are confined to an office or conference room. Clear your mind and get some cardio at the same time. Check with a physician before you begin any exercise program.

4. Deal with Life-Damaging Habits: Poor lifestyle choices account for more misery, suffering, death, and imbalance in our society than any other single cause. The choice to smoke cigarettes, for instance, is the cause of more than 480,000 deaths each year in the United States and 6,000,000 globally. This represents only one lifestyle choice! What about the abuse of alcohol and drugs, as well as poor choices in the areas of food, relationships, and exercise? It has been estimated that more than 70 percent of all disease has a basis in poor lifestyle decisions. It may sound dramatic, but lifestyle decisions can lead you in one of two directions—life or death.

It's hard to fathom how much imbalance life-damaging habits cause. Most of us don't engage in behaviors to harm ourselves. The problem is that we have mistaken certain habits for happiness. We unknowingly exchange a short-term fix for long-term damage. How do we retreat from behaviors we know are hurting us? Mark Twain captured the challenge of moving away from certain behaviors when he said, "Habit is habit, and not to be flung out the window, but coaxed downstairs a step at a time." Here are some steps for coaxing them downstairs:

- Admit that the habit is damaging to you and possibly to others. Go deeply into all the negative effects this habit is having on you. Until you acknowledge the problem, you won't have any genuine motivation to change.
- Get professional and peer support to help you. It's unlikely you can do it on your own, or you would have done it already.
- Continually repeat the first two steps if the habits take hold again or new ones appear.

5. Avoid Taking Yourself So Seriously: Humor and lightheartedness energize mind, body, and spirit. The more rigid and self-centered we are, the more out of balance we become. Imagine yourself in your most secure, strong moments. Aren't these the times you can laugh at yourself and observe life in a playful manner? Letting go of our own rigid, external mask brings joy and energy into our life. Harriet Rochlin wrote in *The Reformer's Apprentice*, "Laughter can be more satisfying than honor; more precious than money; more heart-cleansing than prayer."

In *A Whole New Mind*, Daniel Pink writes about Madan Kataria, a physician in Mumbai, India, who started laughter clubs, believing that laughter can be like a "benevolent virus—that can infect individuals, communities, even nations." With the proliferation of laughter clubs, Dr. Kataria hopes to inculcate an epidemic that will "improve our health, increase our profits, and maybe even bring world peace." Pink also wrote, "Play is emerging from the shadows of frivolousness and assuming a place in the spotlight. . . . Play is becoming an important part of work, business, and personal well-being." I love to watch our Golden Retriever, Leo, let loose on an open field, his pure joy and exhilaration evident in the way he prances, stretches his boundaries, and immerses in his freedom. It's wonderful to witness. Maybe it's time to set your seriousness aside and take a joyous run into your open field!

Treat life like a play. Be concerned about the plot, your fellow actors, and the needs of others. But don't take yourself too seriously. In the broader scheme of things, it's just a role in the cosmic play. *Transformative leaders have clear perspective: they are serious about mission, strategy, execution, and serving people, but not about their role, image, or themselves.*

6. Develop Mind-Body Awareness: Most of us are stuck in our heads. We need to pay more attention to our body's messages. Our body reflects everything that's going on in our lives. It is our primary feedback mechanism to reveal the positive or negative impact of our thoughts, emotions, or choices. Start listening to the wisdom of the body. It speaks through energy: *Do more of that!* It talks through fatigue: *Cut down on that, and give me more rest!* It sends painful messages: *I've been warning you gently, but because you ignored me, I will talk a lot louder. Stop doing that!* Developing awareness of how the mind affects the body and how the body affects the mind is a crucial skill. Fostering mind-body awareness can be one of our most healing and energizing inside out leadership skills.

*7. **Manage Stress More Effectively:*** Stress is primarily a subjective reality. If two people are stressed the same way, one may collapse and the other may thrive on the challenging opportunity. Stress is determined by how we process our world. I recently experienced this firsthand while on a consulting trip to London. I arrived at the airport late for the flight and got onto the plane as the doors were being sealed. To collect myself, I went to the restroom; it was occupied, so I stood outside, took a deep breath, and paused.

> *Our power lies in our small daily choices, one after another, to create eternal ripples in a life well lived.*
> —Mollie Marti

Suddenly, inside the tiny restroom, I heard a tremendous commotion going on, with crashes and pounding noises. My first thought was that someone was having a seizure or heart attack. Just as I was about to get some help, the door flew open. A man, severely physically disabled and with crutches attached to his arms, stood before me. Because his legs were paralyzed, they swung around following the movement of his contorted upper body. In the midst of his noisy struggle to exit the cramped quarters, he looked at me with a knowing smile and said, "I'm just a butterfly freeing myself from my cocoon!" It was a wonderful moment that I will never forget. If only we all could "process our world" with similar dignity, heart, and resilience.

Each time you face a stressful situation or event, achieve balance by asking yourself, "What can I *control* in this situation? What can I do to *influence* this situation? What do I have to *accept* here?" Distress is usually the by-product of wasting energy by trying to control things we can only influence or accept, or accepting things we could influence or control. Take action on what you can control or influence, and more clearly face what you have to accept.

*8. **Nurture Your Close Relationships:*** Few things in life can instantaneously balance us as quickly as love or connection with a close friend. A difficult, stressful day can quickly be put in perspective by the innocence and pure love of a child. Few people can help us sort out a difficult situation as well as a supportive spouse or friend. Close relationships can be our anchors in the sea of change. In fact, according to Robert Waldinger, director of the seventy-five-year

Harvard Study of Adult Development, the most important factor in having a fulfilling, happy, healthy life is the quality and depth of our relationships.

A CEO was given this advice by his wife, to better understand the value of life's most essential relationships: "A few years after you leave your career, most people will forget you, but your family will always remember you."

Past Chairman and CEO of Novartis, Dr. Daniel Vasella, gave this advice to business school graduates: "Be yourself, and don't try to play a role. Tough days never last forever and after follow good days. Your family and friends will support you in difficult times. Therefore, understand and respect also their needs and strike the right balance for yourself and for them."

9. Take Real Vacations: How often have we gone on a vacation only to return more tired and worn out then when we left? As fun as it is to expand our boundaries by experiencing new places, does it provide us with the restorative energy we need? Instead of "emptying our bucket," we fill it up with even more stimulation and activity. Why not try a real vacation next time? Why not get some real rest to provide some life perspective? These are some of the best examples of real vacations:

- *Go to a health spa.* Taking a few days for good food, massage, and rest can turn you around. If you can't actually travel to a spa, consider creating your own spa by unplugging the TV, getting more rest, taking a long walk, getting a massage, reading, or journaling your latest aspiration.
- *Go on a retreat.* Transform your perspective via the gentle, quiet routine of a spiritual or personal retreat. Don't go on a retreat that fills up your day with activities. To advance, you may need to step back first.
- *Go on a vacation by yourself.* If your spouse or significant other is secure enough to let you go, it can be a great way to reconnect with yourself.
- *Stay at home for a week.* Some of my best, most refreshing vacations have been staying at home. If you travel a lot, this can be the most luxurious way to get away.
- *Do a "digital fast."* Consider taking a break from all things digital for a few days. Turn off, tune out, and give up your smartphone, computer, tablet, e-mail, social media, texting, apps, and videos for a few days. If the thought of a digital fast provokes anxiety, then it may be just the remedy needed to refresh you.

10. Integrate More Reflection and Introspection into Your Lifestyle: As leaders, how often do we take time to reflect? In spite of the fact that we are the strategic thinkers behind our organizations, how often do we really step back to rethink ourselves, our lives, and our organizations? On this subject, Larry Perlman, former Chairman and CEO of Ceridian, explained,

> *Learn to unclutter your mind. Learn to simplify your work...your work will become more direct and powerful.*
>
> —John Heider

"I would rather have a senior executive go on a weekend of personal reflection than go to another leadership seminar. Leadership is not about learning theory. It's about finding out how you are going to bring yourself into your work and into your life to make a contribution."

If we aspire to do more, then we must be more. Taking time to reflect—taking time to *be*—is crucial to leaders. It is the still point that everything else revolves around. The more dynamic and effective we want to be in our outer life, the more still and composed we need to be within. The more dynamic the system in nature, the more silent the interior. The eye of the hurricane is silent and still—the center of all the energy.

The ancient *Bhagavad-Gita* captures the essence of resilience: "Established in Being, perform service." This is what real balance and real purpose are all about. Consider integrating meditation, reflection, prayer, reading, writing, music, nature, and any other process that brings energy to your dynamic life.

REFLECTION

BUILDING ENERGY AND RESILIENCE

Step out of the hurried, hectic pace of life. Let these questions guide you to committing yourself to practices that will enhance your energy and resilience.

1. What can you do to improve the quality of your activity or reduce the quantity to bring more resilience to your lifestyle?

2. What can you do to improve the quality or quantity of your rest to revitalize yourself?

3. What habits do you need to replace with more positive behaviors?

4. What are your internal motivators for achieving more resilience?

5. What are your external motivators for achieving more resilience?

6. What is your vision of the more resilient life you want to live?

7. What is your plan to build more energy?

LEADERSHIP GROWTH PLAN

RESILIENCE MASTERY

Take some time now to reflect on a plan for increasing your energy and resilience. Ask yourself: *How can I restore and build my energy?* If you want to take it a step further, ask yourself: *How can I restore and build the energy in my organization?*

1. Areas for Building Awareness:

   - _____
   - _____
   - _____

2. New Commitments to Make:

   - _____
   - _____
   - _____

3. New Practices to Begin:

   - _____
   - _____
   - _____

4. Potential Obstacles:

   - _____
   - _____
   - _____

5. Timeline and Measures of Success:

   - _____
   - _____
   - _____

CHAPTER SEVEN

BEING MASTERY

Leading with Presence

eing is our essence, our deepest presence, and the core of who we are. Being is like a
silent, calm ocean supporting the waves of energy, achievement, and contribution on the
surface. Accessing and expressing Being fosters the deep presence needed to lead with authenticity, equanimity, mindfulness, and calm energy. Although this may be unfamiliar territory
to many people, we can learn practices for leading from this deep state of restful awareness
within us.

PERSONAL JOURNEY INTO BEING

Being Mastery is a lifelong journey that is particularly helpful to *Leadership from the Inside
Out*. Early in my life, I learned to explore Being through meditation. Although meditation
is a technique that works for me, it is just one of many ways to explore this deeper reality.
Many other ways are available to us in our everyday lives. We will consider some of these in
this chapter, as we have throughout the book. Regardless of the technique or techniques we
choose, it's important to understand that these practices are merely bridges to opening ourselves up, "paying attention," as scientist and author Jon Kabat-Zinn would say, and accessing
deeper, more silent levels of ourselves.

For several months in 1972, I lived in a small room on the Atlantic coast of Spain. At least,
that's the superficial description of what I was doing there. What I really was doing was
non-doing. I was learning to Be.

Looking back, this was one of the most intense, valuable experiences of my life. Although I
didn't comprehend it fully at the time, I was fostering an inner silence that would last a lifetime. I was learning to experience deep presence.

Day after day, week after week, month after month, I explored the depths of Being. This journey took me so far into silence and stillness that after the third week, my pulse dropped to thirty-two beats per minute while my eyes were open! The combination of inner wakefulness and physical rest was transformative. For the first time in my life, I comprehended that life evolves from the inside out. I became aware of how my fears and anxieties were created within. I experienced inner blocks, and I learned to free myself from them to permit energy to flow naturally. I discovered a new type of happiness, one that was unattached to any external event, person, memory, or object. Stress, fatigue, and tension were dissolved by the profound restfulness of going within. It became much clearer to me how life is created within and projected outside.

> *I think that what we're seeking is an experience of being alive, so that our life experiences on the purely physical plane will have resonances within our innermost being and reality so that we actually feel the rapture of being alive.*
>
> —Joseph Campbell

During this meditation course, our group gathered each evening with a great teacher, Maharishi Mahesh Yogi. He encouraged us to share our experiences and to ask questions. Spending my days immersed in exploring these inner depths was a rare and wonderful opportunity. Conversing in the evenings with such a wise elder was pure magic. The sessions were free flowing. We covered everything from the purpose of life to higher states of consciousness and the meaning of spirituality.

I particularly remember one evening when Maharishi was guiding us through an exploration of how the inner life supports the outer, and he said, "The son of a millionaire is not born to be poor. Man is born to enjoy. He's born of Bliss, of Consciousness, of Wisdom, of Creativity. It's a matter of choice whether we shiver in the cold on the verandah or are happy in the warmth of the living room. As long as the outer life is connected with the inner values of Being, then all the avenues of outer life will be rich and glorious." Insight and wisdom filled those evenings, during which I received more practical and integrative knowledge crucial to success than during my entire academic career.

GOING TO ANOTHER LEVEL TO RESOLVE LEADERSHIP CHALLENGES

Being present with deeper levels of ourselves to comprehend all sorts of life situations is so natural a process that we may not even be aware of it. Have you ever had the experience of losing your car keys, running frantically around the house, checking over and over all the common places you put them? Exasperated, you give up, sit down, and close your eyes to compose yourself. In this easy, free state of mind, the obscure location of the keys appears. Similarly, have you ever anguished over a very complex problem, and while you were out for a walk, in a relaxed state, the solution rolls out at your feet?

Recently, I was coaching Laura, a CEO who was exceptionally effective in getting results. The idea of going to a deeper level of life by building more silence into her routine was very foreign. Ask anyone—her professional colleagues, family, and friends—and they would tell you, "Laura is a doer." Convinced that her success was all about her steadfast march toward getting more and more done, she became irritated and dismissive of my suggestion that she incorporate some reflection time, or pauses, into her hectic schedule. She countered, "I don't need to pause more; I need to do more."

> *There are only two ways to live your life . . . as though nothing is a miracle . . . or as though everything is a miracle.*
>
> —Albert Einstein

One day when Laura came in for coaching, she seemed distracted and uncomfortable. When I asked if she had something on her mind, she said, "I don't know what happened today. I was completely stumped after struggling with a chronically tough issue. Instead of going another round, I decided to take a break before coming to see you. I went home and took my dog for a walk through the park. I wasn't thinking about anything. I was just happy to be outside, moving, and breathing the fresh air. Suddenly, in a flash, the solution came to me. I was shocked. Where did it come from?"

Like flashes of intuitive insight, awareness of Being—peace, spirit, pause, or whatever you may wish to call it—comes to us in quiet moments. It appears in the silence between our thoughts—the space between the problem and the analysis. As we go within, the power of thought is greater. Just as atomic levels are more powerful than molecular levels, our deeper levels of thought have more energy and clarity. As the mind settles down, it becomes more orderly, more able to comprehend and to handle difficult challenges. As a result, we are able to go beyond the individual issues, combine seemingly unrelated variables, and come up with new solutions or perspectives.

If leadership is the act of going beyond what is, as we have stated earlier in this book, it begins by going beyond what is within ourselves. The inward journey to the center, to the silent experience of Being Mastery, is "Purpose with a capital *P*." You may be thinking that this is way too esoteric. But it's not. Far from esoteric, it may be the most practical, grounding force we can have as people and as leaders.

David Rock, author of *Quiet Leadership*, and Jeffrey Schwartz, scientist and author of *The Mind and the Brain: Neuroplasticity and the Power of Mental Force*, tell us that meditation and other reflective practices are forms of "regular sustained attention." Scientist Richard Davidson compared the brains of Tibetan monks, who are veteran meditators, with the brains of first-year college students and found them markedly different. Research done with pilot groups, who studied and practiced mindfulness meditation for as little as eight weeks, showed a significant increase in focusing attention longer and more quickly when distracted as opposed to a control group, who did not receive training.

> *Real glory springs from the silent conquest of ourselves.*
> —Joseph Thompson

Rock and Schwartz tell us that deeper awareness and quieting the mind—especially the amygdala region, which is stimulated by stress—increases the functioning of the prefrontal cortex. Alarik Arenander, Ph.D., neuroscientist and author of *Upgrading the Executive Brain: Breakthrough Science and Technology of Leadership*, calls this analytical processor region of the brain the "CEO of the brain." Blaise Pascal, the French philosopher and mathematician, wrote, "All men's miseries derive from not being able to sit quietly in a room alone."

Maharishi Mahesh Yogi, the founder of Transcendental Meditation (TM), has said, "The genius of man is hidden in the silence of his awareness, in that settled state of mind, from where every thought emerges. . . . This is not the inert silence of a stone, but a creative silence where all possibilities reside."

Over the years, we have come up with a progressive formula that connects silence to leadership. *With no silence, there is no reflection. With no reflection, there is no vision. With no vision, there is no leadership*. As counterintuitive as it may seem, silence and reflection are actually performance pathways to more expanded vision and more effective innovative leadership.

In the book *Presence: An Exploration of Profound Change in People, Organizations, and Societies*, coauthors Peter Senge, C. Otto Scharmer, Joseph Jaworski, and Betty Sue Flowers consider why it is so difficult for people to effect change. Interviews with over 150 leading scientists, social leaders, and entrepreneurs contributed to the authors' conclusion that we need the ability to view familiar problems from a new perspective in order to better understand how parts and wholes are related. Senge et al. discuss why it is essential to step back to get a much larger perspective of the whole: "When the experience of the past isn't helpful . . . a new kind of learning is needed." They tell us "presencing is when we retreat and reflect . . . [and thereby] allow inner knowing to emerge." Only after that can we "act swiftly with a natural flow." Cultivating a deeper awareness, an inner knowing through the reflective practices of exploring Being, can support the confidence and fluidity needed to lead beyond the known to the unknown. In *Presence*, Scharmer points to something economist Brian Arthur said in an interview: "Managers think that a fast decision is what counts. If the situation is new, slowing down is necessary. . . . Then act fast and with a natural flow that comes from the inner knowing. You have to slow down long enough to really see what's needed."

David Rock and Jeffrey Schwartz tell us that "moments of insight" need to be fostered in leaders at all levels of an organization. This "new kind of knowing" comes from a deeper awareness and requires non-doing—a profound quieting. Steven Baert, CHRO at Novartis, a global life sciences company, shared an aligned way of looking at this: "As results-driven leaders, we must have something to counterbalance all this nonstop action and striving. Developing an inquisitive, thoughtful approach to complex, important issues harnesses our drive by consciously serving our people and patients in a more purposeful manner. As strange as it sounds, slowing down helps us to speed up to what is significant and let go of what is not." If you would like to explore further the principles and practical applications of this critical dynamic for growing self, growing others, and growing innovation, you may find my book *The Pause Principle: Step Back to Lead Forward* helpful.

GETTING THINGS DONE BY NON-DOING

The toughest problems we face are rarely solved on the same level that they were created. The mind needs to go to a more profound, more comprehensive level. It never ceases to amaze me how much "work" we can get done by "non-work." For most leaders, the most innovative ideas and creative solutions usually arise not during traditional work hours but during the quiet, inner moments while swimming, running, walking, taking a drive, or meditating. The mind is loose, settled, relaxed, and able to comprehend the parts and the whole at the same time.

In a *Fortune* commentary, Anne Fisher writes in support of time to reflect: "What scientists have only recently begun to realize is that people may do their best thinking when they are not concentrating on work at all." Fisher cites Dutch psychologists in the journal *Science*, who say, "The unconscious mind is a terrific solver of complex problems when the conscious mind is busy elsewhere or, perhaps better yet, not overtaxed at all."

The president of a consumer products firm related to me how his daily swims were "Zen-like experiences where I peacefully sort out very difficult and complex issues. I don't even go to the pool to 'do' anything. It just happens when I get into that calm, yet aware state." In the *Fortune* article just mentioned, Fisher reminds us that Archimedes discovered the principle of displacement while "lolling in his bathtub." As Wolfgang Amadeus Mozart wrote, "When I am, as it were, completely myself, entirely alone, and of good cheer—say traveling in a carriage or walking after a good meal . . . it is on such occasions that ideas flow best and most abundantly."

THE SEARCH FOR SOMETHING MORE

As leaders, how often do we take the time to relax and reflect? Our job is to be above and beyond the daily grind, but often we are immersed in only the doing. Can we as leaders expect to be ahead of the strategic curve when we rarely get a chance to catch our breath and think in new ways?

In a conversation with Paul Walsh, longtime Chairman and CEO of Diageo, I asked him to share his thoughts on what leaders in the future will require. He quickly responded, "More time to reflect and to think provocatively about current and future dynamics." Another CEO put it this way: "As leaders, our real challenge is to carve out more time to think and more time to be. When we do it, we're more refreshed and more creative. Unfortunately, we get caught up in achieving and sometimes forget where our energy and creativity come from." Leaders are constantly searching for something more. We want more achievement, more happiness, more fulfillment. The crucial thing, however, is how we satisfy this inherent desire for more. Do we attempt to "fill ourselves up" from the outside in? Or are we able to give ourselves something really satisfying from the inside out?

Being Mastery is that satisfying "something" we can give ourselves in a self-sufficient way. It is about learning to transform our state of awareness to greater strength and satisfaction by ourselves. No outside intervention or stimulation is required. We can do it all by ourselves, with no harmful side effects. Imagine having the power to transform yourself physically and emotionally when you are feeling tired and stressed. That's the power of Being. Imagine problems turning to opportunities, irritation to compassion, and alienation to connection. So, why don't we connect more with this state of Being?

> *The soul will bring forth fruit exactly in the measure in which the inner life is developed in it. If there is no inner life, however great may be the zeal, the high intention, the hard work, no fruit will come forth.*
>
> —Charles de Foucauld

> *Within you there is a stillness and sanctuary to which you can retreat at any time and be yourself.*
>
> —Dhammapada

DON'T PLACE DESCARTES BEFORE THE SOURCE

Our fast-moving, ever-connected, never-catch-your-breath, externally focused culture is designed "perfectly" to avoid genuine contact with the deeper levels of ourselves. The background and foreground "noise" of our lives is so dominant that we rarely get a chance to connect with any silence within us. In fact, we have become so stimulation-oriented that even our "fun" and "happiness" have become associated with ever-increasing doses of artificial distraction. While fun, work, achievement, play, and exhilaration are all important parts of a fulfilling life, too often these experiences are an addictive search for the next stimulation, always seeking our next "fix" to make us feel alive. The proliferation of and easy access to increasingly tiny, wireless electronic devices designed to save us time and to entertain us contribute to lives in which we are connected to everything else but ourselves. This type of "I'm stimulated, therefore I am" mentality often lacks the true joy of living. We have become a world of *human doers*, having lost connection to our heritage as *human beings*.

Leaders probably would agree with Descartes: "I think, therefore I am." But Being Mastery has a different view: "I am, therefore I think." To be alive, to be effective, to be fulfilled, first requires a state of Being. Therefore, Being Mastery does not place "Descartes" before the "source."

Thinking is the effect; Being is the cause. Being is consciousness in its pure form, the source of thought. It is not a thought; it is the source of thought. It is not an experience; it is experience itself. *In No Man Is an Island*, Thomas Merton wrote:

> We are warmed by fire, not by the smoke of the fire. We are carried over the sea by ship, not by the wake of a ship. So too, what we are is sought in the depths of our own being, not in our outward reflection of our own acts. We must find our real selves not in the froth stirred up by the impact of our being upon the beings or things around us, but in our own being which is the principle of all our acts.

> I do not need to see myself, I merely need to be myself. I must think and act like a living being, but I must not plunge my whole self into what I think and do.

Leaders who project themselves entirely into activity and seek themselves entirely outside themselves are like madmen who sleep on the sidewalk in front of their houses instead of living inside, where it is more safe and peaceful.

TECHNIQUES TO UNFOLD BEING

To understand the practical relationship of Being Mastery in our lives, we need to look at our everyday experience. Most of us would agree that successful action is based on effective thinking. If our thoughts are clear and focused, then our actions will be precise and effective. But on the days we do not feel well, our thoughts are less effective, our actions less successful. So feeling is more fundamental than thinking; feeling influences thinking, which gives rise to action. Feeling, thinking, and action all have one thing in common—they are always changing. Sometimes we feel great, think clearly, and act effectively. Other times, we do not. But feeling, thinking, and action all have one unchanging "thing" in common: Being. To feel, to think, to act, we first must Be. The pure state of Being underlies all areas of life. The more we awaken our true nature—Being—the more effective our feeling, thinking, and action. It is the foundation, the platform for a more masterful life.

> *Compared to what we ought to be, we are half awake.*
>
> —William James

Another practical way to understand Being Mastery is in terms of the different states of consciousness. Typically we experience three states of consciousness: waking, dreaming, and deep sleep. Each of these states has a unique level of measurable physiological functioning. Being is a distinctly different state of consciousness—a fourth major state. It's a state of restful alertness, where the mind is fully awake in its own nature and the body is deeply rested, even more profoundly than during deep sleep. As we stretch the mind and body to experience broader ranges of their potential, we eventually acquire the natural experience of Being, or pure consciousness, permeating the other three states of consciousness. As a result, we truly begin to live life from the inside out. Every experience we have is in the context of our awakened inner nature.

So how does one experience Being Mastery? There are as many paths to experiencing Being as there are people. Some experience it through meditation, some through prayer, and others through nature, and for others it comes naturally. Franz Kafka wrote: "You need not do anything; you need not leave your room. Remain sitting at your table and listen. You don't even need to wait; just become still, quiet, and solitary, and the world will freely offer itself to you to be unmasked. It has no choice; it will roll in ecstasy at your feet."

Abraham Maslow, in *Toward a Psychology of Being*, explained that self-actualized people had a high frequency of "peak experiences." People described these experiences as moments of great awe and pure, positive happiness, when all doubts, all fears, all inhibitions, all weaknesses, were left behind. They felt one with the world, pleased with it, really belonging to it, instead of being outside, looking in. They had the feeling that they had experienced something foundational—the essence of things. Maslow identified fourteen recurring themes, or "Being-values," experienced by self-actualized people:

- Wholeness
- Perfection
- Completion
- Justice
- Aliveness
- Richness
- Simplicity

- Beauty
- Goodness
- Uniqueness
- Effortlessness
- Playfulness
- Truth
- Self-Sufficiency

Unless these values are an everyday experience for us, we will need some assistance in gaining insights into Being. Although there are many other techniques, one of the best ways I have found is through meditation. As meditation simply means "to think," or as Jon Kabat-Zinn says, "to pay attention," all of us meditate. To arrive at a pure state of Being, we want to learn how to go beyond our thoughts—to transcend meditation. Meditation is a technique for helping us arrive at this state naturally.

I've practiced many forms of meditation over the years. My personal preference is the Transcendental Meditation (TM) program. It's not the only way to meditate, just one way that has worked well for me and many others. I was attracted to it because it was easy to learn and didn't require any belief or behavior changes. I also liked the fact that it was one of the most thoroughly researched human development programs, with more than 600 research studies documenting its benefits to mind, body, and behavior. Among those studies is research to support reduction in high blood pressure, serum cholesterol, hypertension, and anxiety. Studies show that for people who practice TM, "Hospitalization is 87% lower for heart disease . . . and meditators over 40 years old have approximately 70% fewer medical problems than others in their age group."

Another form, mindfulness meditation, and a program called Mindfulness-Based Stress Reduction (MBSR), developed by Jon Kabat-Zinn, are gaining widespread acceptance and are being taught in a range of settings, including corporations and schools. Twenty years ago this was almost unheard of. The MBSR program teaches meditation, gentle yoga, and other practices for living mindfully. Abundant research and experience with MBSR indicate reduced stress and relief from chronic pain, insomnia, and depression, as well as a positive influence on the immune system. The most common feedback is that people feel "more focused." According to David Rock and Jeffrey Schwartz, "Meditation helps the brain overcome the urge to automatically respond to external events," a skill that is vitally important to leaders at all levels, given the barrage of distractions in daily life.

The practical value of meditation can best be understood in terms of its profound rest. Every night when we sleep, we leave the field of activity, close our eyes, and "transcend" our daytime activity. This settling down of mental and physical activity results in rest and stress relief, which prepare us for dynamic action the next day. Profound meditation is similar, with one major difference: we maintain our awareness as we experience inordinately deep rest. When we open our eyes, we feel revitalized, think more clearly, and act more effectively. When we learn to settle into Being, we naturally become more and more ourselves.

It is much like the experience of taking a refreshing bath. If the bath is truly refreshing, you are refreshed. You don't have to convince yourself that you are refreshed; you do not have to create a mood of being refreshed. You don't have to believe that you are refreshed. *You are refreshed.* This is not the power of positive thinking. It is the power of positive Being. As William Penn wrote, "True silence is the rest of the mind; it is to the spirit what sleep is to the body, nourishment and refreshment."

REFLECTION

EXPLORING THE LEADER WITHIN

Take a little break now to explore the leader within. The following reflection is not related to doing TM or applying any other formal meditation technique. It is just meant to be a small taste—an *hors d'oeuvre*—of going within. If you want the full meal, you may want to consider personal meditation instruction.

Find a quiet place and sit comfortably. Close your eyes. Stretch your body so it loosens and relaxes. Let your awareness follow the flow of your breathing, in and out. When your mind wanders, gently come back to your breathing. Observe your awareness settling down. Let your thoughts come and go. Just return to your breathing. If your awareness of your breathing starts to fade, just let your awareness fade. No need to force anything. No need to resist anything. No need to do anything. Just be aware of the entire process in a non-judging manner. If the "bottom drops out" and you find yourself thinking again, you may have just transcended into Being. Just return your awareness gently to your breathing. After fifteen to twenty minutes, lie down for five minutes and then slowly get up. Notice how this calm, centered, refreshed state of awareness could be brought into your leadership . . . and life.

CONNECTING WITH OUR INNER SELF

Several years ago, I gave a keynote entitled "Meditation and the Dynamic Life" at a university. This well-attended event attempted to present new paradigms about meditation as being preparation *for* an effective life, not a retreat *from* life. The audience had so many misconceptions about meditation requiring concentration or contemplation or withdrawal from the world that the session went longer than expected. As I had to speak at another event that evening and had a long distance to travel, I cut short some of the questions, packed my car, and began my drive. Before too long, it occurred to me that if I wanted to be "at my best" for the next speech, I needed to refresh myself. So I pulled the car over near dense woods. I left the car, found a soft, mossy spot, and meditated. As my mind and body repeatedly dove into and out of deep restfulness, my freshness, clarity, and vitality returned.

As I was about to open my eyes and return to the car, I heard footsteps. Cracking my eyes open, I saw a large buck three or four feet away, stomping his hoof and waving his head back and forth. While I was enjoying his display, a second, third, and fourth deer joined us. Before returning to the car, I enjoyed ten to fifteen minutes observing these magnificent forest creatures, who didn't seem the least uncomfortable in my presence. Refreshed and renewed through my meditation, I continued my drive and arrived at my next presentation feeling revitalized. That is why connection with Being is a wonderful preparation for action. It is also a great preparation for seeing life with new eyes. As Marcel Proust wrote, "The real voyage of discovery consists not in seeing new landscapes, but in having new eyes."

> *No amount of human having or human doing can make up for a deficit in human being.*
>
> —John Adams

Although meditation is a great way to connect with our inner potentiality, it is not the only way. Meditation is a technique to bring our mind from the surface of life to the depths of being. What are some other techniques? Because we're talking about a level of life that is the basis of all our experiences, we have the potential to locate that level in any experience. So, what are the best ways to do this? I am sure you have your own paths to Being Mastery, but here are a few that work well for many:

- *Reverence for Nature*

  Most of us, at some time in our lives, have become overwhelmed by the immensity and grandeur of nature. When we stare into the heavens on a star-filled night, gaze over the Grand Canyon, snorkel through tropical waters, or walk along a creek in our neighborhood, we experience a *moment of awe* beyond our intellectual comprehension. David Whyte, the poet and inspiring speaker, suggests that "what we find in nature is the intuitive knowledge that it might be possible to rest into ourselves, to be still." That moment of deep, silent, unbounded appreciation beyond and between our thoughts is the experience of Being. Spend time in nature, and enjoy the profound appreciation and wonder, which stretches and extends our boundaries.

- *Music*

  Music, because it moves us so directly and deeply, is probably the most powerful art form. It can open the gateway to one's soul directly with its organized vibrations. The vibrations that move each of us are different. Handel's *Water Music* or Gregorian chants "take me away." Find the music that soothes and relaxes you the most. (I also love the Rolling Stones, but I listen to them when I want to express energy rather than connect with it.) Dive into soothing music; it can be a wonderful way to explore Being. T.S. Eliot wrote, "Music heard so deeply that it is not heard at all. But you are the music while the music lasts."

- *Present-Moment Awareness*

  Being is infinity contained in the eternally present moment. Thinking about Being in the present is not Being in the present—it is *thinking about* Being in the present. It is not something we create; it is only something we can become aware of. When you're late for an appointment, caught in rush-hour traffic, or missing a deadline, catch your stressed state of mind, and tune in to the present. You will refresh yourself, save wasted energy, and be more focused.

  When you become aware of the silent witness behind all your dynamic activity, Being is present. Gay Hendricks and Kate Ludeman write in *The Corporate Mystic*, "Corporate Mystics put a great deal of attention on learning to be in the present moment, because they have found that this is the only place from which time can be expanded. If you are in the present—not caught up in regret about the past or anxiety about the future—time essentially becomes malleable." If we are always effective in the present moment, can effectiveness and fulfillment escape us?

- *Children at Play*

    How deep is the meditation of a child at play? It is pure Being in action. The joy, energy, focus, spontaneity, and vibrancy of children can teach all of us the way to our goal. John Steinbeck is credited with saying, "Genius is a child chasing a butterfly up a mountain."

- *Love*

    Love is the transcendental glue of the universe. Love unifies and connects everything. It is the vibration of Being in our lives. At the moment of pure love and appreciation, we transcend our limitations and connect with all there is. *Love is the road to Being and the road from Being to the world.*

- *Traumatic Events*

    As difficult as dramatic changes in our lives are, the trauma of these events can shake us up so much that we cope by letting go of everything that seemed so important. In doing so, we can connect with something deeper within ourselves. Consider being more open to the vulnerability of unexpected changes as a pathway to Being Mastery.

> *There is one means of procuring solitude which to me, and I apprehend all men, is effectual, and that is to go to a window and look at the stars. If they do not startle you and call you off from vulgar matters, I know not what will.*
>
> —Ralph Waldo Emerson

- *Inspirational Reading*

    Reading the accounts of people on their journey to realization can be a helpful aid to us on our path. Even though we're reading about other people's experiences, the insights can be helpful and motivating as we progress. Sometimes they provide clarity and validation. Other times, we learn about an area of personal development we need to explore. Once in a while, we become inspired and awaken our essence.

BEING AND EXECUTIVE PRESENCE

Many of the executives I have coached over the years have what could be called *unconscious competence* when it comes to the presence of Being. It's unconscious because they aren't fully aware of it. When I inquire into their experiences of inner silence supporting their effectiveness, they often give me a puzzled look. They may even become very uncomfortable and label such pursuits as "too spiritual." In spite of this lack of awareness, effective people often have a degree of competence in this area. They have what people call "executive presence"—a solid, confident, calm demeanor not easily shaken by external circumstances. Even though they may be experiencing some of the benefits of Being Mastery, they haven't made the connection consciously. Even though they are not fully aware of it, it is their Being—their inner presence—that fosters confidence in others to follow them.

Helping effective people move from unconscious competence to conscious competence is crucial when it comes to Being Mastery. It is one of the most practical ways to impact effectiveness and fulfillment simultaneously. Devoid of conscious competence, our connection to the benefits of Being Mastery is haphazard and sporadic. As a result, we are likely to remain at our current level of realization and thereby limit our external performance. It's much like a naturally talented athlete who needs to become more conscious of her talents to move to the next level. Pausing for Being allows us to play at a new level—the player, the game, and the process of playing are all enhanced simultaneously.

> *Presence is central to our capacity to be self-generative—to choose, in each living moment, who we are and how we respond to life.*
>
> —Doug Silsbee

Jim Secord, longtime CEO of Lakewood Publications and Publisher of *Training* magazine, sees the practical benefits of grounding himself in these principles. Reflecting on the most challenging times in his career, he said, "Had I been unable to ground myself in spiritual principles and practices during the tough times, I wouldn't have been able to rise up to the challenges of leadership."

LEADERSHIP BENEFITS OF BEING MASTERY

Being is the soul of leadership; it is spirit expressing itself through the leader. If you have had the good fortune to be in the presence of leaders such as Nelson Mandela, Maya Angelou, or the Dalai Lama, you probably walked away moved by their sense of peacefulness and joy. The transcendental quality of their silence makes everything they say resound more deeply and clearly in our hearts. This palpable sense of depth and tranquility that is untouched even by very stressful or life-threatening circumstances is the essence of effective leadership.

> *There is no need to go to India to find peace. You will find that deep place of silence right in your room, your garden, or even your bathtub.*
>
> —Elisabeth Kübler-Ross

One of the Dalai Lama's monks, who had been imprisoned and tortured for years by the Chinese after their takeover of Tibet, was interviewed during a visit to Minneapolis. The reporter asked the calm, peaceful monk what he had feared most during his years of abuse. He responded honestly and humbly. "I was most afraid that I would lose my compassion for the Chinese." It was a stunning moment, rich with heart, spirit, and learning for everyone present; this is Being Mastery embodied.

Individuals who have taken the journey to this level of personhood are not only leaders of people and causes but also leaders of life. They are the ones committed to leading our world to a more enriching future, and they are the ones who, by virtue of who they are, can truly honor that commitment. Attaining this level of development, however, need not be the exclusive domain of a few. It is waiting for all of us. It is at the core of who we are.

As leaders, what are some of the practical benefits of Being Mastery in our conscious, everyday experience?

- Our inner calm attracts others to us. People are more comfortable with our increasingly peaceful yet dynamic presence. People tend to seek out our thoughtful advice and counsel.

- We are better equipped to deal with rapid change around us, because we are more calm and centered within.

- Our drive for external success is replaced by a deeper drive for significance. As a result, our actions and behaviors have more meaning, context, and depth.

- We can solve tough, challenging problems. Our minds can get above, below, and around seemingly difficult situations.

- The profound rest of Being gives us the ability to refresh ourselves and allows us to achieve more with less effort.

- We achieve more life balance, because we have the energy and calmness to cope dynamically with life challenges. People sense our balance and trust our grounded, calm demeanor.

- We have the distinct sense that we are growing to become more uniquely and authentically ourselves. Qualities of character flow through us more often and more abundantly.

If we want to do more, we first need to be more. As Emerson wrote, "We but half express ourselves, and are ashamed of that divine idea which each of us represents." Take more time to reflect and to be. Because leaders lead by virtue of who they are, commit to expanding the depth of your character to its most essential level—Being.

FOUR PRINCIPLES OF BEING MASTERY

Keep the following points in mind as you begin to master leading with presence:

1. Take Your Own Journey into Being: Find your own path to unfold Being. It's your road, and only you can travel it. Only you can judge what "vehicles" will help you on your journey. Consider meditation, prayer, reflection, music, nature, and any other ways that seem to resonate with you. Start walking, and the journey is half over.

2. Resolve Life Challenges by Going to a Deeper Level: Problems are rarely solved on their own level. Learn to go to a deeper level to view things in a more comprehensive way. As your mind learns to settle down yet remain alert, the ability to sort through and organize your life will be amazing. *Embrace the power of Being—those transformative moments of pause when the complex becomes clear, and the unsolvable understood.*

3. Consider Learning to Meditate: Consider learning to meditate properly. It may be the best investment in your development you ever make. If you have a particularly strong resistance to spending time with yourself in reflection or meditation, then the need to do so is probably great. Allow the resistance to be there, but still spend the time to do it. As you experience the benefits, the resistance will subside.

4. Integrate Some Reflection into Your Life: Getting on the path to Being Mastery involves committing to a lifestyle that values more solitude, reflection, and meditation. Take some "Being breaks" by investing some time in getting reacquainted with yourself. Enjoy the solitude. Go on some walks. Sort out your priorities. Experience the silence. Reducing the noise of normal living and spending time in nature can help you reconnect. Try not to fill up all your time with endless distractions. Don't just do something—sit there! Enjoy the moonlight on the water, the cry of the loon, the scent of pine in the cool air, the crash of the waves. It will settle you down and bring you closer to yourself. But keep in mind this is not an end in itself. It is preparation for a dynamic, masterful life. It is not an escape but rather a liberation—a process of freeing yourself to connect with the essence of life.

LEADERSHIP GROWTH PLAN
BEING MASTERY

Reflect on the learnings that have surfaced as you read this chapter. Consider some new areas of Awareness, Commitment, and Practice, as well as potential obstacles, resources, and signs or measures of success. Reflect on the question: *How can I bring more peaceful presence into my leadership and my life?*

1. Areas for Building Awareness:

   - _____
   - _____
   - _____

2. New Commitments to Make:

   - _____
   - _____
   - _____

3. New Practices to Begin:

   - _____
   - _____
   - _____

4. Potential Obstacles:

   - _____
   - _____
   - _____

5. Timeline and Measures of Success:

   - _____
   - _____
   - _____

CHAPTER EIGHT

COACHING MASTERY

Leading by Developing Self and Others

Many years ago, a dear friend and I decided to go canoeing on Lake Superior. (You are probably thinking, "Can't you stay off of that fricking lake!?") We were staying in a rustic cabin on a cliff overlooking the lake, and we were hoping for waters calm enough to explore the caves and hidden beaches accessible only by water. For three days, we were disappointed; the water was too rough to venture out. On the fourth day, the lake was totally calm—not a ripple to be seen.

Excited, we packed up our gear and headed out onto the placid lake. We were thrilled to be gliding atop the water on such a perfect day. Our canoeing was effortless and smooth. Peering over the sides of our craft into the chilly depths, we viewed the beautiful yet ominous world that stirred both our curiosity and our vulnerability. Seeing the gigantic slabs of rock and boulders, polished smooth over thousands of years, gave us a fresh yet eerie perspective. We fantasized about draining the lake and exploring the mountains and valleys below. Our first real clearing from the cliffs and rocks came about five miles down the lake at a beautiful lodge. Stopping for a leisurely rest, we lay back in the canoe and caught some sunshine for ten or fifteen minutes.

Suddenly a cold wind, not a cool breeze, jolted us from our reverie. I perked up and noticed the flag at the lodge was standing straight out—a warning signal. We jumped up, grabbed our paddles, and decided to head back. The lake gradually mustered energy. At first, we joked back and forth about the waves and how fun it was. About a mile and a half out, the jokes were over. We were caught in the wild surges of Superior. Because the waves were breaking so high, the most dangerous areas were closest to the rocky cliffs of the shoreline. We had no choice; we had to keep going out farther into the lake for safety. The swells were so high that my friend's head at the front of the canoe dropped beneath the top of them. As we descended over the waves, the canoe landed with a sharp slap. Realizing we were in a life-or-death situation, we encouraged each other, sometimes in not-so-calm voices, and affirmed our resolve to get through this arduous challenge.

> *We delude ourselves into thinking that it is safer to stay in the zone of the predictable. This, however, can be a bad bargain, especially if we want to go all the way to full success in life. . . . The moment we choose to stay in the predictable zone is the moment we sign our death warrant as a creative individual.*
>
> —Gay Hendricks
> and Kate Ludeman

While coping with the formidable waves, I lost my life preserver, which hooked itself under our canoe. It not only slowed us down, but if we capsized . . . you get the picture. We just kept going. We got our second winds, third winds, fourth winds. After a while we were definitely in the "zone"—a calm, focused place amid the raging waters. In fact, we got so absorbed that after four hours of paddling, we actually passed our cabin. Overcome with joy and relief, we glided into our little cove and collapsed on the rocks like two exhausted sea lions after a big night of fishing.

That evening, as we reflected on the wild day, we were astounded at the levels of inner strength and potential we called up. We passed our limits many times. We transcended them so completely that we went to a place of effortlessness, totally unexpected by either of us. How much farther could we have gone? I don't know. All I know is that we went way beyond what we thought was possible. Coaching Mastery allows us to take the real leadership adventure—helping ourselves and others grow beyond our boundaries.

Not long ago, two CEO succession candidates were referred to us for leadership development and coaching. They both had about the same level of experience, and they both had about twenty years of nearly uninterrupted success with Fortune 500 companies. They both excelled on the job. They both also needed to work on their leadership and interpersonal effectiveness if they wanted to continue to advance in their organizations. Each approached his development in dramatically different ways. One person was open to learning and willing to commit to the growth process from the inside out. The other person felt that he already "had it all figured out."

At the start, both candidates exhibited reasonable willingness. After a few days, one executive lost enthusiasm as he got closer to some real feedback on his style and personality. He began to regard the process as "lots of work" and would say, "I'm not sure how relevant it is." He began to miss some appointments. As he pulled back, he began to speculate if the program was "worth it." He became increasingly skilled at fulfilling his prophecy and at rationalizing his lack of benefit.

> *I know of no more encouraging fact than the unquestionable ability of man to elevate his life by conscious endeavor.*
>
> —Henry David Thoreau

The other person stayed with the program. He threw himself into every coaching session. He indulged himself in the self-exploration. He listened to feedback and looked for ways to understand and to apply the information to his career, team, and life. He explored his core meaning and purpose. He projected a new vision for more authentic leadership and for a more authentic life, one congruent with his real values. He refreshed his organization's vision, purpose, and values. He began to read and reflect more. He shared his insights with others. He began to open up with people at work, taking the risk of being more transparent about strengths and vulnerabilities. He started asking for their help and valuing their contributions.

He stayed the course and was selected to be the next CEO. He became a very effective, empowering, agile leader. He was courageous. When the waves became wild and challenging during his sea change, he paddled hard and stayed focused. He never lost sight of his purpose; he believed he could and would go beyond his limits. Within a year, he had made a noticeable and rewarding transition.

The other person? He left the organization six months later. He continued the same rigid pattern of not taking responsibility and projecting his limitations externally. He probably still blames his former company for his misfortunes.

MERGING THREE INTERRELATED COACHING MASTERY STEPS

All traditions throughout the ages have had exceptional coaches. We may have called them advisors, sages, elders, wisdom-keepers, teachers, mentors, shamans, gurus, or masters. No matter what their titles, we have always turned to them to help us look at our lives and behaviors from new, deeper vantage points. These coaches helped their "coachees"—seekers, disciples, students, apprentices—see the world with fresh eyes, transcend what they thought was possible, and glimpse their fullest potential.

We know from our global research that most people rate "coaching and developing others" among the top three most important leadership competencies, according to 360° assessments. However, despite the *rated* importance of this critical competency, it actually scores as the lowest *practiced* competency around the world. No other leadership competency has such a wide gap between importance and practice. We agree that coaching and development are critical to transformative leadership. However, there is just one major problem: we don't practice it! Why? Leaders often tell us that they do not have enough time; they do not know a precise, proven process; and/or they feel it will slow down their immediate performance. Regardless of the reasons, learning a pragmatic, straightforward methodology to coach and develop yourself and others is extremely critical to high-performing leadership.

> *Life is a series of collisions with the future; it is not a sum of what we have seen but what we yearn to be.*
> —José Ortega y Gasset

For coaching to have a lasting, transformative impact, three interrelated foundations need to be constructed: *Building Awareness*, *Building Commitment*, and *Building Practice*. If all three are present and operating, breakthroughs will occur, and growth will be sustained. If any one of the three is absent, the results will dissipate over time. You may learn the best techniques and disciplines to practice, but if you lack commitment, you won't continue your efforts. Similarly, all the enthusiasm and commitment in the world won't get you far if you don't adhere to the right practices. And without awareness of your strengths and weaknesses, how will you know what to commit to or what you need to do?

Now let's apply the three interrelated steps of Coaching Mastery—Building Awareness, Building Commitment, and Building Practice—to developing yourself.

COACHING MASTERY STEP ONE: BUILDING AWARENESS

Because you've taken the journey this far, you've likely built at least some degree of additional self-awareness. Maybe you've even experienced some transformative moments that made you stop and think, nod your head, and ponder their impact. Awareness is the first step on the path of coaching and development. Building Awareness is the process of bringing new information into our field of view. It may include keeping our attention on a newly clarified talent we brought into focus, or it may involve the more painful process of acknowledging that a behavior is unintentionally self-defeating or affecting others in a life-damaging way. Awareness encompasses the *inner discipline* of looking within ourselves to shed light on our strengths and our growth challenges, and the *outer discipline* of observing ourselves through the eyes of others as we engage in making an important behavioral shift.

Consider creating an awareness inventory. Review any leadership assessments you have completed on personality styles or competencies. Consider any other feedback you can think of, like a 360° assessment at work or comments made by people over the years about your strengths, talents, developmental needs, personality, and values. This feedback may have come from colleagues, bosses, people who work with you, friends, or loved ones.

In his groundbreaking book, *Working with Emotional Intelligence*, Daniel Goleman wrote, "People who are self-aware are also better performers. Presumably their self-awareness helps them in a process of continuous improvement. . . . Knowing their strengths and weaknesses and approaching their work accordingly was a competency found in virtually every star performer in a study of several hundred professionals at companies including AT&T and 3M."

Building Awareness requires the willingness to hold a mirror up and take an honest look. Real bravery is required to see, to acknowledge, and to embrace both the positive and negative aspects of who we are. It is well worth the effort. As the memoirist Anais Nin wrote, "Life shrinks or expands in proportion to one's courage." As leaders, our impact shrinks or expands in direct relationship to how courageously we look at our whole selves—light and shadow. *Building Awareness is the path of courage.*

REFLECTION

BUILDING AWARENESS

Take some time to reflect on what has become clearer to you while reading this book.

1. What key themes or learnings emerged for you? Write these down. Consider why these themes have stood out for you.

2. Make a list of what you see as your strengths and a separate list of what you see as your development areas. Reflect on these as a leader, as a member of your team, as a family member, and as a part of your community.

3. Review the StoryLine Reflection Exercise that you did in Chapter Two, Story Mastery. If you have not completed this exercise, take the time to do it now. You will find it at CashmanLeadership.com. It is an excellent tool for reviewing your achievements and challenges, the highs and lows of your career and your life.

COACHING MASTERY STEP TWO: BUILDING COMMITMENT

Awareness opens the doorway to higher levels of performance. However, awareness by itself is not enough. To move toward enduring leadership effectiveness requires motivation born of emotional commitment. Building Commitment begins with comprehending the consequences of our actions. However, it is not enough to *understand intellectually* that if we continue on the same course, we're going to fall short of our goals or hurt ourselves or others. We have to *feel* it. When we have a deep, emotional connection to the impact of a behavior, our life can change permanently. This is why trauma can be such a great change-producing teacher.

Noel Tichy and Warren Bennis put it this way: "Courageous leaders often get their courage from their fear about what will happen if they don't step up and boldly step out." I have seen executives repeatedly ignore their fitness and self-care needs until they were in a hospital bed, fighting for their lives. Once we clearly perceive and emotionally experience both the upside and downside of a behavior, meaningful commitment to transformation begins.

It is important to recognize the consequences of any life-damaging behaviors we may have, but it is equally valuable to understand the life-enriching benefits of doing something more, less, or differently. Motivation happens when we emotionally experience the compelling, positive reasons to do something, as well as the painful reasons to avoid the downside consequence. Both must be apparent to foster the creative tension necessary to sustain our motivation. *What will we gain? What could we lose?* Reflecting at the decisive intersection of these opposing consequences motivates us to take action.

REFLECTION

BUILDING COMMITMENT

If you would like to begin strengthening your commitment muscle, try this exercise. Identify several things you would like to do more, less, or differently in order to improve your life and leadership effectiveness. Make a list of the most important items, and from this list, pick one. (If you immediately know the one thing, you don't need to bother with the list-making process.) Now, envision your future in a two-part drama.

In part one, you have mastered that new habit or behavior and made it part of your life. What does your life look like? How have your surroundings changed? How do you feel? How do people respond to you? What have you gained materially, spiritually, or socially by making this commitment and honoring it? Don't just look at this picture from the outside; immerse yourself in its sights, sounds, and feelings. Try to put yourself completely into your life as it would be. *Feel* it in your body, *feel* it in your heart, *feel* it in your relationships, and *feel* it in your gut.

Part two may not be so much fun, but it is an extremely important part of the process. Envision your life without the new behavior. You did not choose it. Or, you decided to commit to it but did not follow through. How do others perceive you? What have you failed to accomplish, how have you failed to grow because you did not commit and follow through? How do you feel about yourself? What opportunity has been lost? Again, don't be an outside observer and just analyze it intellectually; really feel it. Let your imagination go and envision this dark scenario. Face it. Experience it and see the tough consequences. Now reflect and feel both of these realities: feel the creative tension of the compelling upside gains against the downside losses. Feel both to keep your motivational commitment high.

After considering these two realities, make your choice. Commit to doing it or not doing it. Tell yourself, "This is what I am going to gain if I commit to this course of action, and what I am going to lose if I do not." I would suggest going for something really substantial here. For example, if you didn't align your life to your sense of purpose, where would you end up? Or, if you continue to dominate interactions with people, what is your life going to look like?

From experience, I know that some people get this right away. Others need to take it home as a practice for a few weeks and pay attention to it before they really feel it in their body and experience it in their relationships before the consequences of their actions migrate from their heads to their guts. But once it hits home, behavior starts to change. Learn to challenge your commitment to new behaviors by asking yourself: *What will I gain? What will I lose?*

Aim high with your commitment. Les Brown, a truly inspirational author and speaker, once said, "We don't fail because we aim too high and miss; we fail because we aim too low and hit." Building Commitment entails crafting a vision of the future based on an authentic understanding of who we are, where we stand, and where we want to go. It is about creating a vision—positive and negative—about what is at stake. In their book, *Built to Last*, Jim Collins and Jerry Porras wrote about vision as "knowing 'in your bones' what can or must be done. . . . It isn't forecasting the future, it is creating the future by taking action in the present." *Building Commitment is the path of motivation through vision.*

COACHING MASTERY STEP THREE: BUILDING PRACTICE

Building Practice is the process of consistently engaging in new behaviors to enrich our lives. It is the application phase of growth. While it is crucial to Build Awareness and Commitment, they are not sufficient for transformation; consistent action and new, tangible, pragmatic behaviors are required.

Admiring our great insights and feeling proud of our new commitments will not, in and of themselves, get us to our desired destination. Lao Tzu, who wrote possibly the most profound life and leadership text ever—*Tao Te Ching*—reflected, "A Sage will practice the Tao. A fool will only admire it."

Practice makes potentialities possible. Training & Development magazine published an article in which Jack Zenger, Joe Folkman, and Robert Sherwin make an impressive case for Building

Practice, or what they call "The Promise of Phase 3." In their research, they identified three phases of learning: Phase 1, Pre-Session Work; Phase 2, Learning Events; Phase 3, Follow-Up and Coaching. The results of their study of these three phases were stunning. Organizations typically invested only 10 percent of their resources in Phase 1, or Pre-Session Work, 85 percent of their resources in Phase 2, or Learning Events, and 5 percent in Phase 3, or Follow-Up and Coaching.

> *Coaching involves deep recognition and deep presence: seeing the whole person and the whole situation, we serve their holistic growth with our entire being.*
>
> —Jamen Graves

Wait a minute. Where was the greatest value gained? Fifty percent of the value was found to be in Phase 3, and most organizations spent only 5 percent of their resources there. Studies by the Association for Talent Development yielded similarly dramatic results. Learning events followed by coaching culminated in 73 percent better results than training events alone. Coaching is increasingly making the difference between minimal return on investment and substantial return on investment from leadership and learning programs. This trend is improving, as recent studies have documented that more than 60 percent of all corporate leadership programs now include a coaching component.

Building Practice entails devising new, disciplined ways of behaving to enrich our life and the lives of others. Sometimes practices are an inner discipline, like examining our beliefs from moment to moment to see if they are opening us up or closing us down. Another inner discipline might be to learn to read our physical reactions to monitor our emotional states.

Sometimes practices will be outer disciplines, like starting the day half an hour earlier for more effective planning; showing more appreciation of employees or family members; improving listening skills; or exercising on a regular schedule. Whether it is an inner discipline or an outer discipline, we have to do it consistently. "To keep the lamp burning," Mother Teresa said, "we have to put oil in it." To keep growing, we have to put practice into it. *Building Practice is the path of discipline.* Discipline bridges us to the benefits, and the benefits generate self-sustaining, continued practice.

> *Believe in people and appreciate their gifts: then together you can more clearly envision the future.*
>
> —John Pike

When Pablo Casals, whom many consider the greatest cellist ever, was ninety-two years old, he was practicing five hours a day—more than his best students. One day, a frustrated student approached Casals and asked, "Pablo, why are you practicing five hours a day? You are putting your students to shame. Why are you practicing so hard?" Pablo responded humbly, "I'm practicing so much because I am FINALLY starting to make progress." Pablo was a true master. He did not limit himself by comparing his progress to others. His growth standard involved progressing beyond his previous self.

Locating a practice or behavior that gives you optimal leverage is step one. It is crucial to find a practice that challenges you but also shows tangible benefits, so that you will stick with it or, at the very least, return to it later.

Personally, I have to discipline myself to practice people and interpersonal skills with colleagues. I enjoy it when I do it, but it is usually last on my priority list. I naturally gravitate to creating things that make a difference in people's lives. Slowing down to connect when I am compelled to create requires discipline and practice. Sometimes it is really hard, so I have to make it a practice to walk around the office more—connecting, listening, telling stories, sharing, and learning what is happening. I remind myself to apply my creativity with people, not only with ideas; this

> *Coaching is facilitating self-directed neuroplasticity.*
> —Jeffrey Schwartz

keeps my strengths, interest, and motivation engaged. If I reframe it as a creative and idea-generating process, then it connects to my purpose and motivation to do it. When I practice it in a manner that is genuine and engaging, morale and energy increase. When I don't, an energy-depleting cost is levied.

So, what are the practices and new behaviors that you are going to commit to? Remember, you don't need or want fifty things to practice. Not even ten. If you choose two or three things, well-selected and well-practiced, that is enough to foster transformation. Several years ago, I had the great fortune to meet NBA great, Kobe Bryant. It was early in his amazing career, and he had recently elevated his game to a new level. He was already great, one of the top players in the league. However, his jump shot was just okay, not great. Fortunately, he was aware of this downside. He shared that he decided to practice by shooting 2,000 jump shots per day—four to six hours of continuous shooting daily. He did this routine seven days a week for nine months. The results: his game became nearly unstoppable. His inside game was more dangerous, because he now had an outside game, too.

What do you need to practice 2,000 times per day, or even ten times per day, to take your game to the next level? Do you need to strengthen your "inside game" or your "outside game"?

What are you going to practice? Stop. Don't rush this. Take a pause to answer this key question: What new behavior will you practice that will, over time, move you forward? The entire benefit of this book rests on your thoughtful response. Choose well. Stick with it. *What you practice, you become.*

REFLECTION
BUILDING PRACTICE

Review your reflections on Building Awareness and Building Commitment. Reflect on which behaviors or practices would give you the greatest leverage. Be very specific and pragmatic here.

- If most of your development need is in the people arena, then a practice around listening, receiving, and staying open is likely to yield the greatest returns. You might try a practice of attending meetings with the main purpose of listening, being more open, and asking questions that encourage others to think, problem solve, and innovate.

- If your development need is centered around more courageous expression, your practice may be speaking up the next time you feel inhibition, hesitation, or stress in a meeting. Practice speaking up in a way that is consistent with your values, principles, and purpose.

- If your development need is about energy and resilience, your practice may be a daily meditation and a fitness program to restore your vitality.

Practices, at first glance, seem small, ordinary, and not too exciting. But over time, their benefits accumulate and create a transformative impact. Reflect on and identify the practice that will give you the most leverage to grow.

THE ART OF COACHING OTHERS

With what we've learned about self-coaching, let's transition to the art of coaching others. Emerson wrote, "We mark with light in the memory the few interviews we have had . . . with souls that made our soul wiser; that spoke what we thought; that told us what we knew; that gave us leave to be what we inly were." Indeed, coaching may be the most important of all leadership skills, because helping foster the growth of those around us gives sustainability to our leadership and perpetuates optimal, ongoing value creation.

Coaching is the art of drawing forth potential onto the canvas of high performance. It's the gentle yet firm hand of leadership guiding the way, like a caring friend, helping the "coachee" steer clear of danger or set a more positive course.

Leadership is more than just a job. The leader of a group of any size, from a family, club, congregation, or classroom to a multinational corporation or a nation, sets the tone for all the members of the group. *Leaders touch lives and hold destinies in their hands; it is a sacred calling with sacred responsibility.*

That calling is best honored when a leader sets the highest example of personal and professional behavior and then enlists others to take this challenging path as well. To accomplish both of these tasks, nothing is more vital than coaching. Effective coaching, to bring out the strengths and talents of all the people in the group or organization, serves a dual role. It is a generous contribution to each individual's growth and fulfillment. At the same time, it is one of the most practical strategies for maximizing the effectiveness and success of the group. The more capable and fully developed each individual in your group, the stronger the group. Each person in the group who is not living up to his or her capabilities is dragging the group down, diminishing its effectiveness.

> *You must be the change you wish to see in the world.*
>
> —Mahatma Gandhi

Since 2001, we have worked continuously with Novartis, a $50 billion global life sciences firm formed in 1996 as a result of a merger between Sandoz and Ciba-Geigy. Novartis developed a fast-paced and results-oriented culture. By 2001, the company had hired 70 percent of their senior talent from the outside. Fortunately, the "get results" culture also valued coaching and leadership development.

Significant investments were made to assess, develop, coach, and mentor top talent. Dr. Daniel Vasella, past Novartis Chairman and CEO; Joe Jimenez, current CEO; Steven Baert, CHRO; and Thomas Ebeling, past CEO of two divisions and now CEO of ProSeiben Media, were substantially supportive of and involved in a variety of leadership initiatives. By 2007, only 30 percent of senior talent was hired from the outside. Millions of dollars were saved in recruiting. Millions more were leveraged to produce and sustain results. Thomas Ebeling, one of the most intense, effective, and committed CEO coaches I have ever encountered, commented:

> Coaching, leadership development, and mentoring are not tasks you can just delegate to Human Resources. Coaching is one of the most critical leadership skills for optimizing and sustaining individual and team performance. Investing time in coaching and mentoring gives tremendous return on investment. It impacts results, retention, morale, and talent identification. . . . Over the course of my career, I've learned that coaching is an extremely valuable and energizing investment. Since I am so results-oriented, it is surprising to people when I tell them that coaching and mentoring have been my most satisfying accomplishments.

For many of us, the word *coach* evokes images of a hulking figure in a sweatshirt, blowing a whistle and barking directions to a more or less compliant group of players. But a genuine coach has a far more interesting and refined role than giving orders. If you are on a mountain climbing expedition, struggling with some difficult terrain, lost in a fog or snowstorm, and not able to see the top of the mountain or most of the path ahead, you are grateful for a veteran guide, calling down from above, "Go to the right. Dig in. Watch out for loose rocks. You're doing fine." The guide has perspective, experience, and crucial knowledge that you don't have. Similarly, the players on a sports team, caught up in the moment-to-moment action on the field, have little perspective. An effective coach rises above the playing to get a more complete picture from which to guide optimal approaches.

Some coaches simply assert their expertise. Great coaches blend expertise and facilitation to help the players go beyond their previously held boundaries. In his book, *Masterful Coaching*, Robert Hargrove notes, "When most people think of learning, they don't think in terms of having to change themselves. They tend to think of learning as . . . acquiring ideas, tips, techniques, and so on. Seldom does it occur to them that the problems they are facing are inseparable from who they are or the way they think and interact with other people." Coaching helps us step back to see more of the whole person and more of the whole situation, as well as the dynamics between the two.

A senior team for a global company was struggling. They led the North American operations, which was responsible for 40 percent of the global revenue of the high-technology firm. Sales and profits were flat. The pace of new initiatives was slowing. Energy and morale were deteriorating. The new CEO, full of energy, drive, and strong people skills, was hitting the wall after only four months. Why? The dysfunctional relationships of five key team members were paralyzing the effectiveness of a team of twenty. The problem? All five of the difficult people were highly competitive, bright, and valued in their respective functions. The easy solution, firing all five, wasn't so easy. All five team members had significant things to contribute but viewed the rest of the team as "impossible to work with" and "not trustworthy." While meetings were full of conflict avoidance, team members' off-line comments about one another were toxic.

> *Developing people is a deeply collaborative journey.*
>
> —Dee Gaeddert

The typical event-driven, team-building process would not get to these core dynamics. Instead, we initiated deep, intensive work with each individual. It was imperative that team members each sort out their issues and take personal responsibility. Only then could we begin having authentic conversations and initiate coaching on their interpersonal dynamics. With progress in these areas, we began a larger teaming initiative. In addition, the CEO needed to step in and make some tough calls to transition two people. Over a nine-month period, the team re-engaged, sales and profit were regained, and morale returned. Transformation is not an event but a challenging process of working through the coaching needs of leaders, teams, and organizations simultaneously.

> *It is better to know some of the questions than all of the answers.*
>
> —James Thurber

The leadership and coaching profession needs to develop a new lineage of coaches, ones who are equipped to foster individual, team, and strategic transformation. To accomplish this, coaches need to move from an expert or fix-it model concerned primarily with competencies, learning skills, and techniques to a transformative model focused on fundamentally shifting people's view about themselves, their team, their values, and their sense of purpose.

Influenced by the work of Robert Hargrove, author of *Masterful Coaching*, most coaching today fits within one of the following four categories:

- *Expert Coaching:* building skills, competencies, and knowledge
- *Pattern Coaching:* revealing old patterns and building new patterns of behavior
- *Transformative Coaching:* fostering a fundamental shift in point of view, beliefs, values, identity, and purpose
- *Integrative Coaching:* blending the depth of personal (inside out) work with the complexity of external (outside in) dynamics around team, organizational, marketplace, and societal needs

Most internal coaching programs in organizations deal with Expert Coaching and may refer to this type of coaching as *mentoring*. Most external coaching resources deal with Expert and Pattern Coaching. An increasing number of coaches do Transformative Coaching, but fewer engage in Integrative Coaching. Ideally, as the coaching industry matures, more world-class, enterprise coaches will emerge, who are adept at all levels and can apply them flexibly to the particular needs of leaders, teams, and organizations.

COACHING OTHERS TO BUILD AWARENESS

As leaders, we are constantly faced with the task of Building Awareness. Awareness of changing market conditions, emerging economic realities, new capital needs, cost concerns, and operational issues dominate our time and attention. But often, the greatest task of Building Awareness is in the human, interpersonal domain. Because leadership is such a human endeavor, I would venture to say that 70 percent of business problems today are of a human, interpersonal nature. People problems are typically quite complex, yet when individuals, teams, or managers come to us with their concerns, don't we too easily slip into a reactive, knee-jerk mode, looking for a simple fix?

Helping others Build Awareness requires discipline on the part of the coach to stay out of the expert or fix-it approaches to coaching. If we don't, we will be imposing our awareness onto the coachee instead of building the coachee's awareness from the inside out. One of the most challenging aspects of coaching is to help explore approaches that we might not choose ourselves. Building Awareness requires openness to help those we are coaching in sorting out their own current reality and beginning to chart their own future approaches.

To guide your ability to Build Awareness with people you coach, keep the following principles in mind:

- *Stay open, and bring clarity.* Most answers lie within the person, the team, or the organization; your job is to help clarify and reveal them.
- *Use questions to help the person sort out the current situation.* Before we can move forward with power, we need to know where we stand, understanding both life-enriching and life-damaging behaviors, beliefs, and circumstances. "I've found that I can only change how I act if I stay aware of my beliefs and assumptions," writes Margaret Wheatley, author of *Leadership and the New Science.* Very few people take the time or possess the necessary introspective skills to do this without the gentle prodding of a coach. *Questions are the language of coaching.* They are powerful tools for transformation, because as Bertrand Russell taught, "In all affairs it's a healthy thing now and then to hang a question mark on things you have long taken for granted."
- *Be courageous.* As Robert Hargrove advises, "Be courageous enough to discuss the undiscussable." The coach's job is to shed light on dark regions previously unexplored.
- *Practice speaking directly but with caring.* With compassion, help coachees see their limitations as well as their gifts. Keep in mind: directness without caring will create resistance, while directness with compassion will create openness. Confront in a caring manner.
- *Help coachees explore the differences between their intentions and other people's perceptions.* Discrepancies between how people see themselves and how others perceive them often hold the key to new self-knowledge and overcoming blind spots. Helping people see aspects of themselves through the eyes of others can be challenging but effective. Merge outside-in 360° feedback tools with inside-out personality tools to create a 720° (inside-out/outside-in) process.

> *Building competencies while deepening character is critical to enduring leadership growth.*
>
> —Craig Sneltjes

- *Build awareness by example.* The greatest teachers and coaches teach as much by their being as by their doing. If you want to coach people in authenticity, purpose, or presence, the first step is to become the change you hope to see in them. The *Bhagavad-Gita,* an invaluable ancient handbook on leadership development, guides us: "Whatsoever a great man does, the very same is also done by other men. Whatever standard he sets, the world follows it." Or, as Anne Sophie Swetchine so beautifully put it, "There is a transcendent power in example. We reform others unconsciously when we walk uprightly."

- *Help people uncover and align with what is meaningful and important to them.* As coachees discover their core values, help them explore how aligned or misaligned the various parts of their lives (i.e., personal, family, community, career, spiritual) are with these guiding principles. *An effective transformational coach is both an archaeologist, who helps unearth important artifacts or clues from the past, and an architect, who helps us design a future built on our gifts and deep sense of purpose.*

COACHING OTHERS TO BUILD COMMITMENT

To elicit commitment, we must help people envision the positive and negative outcomes—what they will gain and what they will lose—if they continue on their current path. When one's emotions deeply register both the compelling, positive reasons to change and the damaging behaviors to leave behind, transformation begins. In the words of Margaret Wheatley, "The greatest source of courage is to realize that if we don't act, nothing will change for the better."

To guide your ability to build commitment with people you coach, keep the following principles in mind:

- *Help people sort out consequences.* By guiding people to grasp the life-enriching and life-damaging consequences of their current behavior or path, you help them feel the creative tension between where they want to end up and where they are actually headed as a result of their actions. Helping people envision these alternative futures and make new life choices is the essence of Building Commitment. Remember, the person has to see and feel these consequences for himself or herself, not just see your version of the consequences.
- *Allow your commitment to catalyze their commitment.* Often it is the emotional engagement of the coach that serves as the impetus for transformation to begin. "There comes that mysterious meeting in life when someone acknowledges who we are and what we can be, igniting the circuits of our highest potential," writes Rusty Berkus.
- *Look for openings.* Commitment is far more likely to take place when vulnerability is sufficiently high. Look for these openings, and leverage their growth potential.

Situations that might make people more open to commitment include less-than-positive performance reviews, tough 360° feedback, life traumas, career setbacks, relational breakdowns, broken commitments by others, new or exceptional challenges, need for new skills, lack of preparedness, fear of failure, and new career or life responsibilities. Look for these openings as an opportunity to accelerate progress.

- *Make sure commitment leads to practice.* Commitment without practice is like an explorer who reviews expedition maps but never leaves home. If commitment does not lead to practice, then it is your responsibility as the coach to help the coachee do one of two things: (1) further explore the consequences of staying on his or her current track, in order to achieve a more genuine emotional engagement, leading to actual practice; or (2) find new practices that are more suited to the person.

- *Be patient.* As coaches, we are motivated to help people grow *now*. However, coachees need to unfold at their own pace. If you must be impatient, be impatient with developing your own skills as a coach.

- *Remember the why.* Use the *power of why* to uncover the coachee's underlying fears, assumptions, beliefs, and motivations. Wait for the right opening to ask in a caring manner, "Why?" If one "Why?" doesn't get to the heart of things, you may ask two or three times in a row to dive deeper beneath the surface of the conversation. A technique or process commonly known as "Five Whys" has the potential to get us to the essence of things.

COACHING OTHERS TO BUILD PRACTICE

Building Practice is the third stage of transformational coaching. Without practice, there is no transformation. Practice breathes life into our new awareness and commitment. We can be fully aware of and committed to noble goals, but if we fail to practice them, it is like someone lighting a lamp and then closing his eyes. "In the end," said Max De Pree, "it is important to remember that we cannot become what we need to be by remaining where we were."

A while ago, a somewhat skeptical coaching client came to me with his most recent 360° assessment and a knowing "I told you so" look on his face. When I asked him, "Why the peculiar look?" he said, "I've had the same 360° assessment for the past five years. Every time, the same results! What a worthless process!" I tried to explore with him the specifics of what he actually practiced as part of the process. It was no surprise to find out he had practiced nothing. You know the moral of this story: Nothing practiced, nothing gained.

Beginning practice makes the possible probable; advanced, enduring practice makes the possible real. Practices involve the consistent repetition of new behaviors that transform our lives. Exercise is a practice to build health. Meditation is a practice to unfold our spiritual life. Reflecting at the end of each day on how our interpersonal interactions went is a practice that builds relational effectiveness. For most of us, not letting fears or limiting beliefs sabotage our goals can be a lifelong practice.

For practice to become a habit, it needs to be consistently engaged for at least forty days. A day here and a day there will not bring transformation. At first, our practice requires a discipline to do something we may not be inclined to do. Over time, however, the discipline is replaced by the life-enriching benefits we are gaining; the practice becomes more self-sustaining and requires less effort. Here is the key to practice: if you stop practicing, no problem—just start practicing again.

> *What I have achieved by industry and practice, anyone else with tolerable natural gift and ability can also achieve.*
>
> —Johann Sebastian Bach

To guide your ability to Build Practice with people you coach, keep the following principles in mind:

- *Co-create the practice with the person.* A practice must push boundaries but also be suitable for the individual. Ask the person you are coaching, "What new behavior could you practice that, over time, would move you forward?" Then take time to brainstorm together, to co-create a meaningful practice. Keep the practices simple and defined. Make sure the person wants to give the practice a try.
- *Hold the person accountable.* Define how often the person will do the practice (daily, twice a day, etc.) and for what duration of time (a week, a month, etc.). Meet with the person to audit progress and lack of progress. Hold the person accountable, set new goals, and create new practices, as needed.
- *Avoid intellectualizing.* Thinking about doing something is not the same as doing it, so make sure your practices are behaviors that engage the person in a new action rather than only thinking about behaving in a new way.
- *Just do it . . . or do something else.* While some practices are more dynamic (exercise, asserting our viewpoint, expressing our values) and others are more reflective

(pausing to center ourselves, reflecting on our day), the key to practice is taking action. An initial practice may not be the one that revolutionizes a person's life, but it is the beginning of a process that will lead to a practice that does have an impact. Sometimes the most important contribution a coach can make is to keep people trying new practices and helping them struggle through the challenges that come up, until they settle on an enduring practice, and improvement takes place.

> *If your actions inspire others to dream more, learn more, do more, and become more, you are a leader.*
>
> —John Quincy Adams

BEST PRACTICES FOR PRACTICE

Practicing coaching is a challenge. Disciplining ourselves to slow down and pause to develop others is not easy. While coaching in real time is ideal for coaching effectiveness, it requires discipline to pivot from the transactive immediacies of management to the transformative opportunities of coaching. Some leaders are so passionate about developing others that they not only coach in the moment, but they also develop practices that are more far-reaching.

Paul Van Oyen is CEO of Etex, a $3 billion building materials company based in Brussels. Paul developed a "go-beyond" coaching practice to significantly advance the development of his key team members while also creating deeper intimacy and connection. Once a year, Paul invites each senior team member to take a one-day special trip with him. Each team member selects the date and the place, which can be anywhere in the world. It is their choice. Paul's only caveat is that it be a place that is compelling to them. The place may have a family connection, be a place that inspires them, or be a place they've always wanted to explore.

What is the purpose of the day and the place? It is to share the exploration together, outside and in. As they walk the streets, visit notable sights, and witness small, minor things and impressive ones, they share it all together, and at the same time, they share more of themselves. They talk and get to know more about each other: what is important to them, their significant relationships, and their life stories. The deeper purpose is to create the space and the conditions to foster intimacy through meaningful conversations about life and aspirations for the

> *Coaching is a co-created journey of innovation together.*
>
> —Jane Stevenson

enterprise. In short, it is a rich opportunity to pause together to give personal and business transformation the opportunity to emerge.

Commenting on this practice, Paul reflects, "I didn't set this up to have greater influence with my people. I did it because I care about them and their development. I wanted the free-space to grow together. It is one of the most important practices I have as a CEO to accelerate growth in my team and within myself." What will be your practices for pausing to grow others in your organization?

Commit yourself to a lifelong process of Building Awareness, Commitment, and Practice to inspire authentic leadership in all those you touch. *Become a more generative leader: a leader dedicated to equipping the next generation to both succeed and exceed us.*

PARTING THOUGHTS FOR YOUR JOURNEY AHEAD

After years of coaching leaders behind closed doors, I find it both a challenge and a joy to open the door and take the time to share these principles with you. David Bohm once wrote, "The ability to perceive or think differently is more important than the knowledge gained." In this spirit, I hope this book has been more than just an interesting intellectual excursion. I hope it has been a soul-provoking experience for you. I also hope that you have grown a little since you first opened the cover. But my deepest hope is that, over time, you will breathe life into these principles and live them moment to moment until the inspiration is fully yours.

A dear friend shared a short passage from the *Talmud* that tells the whole story of life and leadership. It goes something like this: "Every blade of grass in all of creation has an angel bent over it passionately whispering three words of encouragement: Grow . . . Grow . . . Grow." That's my wish for you. Grow in courage and authenticity. Grow in influence. Grow in value creation. Become a leader for life.

THE JOURNEY CONTINUES

Twenty years have passed since I completed the first edition. As it is with most things, "being away" for a while and then looking back can bring fresh perspective. For me, this reflective opportunity brought me face-to-face with an essential question: "What is the real purpose of this book?"

Certainly, one purpose of *Leadership from the Inside Out* is to provide growth resources for your personal and leadership transformation. But I hope its contribution is more than that. I hope that it goes beyond helping individuals grow. Imagine a critical mass of authentic leaders, who express their gifts and create life-enriching value through energetic, courageous, purpose-driven leadership. Imagine an organization like that, a community like that, or a nation like that. Envisioning a better world seems less like an idealized fantasy when you think of what a critical mass of authentic, transformative leaders could achieve. As you move forward, I hope that you will accept the challenge not to get lost in your own growth. The purpose of your transformation is to radiate your gifts in the service of others. Growth is much more meaningful and fulfilling when it touches and enriches the lives of others.

As powerful as one authentic leader can be for an organization, a critical mass of leaders growing from the inside out can greatly accelerate an organization's progress. The chairman and CEO of a firm invited me to breakfast to discuss a new coaching candidate. When I arrived at the restaurant, I was surprised to be greeted by the entire executive management team, minus the coaching candidate. In our meeting, we focused on the "issues" of their fellow executive and how each member of the team perceived what he needed in order to improve.

After listening to their concerns, I was confident that we could help the individual, but that was not the real issue. Formulating what I sensed was the actual organizational need, I challenged the team. "What are each of you doing to grow as leaders in order to grow your organization?" In spite of their extremely aggressive business plans, no one could respond to my question. Clarifying my question, I said, "We can help Fred, but the real organizational issue is not to improve Fred's performance. The real issue is: How are you preparing yourselves for success together?"

Leaving the meeting, I felt that although I had isolated their real needs, I had likely lost a potential account. Two days later, however, the chairman and CEO called me and said, "We listened to your counsel and felt you were right on target. I would like to discuss how all the members of our senior team, including me, could engage in coaching along with Fred." Within four months, the entire team was deeply involved in growth together. A critical mass of individuals was now rapidly transforming the organization.

The chairman was now ready to let go of the CEO responsibilities and was using his inner awareness to look with a broader lens at the longer-term future of the company. No member of the senior team wanted the CEO job, so an external search was initiated. Key members of the team began to transform their roles, and new positions were created that energized the company and addressed strategic issues. A common language about leadership, purpose, and growth permeated the organization. A new culture, one that would support growth and transformation, was now on its way. Like this company, leaders and organizations that invest in purpose-driven performance will thrive for decades to come.

I hope that, inspired by these principles, stories, and practices, you will continue the journey we have started. I also hope you will share your blessings with others—share them with your organization, your customers, and your loved ones. Together we can transform our world.

There are stars whose radiance is visible on earth though they have long been extinct. There are people whose brilliance continues to light the world though they are no longer among the living. These lights are particularly bright when the night is dark. They light the way for mankind.

—Hannah Senesh

Notes

This book draws on more than three decades of learning and experience working with thousands of leaders and comprehensive interviews with more than 100 CEOs. In some cases, clients requested anonymity, and we respected those requests. For all others, we cited their names, positions, and companies in the text. The many quotations throughout the book come from a variety of sources: conversations, interviews, books, articles, news and talk shows, my own file of favorite quotes, and quotation sites.

CHAPTER ONE: PERSONAL MASTERY

Youth Frontiers is a nonpartisan, nonprofit organization dedicated to improving school climate by building character through teaching students to incorporate kindness, courage, respect, leadership, and wisdom into their daily lives. Joe Cavanaugh is founder and CEO.

The reference to "top ten career stallers and stoppers" is from M. M. Lombardo and R. W. Eichinger, "Top Ten Career Stallers and Stoppers," *The Leadership Architect: Norms and Validity Report*, 4th ed. (Minneapolis: Lominger International, Korn Ferry, 2003).

The mention of the connection of agile growth, an evolving decision-making and leadership style, to career and leadership advancement is from a study by Kenneth R. Brousseau, Michael J. Driver, Gary Hourihan, and Rikard Larsson, "The Seasoned Executive's Decision-Making Style," *Harvard Business Review* (February 2006): 111–121.

The research study by David Zes and Dana Landis was the first to correlate organizational financial performance and leader self-awareness. To read more, see: David Zes and Dana Landis, "A Better Return on Self-Awareness," *Briefings*, Korn Ferry Institute (November 2013). You may also want to go to an article, "Return on Self-Awareness," published March 2013 in my Forbes.com column and accessible at CashmanLeadership.com, on the implications of this research.

You can find the classic line from *Hamlet* in Act IV, Scene V, William Shakespeare, *Hamlet*.

Jim Collins's research on "Level 5 leaders," and in particular what seems like combinations of paradoxical traits, comes from: Jim Collins, *Good to Great: Why Some Companies Make the Leap . . . and Others Don't* (New York: HarperCollins, 2001), 27–40.

You can find more information on emotional intelligence and leadership in these referenced sources: Daniel Goleman, *Working with Emotional Intelligence* (New York: Bantam, 1998), 26–27. Daniel Goleman, Richard Boyatzis, and Annie McKee, *Primal Leadership: Learning to Lead with Emotional Intelligence* (Boston: Harvard Business School Press, 2004), 94.

You can read more about today's "flat world" in Thomas L. Friedman's book *The World Is Flat* (New York: Farrar, Straus, Giroux, 2005).

During the writing of the second edition of this book, we saw an interview Charlie Rose did with Howard Schultz, in which Rose asked, "What's the most important quality today for leadership?" The book quotes mentioned come from: Howard Schultz and Dori Jones Yang, *Pour Your Heart Into It: How Starbucks Built a Company One Cup at a Time* (New York: Hyperion, 1997), 147–152.

The quote from Jeffrey Immelt was excerpted from an interview on *Fareed Zakaria GPS*, a CNN news show, on April 2, 2017.

For more on "The Study of Character," see Terry Bacon, *The Elements of Power* (AMACOM, 2011), 3, 127, 115–119.

You can find more on "courage," and other differentiating competencies in C-suite and midlevel management, in this summary of research: James Lewis, "Finding the Keys to the Corner Office," *Briefings*, Korn Ferry Institute (February 2017).

The Korn Ferry Hay Group database is the source of the data on connection between leader influence on team climate and team performance, and the *Businessweek* reference is from the August 2007 issue.

CHAPTER TWO: STORY MASTERY

The documentary on Shaquille O'Neal and his unique relationship with his coach and friend, Dale Brown, is an SEC Storied documentary, *Shaq and Dale*, 2015.

To learn more about the "Hero's Journey," read Joseph Campbell's *The Hero with a Thousand Faces* (Novato, CA: New World Library, 2008). This book was first published in 1949, and there have been many editions. You may also want to read, listen to, or watch *The Power of Myth*, a series of interviews that Bill Moyers did with Joseph Campbell on PBS, which is also available as a book: Joseph Campbell with Bill Moyers, *The Power of Myth* (New York: Doubleday, 1988). It is also available as an audiobook and on DVD.

The Ken Burns quote is from a documentary on the award-winning documentarian: Redglass Pictures, *Ken Burns On Story*, 2012.

If you want to learn more about oxytocin and Paul Zak's research, go to: Paul Zak, "Why Your Brain Loves Good Storytelling," *Harvard Business Review* (October 2014).

For more on the power of sharing stories on teams and the impact on team performance, read: Francesco Gino, "Teams Who Share Personal Stories Are More Effective," *Harvard Business Review* (April 2016).

A book by Derek Thompson, *Hit Makers: The Science of Popularity in an Age of Distraction* (New York: Penguin Random House, 2017), influenced my writing on Destructive Stories.

To learn more about the research on the impact of trauma, read: Tori Rodriguez, "Descendants of Holocaust Survivors Have Altered Stress Hormones," *Scientific American*, March 2015. Or go to PBS News Hour online to view or read a segment on the same research, "Trauma effects may linger in body chemistry of next generation," August 2015.

John Mark Green's poem was accessed at facebook.com/JohnMarkGreenPoetry/ and is reprinted with permission: "Burn Our Masks at Midnight" © 2015 by John Mark Green.

CHAPTER THREE: PURPOSE MASTERY

The Huffington Post wrote about Paul Polman's purpose-driven leadership in the following article: Alexandre Mars, "Doing Well By Doing Good: An Interview With Paul Polman, CEO of Unilever," *The Huffington Post* (May 2016). Go to www.unilever.com to see more on Unilever's purpose statement and values.

The insight by Bob Eichinger and Michael Lombardo on the correlation between "inspiring missions" and improvement in the marketplace comes from: *FYI, For Your Improvement* (Minneapolis: Lominger Limited, 2004), 386. The reference to "core legacy" is from: Jim Collins, *Good to Great: Why Some Companies Make the Leap . . . and Others Don't* (New York: HarperCollins, 2001), 193–197. Howard Schultz's quote on Core Purpose is from: Howard Schultz and Dori Jones Yang, *Pour Your Heart Into It: How Starbucks Built a Company One Cup at a Time* (New York: Hyperion, 1997), 81.

We referenced a significant study on how well purpose-driven companies in the consumer sector did compared to non-purpose-driven companies in the same sector. To read more of the study's findings, go to: Elaine Dinos, Janet Feldman, and Rick Lash, "People on a Mission," Korn Ferry Institute (December 2016), 2–15. The researchers also conducted interviews, including one with David Lubetzky, founder and CEO of KIND Snacks, parts of which we related. Another article on the success of purpose-driven companies that we cited is: Simon Caulkin, "Companies with a purpose beyond profit tend to make more money," *Financial Times* (January 2016).

To further explain Core Talents, we referred to: Mihaly Csikszentmihalyi, *Flow: The Psychology of Optimal Experience* (New York: Harper Perennial, 1991), 43–70; and to: Martin E. P. Seligman, *Authentic Happiness: Using the New Positive Psychology to Realize Your Potential for Lasting Fulfillment* (New York: Free Press, 2004), 166.

CHAPTER FOUR: INTERPERSONAL MASTERY

The research on the correlation between engagement and revenue growth is from: James Lewis, "Finding the Keys to the Corner Office," *Briefings*, Korn Ferry Institute (February 2017). Stuart Crandell, mentioned in the text, assisted with the research but was not an author on the article. Another source is: William Werhane and Mark Royal, "Engaging and Enabling Employees for Company Success," *Workspan* (October 2009). You can find the reference to Zenger and Folkman's results in: John H. Zenger and Joseph Folkman, *The Extraordinary Leader: Turning Good Managers into Great Leaders* (New York: McGraw-Hill, 2002), 149–150.

The information from the Saratoga Institute study derives from: Leigh Branham, *The 7 Hidden Reasons Employees Leave: How to Recognize the Subtle Signs and Act Before It's Too Late*, Saratoga Institute (New York: AMACOM, 2005).

The book *Presence* is the result of two years of conversations between the authors on many topics related to people and change. Intentional work is one topic. For further reading: Peter Senge, C. Otto Scharmer, Joseph Jaworski, and Betty Sue Flowers, *Presence: An Exploration of Profound Change in People, Organizations, and Society* (New York: Doubleday Currency, 2005), 141.

An article by Rick Lash, "Motives and Leadership," Hay Group (2015), clarifies McClelland's work in motives, Personalized Power, and Socialized Power in particular.

On the issue of executives and high potentials receiving less specific feedback, we referenced: Bob Eichinger, Michael M. Lombardo, and Dave Ulrich, *100 Things You Need to Know: Best People Practices for Managers & HR* (Minneapolis: Lominger Limited, 2006), 193.

My colleague Andrés Tapia and I have had many discussions and collaborations because of the integral alignment of self-awareness for inclusive leadership and organizations. For more on this topic read: Andrés T. Tapia, *The Inclusion Paradox: The Post Obama Era and the Transformation of Global Diversity.* (Los Angeles: Korn Ferry Institute, 2016).

Lack of listening is a serious blind spot for many leaders. To read more, look up: Kelly E. See, Elizabeth Wolfe Morrison, Naomi B. Rothman, and Jack B. Soll, "The Detrimental Effects of Power on Confidence, Advice Taking, and Accuracy," *Organizational Behavior and Human Decision Processes* (2011), 1–12; and: Jack Zenger and Joseph Folkman, "What Great Listeners Actually Do," *Harvard Business Review* (July 2016). You will also find practices for authentic listening in: Kevin Cashman, *The Pause Principle: Step Back to Lead Forward* (San Francisco: Berrett-Koehler, 2012), 88–91.

CHAPTER FIVE: CHANGE MASTERY

References to much of what we have learned about the issues facing leaders and the competencies needed come from these sources: Center for Creative Leadership research presented at Conference Board Executive Coaching Conference, February 2008; M. M. Lombardo and R. W. Eichinger, *Preventing Derailment: What to Do Before It's Too Late* (Greensboro, NC: Center for Creative Leadership, 1989); M. M. Lombardo and R. W. Eichinger: "High Potentials as High Learners," *Human Resource Management* (2000), 39, 321–320; R. J. Sternberg, R. K. Wagner, W. M. Williams, and J. A. Horvath, "Testing Common Sense," *American Psychologist* (1995), 50, 912–927; Daniel Goleman, *Emotional Intelligence: Why It Can Matter More Than IQ* (New York: Bantam Books, 1995); M. M. Lombardo and R. W. Eichinger, *FYI: For Your Improvement* (Minneapolis: Lominger Limited, 2004); M. M. Lombardo and R. W. Eichinger, "High Potentials as High Learners," *Human Resource Management* (2000), 39, 321–329; A. H. Church and E. I. Deroisiers, "Talent Management: Will the High Potentials Please Stand Up?" (symposium presented at the Society for Industrial and Organizational Psychology Conference, Dallas, 2006); J. A. Connolly and C. Viswesvaran, "Assessing the Construct Validity of a Measure of Learning Agility" (presentation at the Seventeenth Annual Conference of the Society for Industrial and Organizational Psychology, Toronto, April 2002); James L. Lewis, "The Rules of Engagement: Four Specific Traits Predict High Engagement among Executives," Korn Ferry Institute (2013).

You can read more about the data collected in the study on C-suite executives and prevalent competencies in those who are highly engaged versus less engaged peers here: James Lewis, "Finding the Keys to the Corner Office," *Briefings*, Korn Ferry Institute (February 2017).

BNP Paribas and Scorpio Partnership annually publish a report of an international survey of entrepreneurs. The "BNP Paribas Global Entrepreneur's Report 2016" identified the "Emergence of the

Millennipreneur." In the 2017 report, it identified five groups: the Ultrapreneur, the Serialpreneur, the Millennipreneur, the Womanpreneur, and the Boomerpreneur.

The data on failed change initiatives comes from: A.T. Kearney, *After the Merger: Seven Rules for Successful Post-Merger Integration* (2000); Stuart Kliman and Stuart Price, "New Alliance Management Study - Success rates increase but challenges remain," Vantage Partners (2015); "Diminished Returns," *Bloomberg Businessweek* (2007); Jonathan Hughes and Jeff Weiss, "Simple Rules for Making Alliances Work," *Harvard Business Review* (November 2007).

For more on the science behind leading successful change initiatives, see: David Rock and Jeffrey Schwartz, "The Neuroscience of Leadership," *strategy+business* (2006).

There is considerable research on the benefits of mindfulness practices. Go to www.umassmed.edu/cfm/ for the University of Massachusetts Center for Mindfulness. The focus of Dr. Richard Davidson's work is on neural emotion and emotional style. One study on the relationship between meditation and regulation of attention is by Antoine Lutz, Heleen A. Slagter, John D. Dunne, and Richard J. Davidson, "Attention regulation and monitoring in meditation," *Trends in Cognitive Science* (April 2008), 163–169.

You can read more about Daniel Goleman's work on the importance of leaders developing awareness and focusing attention, both their own and others', in: Daniel Goleman, "The Focused Leader," *Harvard Business Review* (December 2013).

CHAPTER SIX: RESILIENCE MASTERY

The original E. B. White quote, with which I took liberties, is: "I arise in the morning torn between a desire to improve (or save) the world and a desire to enjoy (or savor) the world. This makes it hard to plan the day."

For more on the perception of fit, healthy leaders, see: "Study: Slimmer CEOs are often considered better leaders," *Advisory Board* (January 2013); and: Leslie Kwoh, "Want to Be CEO? What's Your BMI?" *The Wall Street Journal* (January 2013).

For more about Arianna Huffington's personal health crisis and her advocacy of sleep and related aspects of well-being, see: Paul Raeburn, "Arianna Huffington: Collapse from exhaustion was 'wake-up call'," Today.com, (May 2014); Rina Raphael, "Arianna Huffington's Recipe for a Great Night's Sleep," FastCompany.com (June 2016); and: Arianna Huffington, *The Sleep Revolution: Transforming Your Life, One Night at a Time* (New York: Harmony, 2017).

Brian Cornell's health and fitness comments were extracted from: Jonathan Dahl, "Targeting Transformation," *Briefings*, Korn Ferry Institute (November 2016.)

To read more on the research supporting a shift from time to energy, see: Tony Schwartz and Catherine McCarthy, "Manage Your Energy, Not Your Time," *Harvard Business Review* (October 2007).

The referenced research on 100-year-olds is from: L. W. Poon, Ph.D., and S. L. K. Cheung, Ph.D., "Centenarian research in the past two decades," *Asian Journal of Gerontology & Geriatrics* 7:1 (June 2012).

You can read more on engagement and the principles of stress and recovery in: James Loehr and Jack Groppel, "Stress & Recovery: Important Keys to Engagement," *Chief Learning Officer* (September 2004).

To read more about the benefit of laughter and Dr. Kataria's laughter clubs, see: Daniel H. Pink, *A Whole New Mind: Moving from the Information Age to the Conceptual Age* (New York: Penguin, 2005), 177–197.

The Study of Adult Development is a longitudinal study that has followed two groups of men since 1939. We referenced the following article: Melanie Curtin, "This 75-Year Harvard Study Found the 1 Secret to Leading a Fulfilling Life," *Inc.* (February 2017). You can learn more by visiting adultdevelopmentstudy.org.

CHAPTER SEVEN: BEING MASTERY

On meditation as "paying attention," read: Jon Kabat-Zinn, *Wherever You Go, There You Are: Mindfulness Meditation in Everyday Life* (New York: Hyperion, 1994), 4–5.

Maharishi Mahesh Yogi was the founder of TM and one of my greatest teachers. *Maharishi Mahesh Yogi: The Definitive Biography* by Jack Forem, his longtime student, will be released in 2018.

The reference to reflective practices as "regular sustained attention," is from: David Rock and Jeffrey Schwartz, "Why Neuroscience Matters to Executives," *strategy+business* (April 2007), which can also tell you more on quieting the mind and the amygdala region.

For more about Richard Davidson, read: Kathy Gilsinan, "The Buddhist and the Neuroscientist: What compassion does to the brain," *The Atlantic* (July 2015). For Davidson's paper on the study of attention regulation, see: Antoine Lutz, Heleen A. Slagter, John D. Dunne, and Richard J. Davidson, "Attention regulation and monitoring in meditation," *Trends in Cognitive Science* (April 2008), 163–169. Another paper on the study of the neuroplasticity of the brain is: Richard Davidson and Antoine Lutz, "Buddha's Brain: Neuroplasticity and Meditation," *IEEE Signal Processing Magazine* (January 2008).

The following work explains why we need to look at familiar problems from a new perspective: Peter Senge, C. Otto Scharmer, Joseph Jaworski, and Betty Sue Flowers, *Presence: An Exploration of Profound Change in People, Organizations, and Society* (New York: Doubleday Currency, 2005), 85–91.

The reference to "moments of insight" is from: David Rock and Jeffrey Schwartz, "The Neuroscience of Leadership," *strategy+business* (May 2006). Steven Baert's insight was part of an interview he did with me for an article: Kevin Cashman, "Pauses Really Do Refresh," Korn Ferry Institute, *Briefings* (August 2015).

In the section "Getting Things Done by Non-Doing," we cite: Anne Fisher, "Be Smarter at Work, Slack Off," *CNN Money* (March 2006).

Studies on the benefits of TM, including improvement in brain activity and intelligence, as well as metabolic functions, include the following: M. C. Dillbeck et al., "Frontal EEG Coherence, H-Reflex Recovery, Concept Learning, and the TM-Sidhi Program," *International Journal of Neuroscience* 15:3 (1981), 151–157; M. C. Dillbeck, "Meditation and Flexibility of Visual Perception and Verbal Problem-Solving," *Memory & Cognition* 10:3 (1982), 207–215; M. C. Dillbeck et al., "Longitudinal Effects of the Transcendental Meditation and TM-Sidhi Program on Cognitive Ability and Cognitive Style," *Perceptual and Motor Skills* 62:3 (1986), 731–738; S. Yamamoto et al., "Medial Prefrontal Cortex and Anterior Cingulate Cortex in the Generation of Alpha Activity Induced by Transcendental Meditation: A Magnetoencephalographic Study," *Acta Medica Okayama* 60:1 (2006), 51–58; J. Anderson et al., "Blood Pressure Response to Transcendental Meditation: A Meta-analysis," *American Journal of Hypertension* 21:3 (2008), 310–316; V. Barnes et al., "Stress, Stress Reduction, and Hypertension in African Americans: An Updated Review," *Journal of the National Medical Association* 89:7 (1997), 464–476.

The following book is used in the Mindfulness-Based Stress Reduction (MBSR) Program: Jon Kabat-Zinn, *Full Catastrophe Living: Using the Wisdom of Your Body and Mind to Face Stress, Pain, and Illness* (New York: Bantam Dell, 2005). You will discover additional information on mindfulness meditation at the University of Massachusetts Center for Mindfulness website. The quote from David Rock and Jeffrey Schwartz on how meditation helps the brain is from "Why Neuroscience Matters to Executives," *strategy+business* (April 2007).

CHAPTER EIGHT: COACHING MASTERY

Daniel Goleman's statement on self-awareness and performance is from his *Working with Emotional Intelligence* (New York: Bantam, 1998), 67.

The statement by Noel Tichy and Warren Bennis is from "Wise Leaders Cultivate Two Traits," *Leadership Excellence Essentials* (June 2007), 3.

For the article explaining how critical Building Practice is, see: Jack Zenger, Joe Folkman, and Robert Sherwin, "The Promise of Phase 3," *Training and Development* (January 2005), 31–34.

Robert Hargrove's work has been an important influence. To learn more, read: Robert Hargrove, *Masterful Coaching* (San Francisco: Jossey-Bass, 1995), 27.

BIBLIOGRAPHY

The following is a combined list of resources used and recommended readings:

Arbinger Institute. *Leadership and Self-Deception: Getting Out of the Box.* San Francisco: Berrett-Koehler, 2002.

Arenander, Alarik T., and Craig Pearson. *Upgrading the Executive Brain: Breakthrough Science and Technology of Leadership.* www.theleadersbrain.org.

Bacon, Terry R. *The Elements of Influence: The Art of Getting Others to Follow Your Lead.* New York: AMACOM, 2011.

Bacon, Terry R. *The Elements of Power: Lessons on Leadership and Influence.* New York: AMACOM, 2011.

Bacon, Terry R., Ph.D., and Laurie Voss, Ph.D. *Adaptive Coaching: The Art and Practice of a Client-Centered Approach to Performance Improvement.* London: Nicholas Brealey, 2011.

Badaraco, Joseph L., Jr. *Questions of Character: Illuminating the Heart of Leadership through Literature.* Brighton: Harvard Business School Press, 2006.

Begley, Sharon. *Train Your Mind, Change Your Brain: How a New Science Reveals Our Extraordinary Potential to Transform Ourselves.* New York: Ballantine, 2007.

Bennis, Warren. *On Becoming a Leader.* Reading: Addison-Wesley, 1990.

Bennis, Warren, and Patricia Ward Biederman. *Organizing Genius: The Secrets of Creative Collaboration.* Reading: Addison-Wesley, 1996.

Bennis, Warren, and Burton Nanus. *Leaders: The Strategies for Taking Charge.* New York: Harper Business, 1985.

Bennis, Warren, and Robert J. Thomas. *Leading for a Lifetime: How Defining Moments Shape Leaders of Today and Tomorrow.* Cambridge: Harvard Business School Press, 2007.

Block, Peter. *Stewardship: Choosing Service over Self-Interest.* San Francisco: Berrett-Koehler, 1996.

Bolman, Lee, and Terrance E. Deal. *Leading with Soul: An Uncommon Journey to Spirit.* San Francisco: Jossey-Bass, 1994.

Boyatzis, Richard E., and Annie McKee. *Resonant Leadership: Renewing Yourself and Connecting with Others through Mindfulness, Hope, and Compassion.* Cambridge: Harvard Business School Press, 2005.

Branden, Nathaniel. *Six Pillars of Self-Esteem.* New York: Bantam Books, 1995.

Bridges, William. *Transitions: Making Sense of Life's Changes.* Boston: Da Capo Press, 2004.

Brousseau, Kenneth R., Michael J. Driver, Gary Hourihan, and Rikard Larsson. "The Seasoned Executive's Decision-Making Style," *Harvard Business Review* (February 2006); 111–121.

Burnison, Gary. *The Twelve Absolutes of Leadership.* New York: McGraw-Hill, 2013.

Byron, Thomas. *Dhammapada: The Sayings of the Buddha.* Boston: Shambhala, 1976.

Campbell, Joseph. *The Hero with a Thousand Faces.* Novato: New World Library, 2008.

Campbell, Joseph. *The Power of Myth.* New York: Doubleday, 1988.

Cashman, Kevin. *The Pause Principle: Step Back to Lead Forward.* San Francisco: Berrett-Koehler, 2012.

Cashman, Kevin, and Jack Forem. *Awakening the Leader Within: A Story of Transformation.* Hoboken: John Wiley & Sons, 2003.

Cavanaugh, Joseph. "Respectfully, Joe Cavanaugh" (video). St. Paul: Kelley Productions and Twin Cities Public Television, 1994.

Charan, Ram, and Bill Conaty. *The Talent Masters: Why Smart Leaders Put People Before Numbers.* New York: Crown, 2010.

Charan, Ram, Stephen Drotter, and James Noel. *The Leadership Pipeline: How to Build the Leadership Powered Company.* San Francisco: Jossey-Bass, 2001.

Ciampa, Dan, and David L. Dotlich. *Transitions at the Top: What Organizations Must Do to Make Sure New Leaders Succeed.* San Francisco: Jossey-Bass, 2015.

Collins, Jim. *Good to Great: Why Some Companies Make the Leap . . . and Others Don't.* New York: HarperCollins, 2001.

Collins, Jim, and Jerry Porras. *Built to Last: Successful Habits of Visionary Companies.* New York: HarperCollins, 1994.

Connolly, Mickey, and Richard Rianoshek, Ph.D. *The Communication Catalyst: The Fast (But Not Stupid) Track to Value for Customers, Investors, and Employees.* Chicago: Kaplan/Conversant Solutions, 2002.

Costa, John Dalla. *The Ethical Imperative: Why Moral Leadership Is Good Business.* Cambridge: Perseus, 1998.

Csikszentmihalyi, Mihaly. *Flow: The Psychology of Optimal Experience.* New York: Harper Perennial, 1991.

DeFoore, Bill, and John Renesch, eds. *The New Bottom Line: Bringing Heart & Soul to Business.* San Francisco: New Leaders Press, 1996.

Dinos, Elaine, Janet Feldman, and Rick Lash. "People on a Mission." Korn Ferry Institute (December 2016).

Dotlich, David, Ph.D., Peter Cairo, Ph.D., and Stephen Rhinesmith, Ph.D. *Head, Heart and Guts: How the World's Best Companies Develop Leaders.* San Francisco: Jossey-Bass, 2006.

Driver, Michael J., Ken R. Brousseau, and Phillip Hunsaker. *The Dynamic Decision Maker: Five Decision Styles for Executive and Business Success.* New York: Excel, 1998.

Eichinger, Robert W., Michael M. Lombardo, and Dave Ulrich. *100 Things You Need to Know: Best People Practices for Managers & HR.* Minneapolis: Lominger Limited, 2006.

Einstein, Albert. *Einstein on Humanism: Collected Essays of Albert Einstein.* Secaucus: Carol Publishing, 1993.

Emerson, Ralph Waldo. *The Collected Works of Ralph Waldo Emerson.* Cambridge: Belknap, 1984.

Flaherty, James. *Coaching: Evoking Excellence in Others.* London: Routledge, 2011.

Forem, Jack. *Transcendental Meditation: The Essential Teachings of Maharishi Mahesh Yogi.* Second Edition. Carlsbad: Hay House, 2013.

Friedman, Thomas L. *The World Is Flat.* New York: Farrar, Straus and Giroux, 2005.

Garfield, Charles. *Peak Performance.* New York: Warner Books, 1989.

George, Bill, and Peter Sims. *True North: Discover Your Authentic Leadership.* San Francisco: Jossey-Bass, 2007.

Goleman, Daniel. *Emotional Intelligence: Why It Can Matter More Than IQ.* New York: Bantam, 1995.

Goleman, Daniel. *Focus: The Hidden Driver of Excellence.* New York: HarperCollins, 2013.

Goleman, Daniel. "The Focused Leader." *Harvard Business Review* (December, 2013).

Goleman, Daniel. *Social Intelligence: The New Science of Human Relationships.* New York: Bantam, 2006.

Goleman, Daniel. *Working with Emotional Intelligence.* New York: Bantam, 1998.

Goleman, Daniel, Richard Boyatzis, and Annie McKee. *Primal Leadership: Learning to Lead with Emotional Intelligence.* Boston: Harvard Business School Press, 2004.

Goss, Tracy. *The Last Word on Power: Executive Re-invention for Leaders Who Must Make the Impossible Happen.* New York: Bantam Doubleday Dell, 1996.

Greenleaf, Robert K. *Servant Leadership: A Journey into the Nature of Legitimate Power and Greatness.* Mahwah: Paulist Press, 1977.

Groppel, Jack L., and Bob Andelman. *The Corporate Athlete: How to Achieve Maximal Performance in Business and Life.* New York: John Wiley & Sons, 1999.

Halpern, Belle Linda, and Kathy Lubar. *Leadership Presence: Dramatic Techniques to Reach Out, Motivate, and Inspire.* New York: Gotham Books, 2004.

Hargrove, Robert. *Masterful Coaching.* San Francisco: Jossey-Bass, 1995.

Hawley, John A. *Reawakening the Spirit in Work.* New York: Simon & Schuster, 1995.

Heider, Joseph. *Tao of Leadership.* New York: Bantam Books, 1986.

Hendricks, Gay, and Kate Ludeman. *The Corporate Mystic: A Guidebook for Visionaries with Their Feet on the Ground.* New York: Bantam Books, 1996.

Hillman, James. *The Soul's Code: In Search of Character and Calling.* New York: Random House, 1996.

Huffington, Arianna. *The Sleep Revolution: Transforming Your Life, One Night at a Time.* New York: Harmony, 2016.

Huffington, Arianna. *Thrive: The Third Metric to Redefining Success and Creating a Life of Well-Being, Wisdom, and Wonder.* New York: Harmony, 2014.

Hurst, Aaron. *The Purpose Economy: How Your Desire for Impact, Personal Growth and Community Is Changing the World.* Boise: Elevate, 2014.

Jaworski, Joseph. *Synchronicity: The Inner Path of Leadership.* San Francisco: Berrett-Koehler, 1996.

Jung, C.G. *Basic Writings of C.G. Jung.* New York: Random House, 1993.

Kabat-Zinn, Jon. *Coming to Our Senses: Healing Ourselves and the World through Mindfulness.* New York: Hyperion, 2005.

Kabat-Zinn, Jon. *Wherever You Go, There You Are: Mindfulness Meditation in Everyday Life.* New York: Hyperion, 1994.

Kets de Vries, Manfred. *Leaders, Fools and Impostors: Essays on the Psychology of Leadership.* San Francisco: Jossey-Bass, 1993.

Kimsey-House, Henry, and Karen Kimsey-House. *Co-Active Coaching: Changing Business, Transforming Lives.* Third Edition. London: Nicholas Brealey, 2011.

Kouzes, James M., and Barry Z. Posner. *The Leadership Challenge.* San Francisco: Jossey-Bass, 2007.

Landsberg, Max. *Mastering Coaching.* London: Profile Books, 2016.

Leider, Richard. *The Power of Purpose: Creating Meaning in Your Life and Work.* Oakland: Berrett-Koehler, 2015.

Lewis, James, Ph.D. "Finding the Keys to the Corner Office." *Briefings* (Korn Ferry Institute, February 2017).

Lewis, James L. Ph.D. "The Rules of Engagement: Four Specific Traits Predict High Engagement among Executives." Korn Ferry Institute (2013).

Lipton, Bruce. *The Biology of Belief.* Carlsbad: Hay House, 2016.

Loehr, Jim, and Tony Schwartz. *The Power of Full Engagement.* New York: Simon & Schuster, 2003.

Lombardo, Michael, and Robert W. Eichinger. *FYI: For Your Improvement.* Third Edition. Los Angeles: Korn Ferry Institute, 2017.

Laudicina, Paul. *Beating the Global Odds.* New York: Wiley, 2012.

Lowen, Alexander. *Narcissism: Denial of the True Self.* New York: Collier Books, 1995.

Maharishi Mahesh Yogi. *Maharishi Mahesh Yogi on the Bhagavad-Gita: A New Translation and Commentary.* Fairfield: Enlightenment Press, 1967.

Maslow, Abraham. *Toward a Psychology of Being.* New York: Van Nostrand-Rheinhold, 1968.

Maxwell, John. *Intentional Living: Choosing a Life That Matters.* New York: Center Street, 2015.

McClelland, David. *The Achieving Society.* Eastford: Martino Fine Books, 2010.

Melrose, Ken. *Making the Grass Greener on Your Side.* San Francisco: Berrett-Koehler, 1995.

Merton, Thomas. *No Man Is an Island.* New York: Walker, 1986.

Morris, Tom. *True Success: A New Philosophy of Excellence.* New York: Putnam, 1994.

Mourkogiannis, Nikos. *Purpose: The Starting Point of Great Companies.* New York: Palgrave Macmillan, 2006.

O'Neil, John. *Success and Your Shadow.* Boulder: Sounds True Audio, 1995.

Orsborn, Carol. *Inner Excellence: Spiritual Principles of Life-Driven Business.* San Rafael: New World Library, 1992.

Parry, Danaan. *Warriors of the Heart.* Bainbridge Island: Earthstewards Network, 1997.

Patnaude, Jeff. *Leading from the Maze: A Personal Pathway to Leadership.* Berkeley: Ten Speed Press, 1996.

Pearman, Roger R., Michael M. Lombardo, and Robert W. Eichinger. *You: Being More Effective in Your MBTI Type.* Minneapolis: Lominger Limited, 2005.

Pink, Daniel H. *A Whole New Mind: Moving from the Information Age to the Conceptual Age.* New York: Penguin, 2005.

Pontefract, Dan. *The Purpose Effect: Building Meaning in Yourself, Your Role, and Your Organization.* Boise: Elevate, 2016.

Pritz, Alan L. *Meditation as a Way of Life: Philosophy and Practice.* Wheaton: Quest Books, 2014.

Rechtschaffen, Stephan. *Time Shifting: Creating More Time to Enjoy Your Life.* New York: Doubleday Currency, 1996.

Rock, David. *Quiet Leadership: Six Steps to Transforming Performance at Work.* New York: Harper Collins, 2006.

Scharmer, C. Otto. *Theory U: Leading from the Future as It Emerges.* San Francisco: Berrett-Koehler, 2009.

Schneider, Bruce D. *Energy Leadership: Transforming Your Workplace and Your Life from the Core.* Hoboken: John Wiley & Sons, 2007.

Schultz, Howard, and Dori Jones Yang. *Pour Your Heart into It: How Starbucks Built a Company One Cup at a Time.* New York: Hyperion, 1997.

Schwartz, Tony, and Catherine McCarthy. "Manage Your Energy, Not Your Time." *Harvard Business Review* (October 2007).

Segal, Jeanne. *Raising Your Emotional Intelligence: A Practical Guide.* New York: Henry Holt, 1997.

Seligman, Martin E. P., Ph.D. *Authentic Happiness: Using the New Positive Psychology to Realize Your Potential for Lasting Fulfillment.* New York: Free Press, 2004.

Seligman, Martin E.P. *Learned Optimism: How to Change Your Mind and Your Life.* New York: Vintage, 2006.

Senge, Peter M. *The Fifth Discipline: The Art and Practice of the Learning Organization.* New York: Doubleday Currency, 1994.

Senge, Peter, C. Otto Scharmer, Joseph Jaworski, and Betty Sue Flowers. *Presence: An Exploration of Profound Change in People, Organizations, and Society.* New York: Doubleday Currency, 2005.

Siegel, Daniel J. *The Developing Mind: How Relationships and the Brain Interact to Shape Who We Are.* New York: Guilford Press, 1999.

Silsbee, Doug. *Presence-Based Coaching: Cultivating Self-Generative Leaders Through Mind, Body, and Heart.* San Francisco: Jossey-Bass, 2008.

Sinek, Simon. *Start with Why: How Great Leaders Inspire Everyone to Take Action.* New York: Portfolio Penguin, 2011.

Stahl, Jack. *Lessons on Leadership: The 7 Fundamental Management Skills for Leaders at All Levels.* New York: Kaplan, 2007.

Suzuki, D.T. *Essays in Zen Buddhism.* New York: Grove/Atlantic, 1989.

Tapia, Andrés T. *The Inclusion Paradox: The Post Obama Era and the Transformation of Global Diversity.* Third Edition. Los Angeles: Korn Ferry Institute, 2016.

Teilhard de Chardin, Pierre. *The Phenomenon of Man.* San Bernardino: Bongo Press, 1994.

Thompson, Derek. *Hit Makers: The Science of Popularity in an Age of Distraction.* New York: Penguin Press, 2017.

Tichy, Noel M. *The Leadership Engine: How Winning Companies Build Leaders at Every Level.* New York: Harper Collins, 2002.

Tichy, Noel M., and Warren Bennis. *Judgment: How Winning Leaders Make Great Calls.* New York: Portfolio, 2007.

Tzu, Lao, translated by Brian Walker. *The Tao Te Ching of Lao Tzu.* New York: St. Martin's Press, 1996.

Useem, Michael. *The Leadership Moment: Nine True Stories of Triumph and Disaster and Their Lessons for Us All.* New York: Three Rivers Press, 1998.

Wageman, Ruth, Debra A. Nunes, James A. Burruss, and J. Richard Hackman. *Senior Leadership Teams: What It Takes to Make Them Great.* Boston: Harvard Business School, 2008.

Whitelaw, Ginny. *The Zen Leader: 10 Ways to Go from Barely Managing to Leading Fearlessly.* Wayne: Career Press, 2012.

Whyte, David. *The Heart Aroused: Poetry and the Preservation of the Soul in Corporate America.* New York: Doubleday Currency, 1994.

Wilber, Ken. *One Taste: Daily Reflections on Integral Spirituality.* Boulder: Shambhala, 2000.

Wilber, Ken. *No Boundary.* Boston: Shambhala, 1979.

Zenger, John H., and Joseph Folkman. *The Extraordinary Leader: Turning Good Managers into Great Leaders.* New York: McGraw-Hill, 2002.

ACKNOWLEDGMENTS

Venturing further into life, there is a commensurate awareness of how deeply others have formed, shaped, and inspired me. I feel fortunate to be surrounded by so many passionate, brilliant, and knowledgeable people. It is a privilege to pause now to express my deep appreciation.

To my colleagues at Korn Ferry, I want to express my most heartfelt thanks to each and every one of you. I am so blessed to have the opportunity to collaborate and innovate with so many of you. The depth and diversity of your knowledge is mind-boggling and heart-inspiring.

First, I want to thank current and past Korn Ferry Minneapolis colleagues. We have grown from a small group to one of the biggest concentrations of talent consultants anywhere, as the PDI Ninth House, Lominger, and LeaderSource's offices came together in Minneapolis. Deepest thanks to Janet Feldman, Dee Gaeddert, Sidney Reisberg, Bill McCarthy, Bob Eichinger, Karin Lucas, Dina Rauker, Anne Tessien, John Pike, Craig Sneltjes, Chuck Feltz, Terry Enlow, Stu Crandell, RJ Heckman, Lee Artimovich, Kraig King, Barb Lubinski, Susan Brock, Jeff Schwartz, Dave Pearce, Tracy Kurschner, Marlys Aukee, Patrick Walsh, Lisa Peterson, Sara Larson, Cathy Winter, Anna Waters, Ken De Meuse, George Hallenbeck, Renée Garpestad, Pat Mulvehill, Katie Cooney, David Brings, Doug Menikheim, Joe Eastman, Jim Lewis, Paul Cimmerer, and so many others for being such extraordinary consulting colleagues over the years. So many Minneapolis people have supported the production of each edition of this book over the years, but special thanks to Shelley Lent, Angie Keranen, Matt Bertram, Faye Way, Sherri Rogalski, Kate Smith, Karissa Ernst, Joan Davis, Barbara Nelson, Sandee Johnson, Kari Block, and Sue Puncochar. As you all know, without your organizing genius, I would be lost!

Thanking all my colleagues outside of Minneapolis is a challenge. There is only one place to begin my gratitude: Gary Burnison. Your vision for Korn Ferry has been unwavering, and I am so grateful you invited me to play a role in this amazing growth journey. Thanks to all my current and former global colleagues: Lewis Rusen, Jane Stevenson, Stephen Kaye, Mark Arian, Ron Johnson, Mike Distefano, Jonathan Dahl, Linda Hyman, Bernard Zen-Ruffinen,

Jean-Marc Laouchez, Doug Charles, David Wise, Christoph la Garde, James Ringer, Becky Sanderson, David Dotlich, Andrés Tapia, Anthony Lo Pinto, Brigitte Morel-Curran, Jamen Graves, Naomi Sutherland, Bob Mintz, Bill Westwod, David Lange, Evelyn Orr, Ilene Gochman, Mike Hyter, Scott Kingdom, Mark Pierce, Sergio Averbach, Arvi Dhesi, Jim Peters, Tierney Remick, Richard Emerton, Catherine McCarthy, Jack MacPhail, Addy Chulef, Don Spetner, Terry Bacon, and Ken Brousseau. Special thanks to Rick Lash for his expertise and wisdom regarding legacy Hay Group research. Thanks to all 7,000 of my Korn Ferry colleagues for your inspiration and leadership.

Deep thanks to the thousands of clients I have been privileged to serve over the past thirty years. I wish I could name all of you, but that would fill another book. Working with you has inspired me to share many of your transformative journeys. I hope that I have represented you well. I am so grateful for your generosity, trust, gratitude, and energetic enthusiasm. Your character-rich stories continually move me and sustain me.

Heartfelt thanks to the late Warren Bennis, whom I consider the "godfather of leadership development," a model of the personal and leadership presence I can only aspire to attain. I want to acknowledge the prodigious, influential work of: Jim Collins, author of *Good to Great*, for your breakthrough work on authenticity and Level 5 leaders; Daniel Goleman, for bringing your body of work on emotional intelligence, focus, and consciousness to the world's attention; Jack Zenger and Joseph Folkman, authors of *Extraordinary Leader*, for your extensive research contributions; Peter Senge, author of the classic *The Fifth Discipline*, for your foundational, innovative thought leadership on the organization as a learning system; Robert Hargrove, author of *Masterful Coaching*, for your meaningful contribution in the field of coaching; Bob Eichinger and Michael Lombardo, for your breakthrough thinking on competencies and leadership and for your best-selling book, *The Leadership Machine*; and to all the Hay Group colleagues for being pioneers in motives, assessment, engagement, reward, leadership styles, and culture.

I'd especially like to thank the late David McClelland for his trailblazing thought leadership on human motivation and for his amazing book, *The Achieving Society*. Gratitude also to: Lowell Hellervik, Stu Crandell, and RJ Heckman, for your precise research and practice in leadership assessment; and to Richard Leider, for his extraordinary work on purpose and transition, and particularly for his book, *The Power of Purpose*. All of you truly are authentic leaders whose influence and value creation has been felt around the world.

Thanks to the 100+ CEOs and other executives who took the time to share your thoughts, stories, and life experiences over the years and across three editions. Our exchanges have been enlightening and provocative. Special thanks to Paul Walsh, Ken Melrose, Daniel Vasella, Thomas Ebeling, Joerg Reinhardt, Brian McNamara, Stuart Parker, Richard Nolan, Brad Hewitt, Bruce Nicholson, Alex Gorsky, Bill George, Jeff George, Marijn Dekkers, David MacLennan, Paul Van Oyen, Werner Bauman, Andreas Guenther, Andreas Fibig, Patrick Thomas, David Meek, Kurt Graves, Ludwig Hantson, Anne-Marie Law, Paul Laudicina, Steve Reinemund, Jack Stahl, Dona Young, Laura Karet, Brian Cornell, Stephanie Lundquist, David Epstein, Deborah Dunsire, Steven Baert, Mike Ball, Merrick McCracken, Jurgen Brokatsky-Geiger, Chris Howarth, Diana Pierce, Corey Seitz, Mike Moshier, Joanne Chang, Vikramaditya Bajpai, Rahul Sharma, Roger Lacey, David Wessner, Joe Cavanaugh, Mike Peel, Kevin Wilde, Marc Belton, Gus Blanchard, Larry Perlman, Jim Secord, Ron James, David Prosser, John Hetterick, Al Schuman, Bob Kidder, Rob Hawthorne, Mike Paxton, John Sundet, Tom Gegax, and many others.

Thanks to Ken Shelton, Trent Price, Robert Chapman, and the entire Executive Excellence team for publishing the original edition. Your guidance, persistence, and confidence were crucial to this book when, more than twenty years ago, others found it "too cutting edge." Thanks for partnering with me.

Thanks to everyone at Berrett-Koehler Publishers—Steve Piersanti, Jeevan Simvasubramaniam, Johanna Vondeling, Neal Maillet, David Marshall, Kristen Franz, Katie Sheehan, Michael Crowley, Maria Jesús Aguilo, Lassel Whipple, Courtney Schonfeld, Liz McKellar, Shabnam Banerjee-McFarland, and many others on your purpose-driven, hard-working team, especially Linda Jupiter, our production manager, and Peter Berry, our exceptional copyeditor. I am proud to be a part of the Berrett-Koehler community. You distinguish yourself not only by the authors and books you choose to publish but also by your courage, character, mission, commitment, and practices to live consciously and authentically, according to the ideas that you put out into the world. You are truly authentic leaders, breathing life into your purpose and creating enduring value. I appreciate your professionalism, your genuine ardor for my work, and the endless good humor with which you do yours.

Thanks to Margie Adler for editing and research help on all three editions. We had a great time working on the first one, but these last two editions would not have happened without you. I am grateful for your authentic passion and commitment to the principles in these pages and for your clarity, purpose-driven persistence, calmness, endurance, and brilliance. I could not have had a better writing partner for this project. Endless thanks!

Thanks to Peggy Lauritsen and her design team for the original cover and text design. For your excellent public relations efforts on the original, thanks to Fred and Sarah Bell Haberman; your excitement and belief in this book always lifted me up. Thanks to Kohnstamm Communications and to our current public relations team, Cave Henricks for your vision, creativity, passion, commitment, and professionalism. Big thanks go to Korn Ferry's marketing and communications team, in particular Jonathan Dahl, Mike Distefano, Tracy Kurschner, Dan Gugler, Derek Fromson, and Russel Pearlman. Your creativity and support are greatly appreciated.

Thanks to writer-author Jack Forem, for your encouragement and friendship. It was your confidence from the moment you told me that I was a "really good writer" that sustained me through a couple of years of drafts. Special thanks to book agent Bob Silverstein, for rejecting my initial manuscript twenty-two years ago and then sharing with me that I needed to "find my voice." Although I was devastated at first, it was the best feedback I received; it literally transformed my entire approach to writing.

My love and gratitude to Soraya, my wife, who prepares multiple places at home for me to write, because I like to shift spontaneously from office to meditation room to fireplace, or from kitchen table to dining room, as energy moves me. From a family of artists, and a wise psycho-spiritual-healer and artist in her own right, Soraya knows the value of fostering the creative process. The quiet, nurturing space you created often was a great challenge for you, but it was so appreciated by me. Thank you for your help and for your love. Heartfelt thanks to Tahiel, my son, best buddy, my close friend and fellow spiritual traveler. You are an amazing and creative person, truly wise beyond your years, and often my very insightful life coach.

It is impossible to put into words my gratitude for the teacher who most influenced my heart, mind, and soul—Maharishi Mahesh Yogi. In the last few days of my finishing the second edition of this book, this great sage and world teacher left his body. I must acknowledge that there would be no *Leadership from the Inside Out* without Maharishi's inner and outer guidance. His wisdom and practice completely transformed my life. The last time I sat with him, he said, "Bring peace and happiness to the world." I hope I have been a worthy student. Another world teacher I want to thank is Chunyi Lin, founder of Spring Forest Qigong and author of *Born a Healer*. Your wisdom, inspiration, and friendship have been a living model of inside out transformation.

My most important thanks go to you, the reader. I wrote this book for you—leaders, who are learners, willing to take the courageous steps to personal transformation. Thanks for the privilege of taking this sacred growth journey together.

INDEX

ABOUT KEVIN CASHMAN

Kevin is a best-selling author, top-ten thought leader, world-class keynote speaker, global CEO coach, and pioneer of the "grow the whole person to grow the whole leader" approach to transformative leadership. He is the founder of LeaderSource Ltd., *Executive to Leader Institute*, and the *Chief Executive Institute*, which are recognized as leadership development programs globally. In 2006, LeaderSource was acquired by Korn Ferry, where Kevin is now Senior Partner, CEO and Executive Development.

Kevin has advised thousands of CEOs, senior executives, and senior teams in more than eighty countries. He is an accomplished thought leader on personal, team, and organizational transformation. He has written six books, including *Awakening the Leader Within* and *Leadership from the Inside Out*, which was named the number-one best-selling business book of 2000 by CEO-READ, a classic international best seller, and is currently used at over 150 universities globally. His book *The Pause Principle: Step Back to Lead Forward* has been recognized as a Business Book of the Year Finalist by both ForeWord Reviews and CEO-READ.

Kevin has written scores of articles on leadership and talent management and has been featured in *The Wall Street Journal*, *Chief Executive*, *Bloomberg*, *Human Resource Executive*, *Fast Company*, *strategy+business*, *Directors & Boards*, National Public Radio, *Oprah*, and other national media. He is a leadership columnist for Forbes.com and has been recognized multiple times as one of the "Top 10 Thought Leaders" by *Leadership Excellence* and one of the "Top 10 Executive Coaches" by GlobalGurus.org. Kevin was honored to be the first leadership consultant to receive a Lifetime Achievement Award from the Association of Executive Search and Leadership Consultants for his contributions in transforming the talent industry through leadership development.

Kevin holds a degree in psychology from St. John's University and has been an adjunct professor for the University of Minnesota Executive Education program. He is a former advisory board member for HR.com; a Senior Fellow on the Caux Round Table for Moral Capitalism; and a past board member for the University of St. Thomas Center for Ethical Business Cultures, which fosters ethical leadership worldwide.

For more information on Keynote Speaking, CEO Development and Executive Development programs, visit CashmanLeadership.com.

ABOUT KORN FERRY

Korn Ferry is dedicated to one purpose: *releasing the full power and potential of people.* Inspired by this mission, Korn Ferry has grown to become the world's largest and most fully integrated talent management firm. With 130+ offices and 7,000 colleagues across the globe, Korn Ferry now serves 93 percent of the Fortune 100 companies. Every month, Korn Ferry touches the careers of 100,000+ professionals as it attracts, develops, engages, and rewards key talent.

In 2007, Korn Ferry acquired LeaderSource (founded by Kevin Cashman), including its *Chief Executive Institute*, *Executive to Leader Institute*, and *LeaderSuccession* programs, now available globally. Kevin is responsible for overseeing the CEO Development and Executive Development offerings worldwide.

For more information, contact Kevin at Kevin.Cashman@KornFerry.com; visit his website at CashmanLeadership.com; or visit the Korn Ferry website at KornFerry.com.

Another Book by Kevin Cashman
The Pause Principle
Step Back to Lead Forward

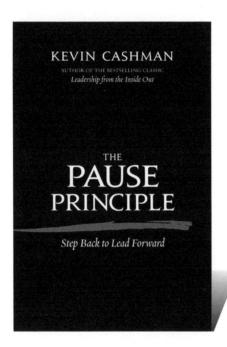

We live and lead in an increasingly volatile, uncertain, complex, and ambiguous world. But paradoxically, Kevin Cashman contends that leaders today must not merely act more quickly but pause more deeply. Pausing is a powerful methodology to imbue continuous growth in three critical domains: personal leadership, development of others, and fostering of innovation cultures. Drawing on decades of experience working with senior leaders, personal stories, and research in psychology, neuroscience, and leadership development, Cashman focuses our attention on our inherent power to ground our leadership and our organizations in authenticity, generativity, and purposeful transformation. You and your organization will learn to move from management speed and transaction to leadership significance and transformation. *The Pause Principle* offers break-through practices for leading as a whole person, harnessing one's drive to create more compelling, creative, and sustainable futures.

Paperback, 176 pages, ISBN 978-1-60994-532-9
PDF ebook ISBN 978-1-60994-533-6
ePub ebook ISBN 978-1-60994-534-3
Digital audiobook ISBN 978-1-62656-016-1

Berrett–Koehler Publishers, Inc.
www.bkconnection.com

800.929.2929

Berrett–Koehler
Publishers

Berrett-Koehler is an independent publisher dedicated to an ambitious mission: *Connecting people and ideas to create a world that works for all.*

We believe that the solutions to the world's problems will come from all of us, working at all levels: in our organizations, in our society, and in our own lives. Our BK Business books help people make their organizations more humane, democratic, diverse, and effective (we don't think there's any contradiction there). Our BK Currents books offer pathways to creating a more just, equitable, and sustainable society. Our BK Life books help people create positive change in their lives and align their personal practices with their aspirations for a better world.

All of our books are designed to bring people seeking positive change together around the ideas that empower them to see and shape the world in a new way.

And we strive to practice what we preach. At the core of our approach is Stewardship, a deep sense of responsibility to administer the company for the benefit of all of our stakeholder groups including authors, customers, employees, investors, service providers, and the communities and environment around us. Everything we do is built around this and our other key values of quality, partnership, inclusion, and sustainability.

This is why we are both a B-Corporation and a California Benefit Corporation—a certification and a for-profit legal status that require us to adhere to the highest standards for corporate, social, and environmental performance.

We are grateful to our readers, authors, and other friends of the company who consider themselves to be part of the BK Community. We hope that you, too, will join us in our mission.

A BK Business Book

We hope you enjoy this BK Business book. BK Business books pioneer new leadership and management practices and socially responsible approaches to business. They are designed to provide you with groundbreaking and practical tools to transform your work and organizations while upholding the triple bottom line of people, planet, and profits. High-five!

To find out more, visit **www.bkconnection.com**.

Berrett–Koehler
Publishers

Connecting people and ideas
to create a world that works for all

Dear Reader,

Thank you for picking up this book and joining our worldwide community of Berrett-Koehler readers. We share ideas that bring positive change into people's lives, organizations, and society.

To welcome you, we'd like to offer you a free e-book. You can pick from among twelve of our bestselling books by entering the promotional code **BKP92E** here: http://www.bkconnection.com/welcome.

When you claim your free e-book, we'll also send you a copy of our e-newsletter, the *BK Communiqué*. Although you're free to unsubscribe, there are many benefits to sticking around. In every issue of our newsletter you'll find

- A free e-book
- Tips from famous authors
- Discounts on spotlight titles
- Hilarious insider publishing news
- A chance to win a prize for answering a riddle

Best of all, our readers tell us, "Your newsletter is the only one I actually read." So claim your gift today, and please stay in touch!

Sincerely,

Charlotte Ashlock
Steward of the BK Website

Questions? Comments? Contact me at bkcommunity@bkpub.com.

MIX
From responsible sources
FSC® C113845
www.fsc.org

Certified
Corporation
bcorporation.net